JEAN GENET AND
THE SEMIOTICS
OF PERFORMANCE

Advances in Semiotics

Thomas A. Sebeok, General Editor

JEAN GENET AND THE SEMIOTICS OF PERFORMANCE

L A U R A   O S W A L D

INDIANA UNIVERSITY PRESS

Bloomington and Indianapolis

A version of Chapter IV has been published in *Enclitic*, VII, No.
2 (1983). Chapter V has been published in *Poetics
Today*, Vol. 8:2 (1987).

Manufactured in the United States of America

Library of Congress Cataloging-in-Publication Data

Oswald, Laura.
  Jean Genet and the semiotics of performance.

  (Advances in semiotics)
  Bibliography: p.
  Includes index.
    1. Genet, Jean, 1910-   —Criticism and interpre-
tation.   2. Semiotics and literature.   I. Title.
  II. Series.
  PQ2613.E53Z795   1989   848'.91209   88–45447
  ISBN 0–253–33152–8

    1 2 3 4 5 93 92 91 90 89

For Michael, Julia, and Nicolas Koenigsknecht

Contents

A Note on Authorship

Genet's work offers valuable testimony to the ways in which literary texts are betrayed as they pass through the hands of editors, translators, and censors. There are at least two versions of Genet's novels, *Notre-Dame-des-fleurs*, *Miracle de la rose*, and *Pompes funèbres*: cut and uncut. The Marc Barbézat, l'Arbalète editions of *Notre-Dame-des-fleurs* (1948) and *Miracle de la rose* (1946), and an anonymously published, special edition of *Pompes funèbres* (1948),[1] contain passages which have been censored from the later, Gallimard editions published in the 1950s. Ironically, the incomplete, censored versions form part of the *Oeuvres complètes* of Jean Genet, the most widely known collection of his works, which includes Sartre's monumental "introduction," *Saint Genêt*.

While all of the censored passages contain profane language or depict illicit sex acts, it is not always clear why some were cut and others uncut from the Gallimard edition. Political motives could explain why a sex scene involving two German soldiers during the occupation of France is included in *Pompes funèbres*, while a similar scene between two French men is censored; or why profane words are included when they describe other criminals in *Miracle de la rose*, but excluded when they refer to guards. The danger lies in the fact that the censor's hand barely leaves a trace in the Gallimard edition. At times, where entire pages have been cut, there remains an unmarked passage from one sentence to the next or one paragraph to the next. Any gaps in the text blend imperceptibly into Genet's fragmented, non-linear style of narration.

I am grateful to the Grove Press for permitting me to reproduce passages from Bernard Frechtman's English translation of Genet's work. However, since this translation was based on the Gallimard edition, it passes on to Anglophone readers the same, censored version of Genet's novels. When necessary, I translated the original texts directly from French. By including uncensored material in my own analysis of Genet's language, I do not intend to shock or tease the reader, but to restore to the texts their original, raw poetry.

Frechtman's is by and large an adequate translation, but it leans toward clarifying the meaning of words at the expense of the work of the signifier, including the effects of rime and alliteration. Consequently, Frechtman often misses the erotic dimension of word-play in Genet's style, obscuring the point that Genet practices perversion first and foremost with reference to languages of authority, notably standard French. In other instances, the violence done to syntax and meaning by criminal argot simply escapes translation and has no counterpart in the American slang used in the English version.

Finally, Genet's last work, *Un Captif amoureux*, published shortly after his death, poses extremely interesting problems of authorship. Having worked long and closely with Genet's literary language, I have the impression that *Un Captif amoureux* was authored by two different writers. While one recognizes Genet in lyrical passages which seize the cruel beauty of human existence in paradoxical figures, one cannot identify the voice speaking in the more didactic passages, which give almost journalistic accounts of Middle East politics and the history of the Palestinian Liberation Movement. It is not unlikely that Genet's last work, which has provoked a great deal of gossip in the press but not much critical reading, was written cooperatively, though the nature of such collaboration and Genet's part in it will never be known. Genet mentions in *Un Captif amoureux* that he dismissed a suggestion of Arafat's to write a book about the movement. The question remains whether Genet was indeed co-opted by one Palestinian group or another to author a book which would draw attention to their cause, or whether Genet deliberately surrendered his authority over the narration in keeping with his systematic challenge to systems of authority.

Now that Gallimard is planning to reedit *Un Captif amoureux* (along what lines?), perhaps the traces of another voice, another author, will be erased for all time, leaving us with the appearance of a false unity, a shallow beauty.

NOTE:

1. According to Jean-Bernard Moraly, this edition was published anonymously by Paul Morhien and financed by Jean Cocteau. "Les Cinq vies de Jean Genet," in *Les Nègres au port de la lune*. ed. C.D.N. Bordeaux. (Paris: Editions de la Différence, 1988), p. 25.

Mon 6/27/22

Acknowledgements

This book has its roots in my doctoral dissertation, directed by Michel Beaujour and submitted to New York University in 1981. I am grateful to Professor Beaujour for his challenging guidance as teacher and scholar. I also thank Christian Metz, whose seminars at the Ecole des hautes études en sciences sociales in Paris are a testing ground for state of the art research in semiotic study, and whose writing sets the standards for intellectual rigor. Furthermore, I am indebted to Professor Thomas Sebeok, both for bringing this book to the attention of the Indiana University Press and for his ongoing interest in and support of my work.

I thank Richard Avedon for generously allowing me to reproduce his protrait of Genet on the jacket of the book. The frame around the image seems to imprison Genet on the stage of photographic representation, calling attention to a performative dimension of photography which anticipates my own theoretical concerns.

My thanks go to John Aubrey and Karen Skubish of the Newberry Library of Chicago, who shared their fellowship and provided research support during the early stages of the book, and to the staffs of the Anthology Film Archive, the Museum of Modern Art, and the Northwestern University Library for their knowledgeable assistance. I thank Professors Carol Avins, Maria Breuer, and Tom Conley for their suggestions and encouragement.

Three of my students at Northwestern University, Deborah Finkelstein, Sarah Rich, and Nathalie Bullock, made important editorial comments on the final copy of the manuscript. Doreen Patterson Robinson cared for my children while I devoted substantial stretches of time to writing and research. And Melinda Oswald Kamick contributed valuable secretarial skills in preparing different stages of the manuscript.

And finally, my warm regards go to my friends, Sheila Lesensky, Priscilla Clark, and Diane Burgin, for lending an ear and sharing my enthusiasm for this work.

Introduction

Jean Genet, the *enfant terrible* of the French theater, died on April 15, 1986, leaving a literary legacy which spans five decades and includes plays, novels, films, poems, and political essays. Though important criticism has addressed the originality of Genet's theater,[1] and though Jean-Paul Sartre wrote a major study of Genet's novels,[2] to date no one has traced the evolution of Genet's famous "theater of the double" out of his early work with narrative or cinematic point of view, or negotiated relations between Genet's poetics and his militant politics. Nor, moreover, has Genet been comfortably situated in any of the major trends in modernism, though he has been loosely associated with surrealism, existentialism, and postmodernism.[3]

The problem with Genet for literary criticism is that his work systematically calls into question discourses of authority, including those of scholars and literary critics. An *hors-la-loi*, Genet wrote from the margins of dominant, heterosexual culture about events and in a language which could ruffle the complacency of the most sophisticated reader. Genet's work also eludes the classifications and definitions we use to make sense of literary history. Even the label "avant-garde" fails to account for the movement of Genet's pen, since literary avant-gardes, by definition, prepare the ground for the future of mainstream literature, and are eventually assimilated into dominant styles of discourse. Genet's work resists this kind of assimilation. From the early novels written in prison to his final prose-poem-journal, *Un Captif amoureux*, Genet consistently challenges the integrity and specificity of genres and representational modes, merging as he does the novelistic, the cinematic, and the dramatic in any given work.

While I maintain that no single formal grid or critical formula can contain Genet's writing, I argue that his struggle to be heard beyond the borders of dominant culture raises, consistently and urgently, the question of the speaking subject's place in socially constituted discourses. In order to track the effects of this struggle in Genet's novels, plays, and film, I propose an approach which investigates the act which allows subjects to participate in dominant discourse, an act of performance. The notion of performance is posed here as a question rather than as a closed theoretical system, and puts into play relations between semiotics and philosophy while testing the limits of both disciplines with reference to the works themselves.

Mine is a rather broad approach, yet unlike the narrow theoretical models which structural poetics borrows from linguistics, it respects the complexity of the question of literature in the framework of a rigorous scientific investigation. By focussing on the question of how subjects become something for someone else, in performance, rather than on the form and function of structural models, I discover a means of tracing the movement of the mask in Genet's work, a figure which transcends the semiotic specificity of theater and drama and places in question the subject of Genet's novels and film.

This kind of approach accounts for trends not only in Genet's work, but in contemporary French literature generally. Other postwar writers, including Beckett, Robbe-Grillet, and Duras, move regularly between work in cinema or the novel and theater, while novelists such as Simon and Sarraute borrow semiotic operations such as montage or role-play from cinema or theater respectively, in constructing a hybrid form of the novel.[4] Performance constitutes the main event with such writers, moving the subject of narrative, cinematic, and theatrical representation in a kind of philosophical or psychological mise-en-scène.

In the 1930s, Antonin Artaud, anticipating our contemporary concern for performance, called for a "theater of cruelty" which would overthrow the authority of the text over mise-en-scène and place the human subject on stage in the place of dramatic characters. He called for the devalorization not only of the dramatist, but of the very notion of authorship, including the controlling point of view of the *metteur en scène*. In *Le Théâtre et son double*, performance is never very far from the human body, from the staging of life in perpetual crisis, life which is irreducible to a semiotic system or "work," whose spontaneity can only be described as a "happening."[5] Artaud offers no technical prescriptions for producing this kind of theater, except to say that the theater of cruelty destroys the borders between art and life and resists formulation into a prepared text or schema.[6] He declares (guerilla) war on Western culture and the Aristotelian tradition, which define representation in terms of its ability to imitate universal truths about Man.

While Artaud claims to examine theater as a question, "philosophically and in its essence," he also calls for the articulation of a purely theatrical "language" in terms of the material specificity of performance. "This physical and concrete language to which I allude is truly theatrical only to the extent that the thoughts it expresses elude spoken language"(p. 45, my translation).

In *Le Théâtre et son double* Artaud states something of the complexity of the issues at hand in my book, and suggests how semiotics and philosophy overlap in the question of performance. Artaud seeks a language of the stage which would privilege movement over mimesis, space over speech, spectacle over meaning, vision over voice. In the same gesture he poses a philosophical challenge to the means and ends of Western culture and the ideology of the "same." He places in question metaphysical hierarchies which in Aristotle grant primacy to the closure of being and meaning in dramatic discourse and to the unity of poetic signifier and signified in the image.

Artaud seems to be unaware of the profound implications of the theater of cruelty for metaphysical philosophy. While he attacks the Aristotelian tradition in poetics, he praises oriental theater for its "metaphysical" dimension and calls for a substitution of metaphysics for the psychological approach to theater in the West. What Artaud seems to be addressing in the notion of "metaphysical" theater is theater focussed on the spectating subject's response to mise-en-scène, which he defines as "a language in space and in movement" (p. 55, my translation). Unlike the spectator's identification with the personal identities of characters, metaphysical theater would be the scene of the transcendental subject's performance in the space of spectacle.[7] Theater must "call into question, organically, man, his ideas about reality, and his poetic place in reality" (p. 110, my translation).

Moreover, Artaud's writings transcend the realm of theater per se and point to the broader question of the subject's performance in poetic discourse. In the following statement from *La Cruelle raison poétique*, Blanchot summarizes the implications of Artaud's work for modern poetry and poetics:

> Artaud has left us a major document which is nothing other than a Poetics. I recognize that he speaks there of theater, but what is at issue is the very

essence of poetry, namely that poetry cannot be achieved without refusing limited genres and affirming a more original language . . . it is no longer a question of the real space presented to us by the stage, but of *another* space.[8]

Artaud did not finally articulate a "language of theater" in terms of semiotic codes or sign functions, nor did he bring philosophical tradition to bear on the question of metaphysical theater, but set the stage for investigating a general semiotics of performance. Moreover, Artaud instigated a revolution which is currently eroding the Aristotelian tradition in Western poetry and poetics. In Artaud we discover not only a radical poetics of modern theater, but a theatrical model for modern poetry.

Artaud had considerable influence on Genet. The theater of cruelty resounds in Genet's ideal of "theater about theater,"[9] a call for the destruction of characters, for a theater which places the spectator on stage. This concept of theater shows up in his novels and film in terms of dramatic spacing, role-play, and mistaken identity.

The structuralist bent of semiotics has been the greatest barrier to a theoretical account of this phenomenon, insofar as structuralism posits the autonomy of each representational mode with regard to the others as the condition of possibility of semiotic analysis. This premise derives from still another assumption, namely that a "scientific" study of discourse can only be achieved by segmenting it into minimal units structured according to a model for closure between the form, the meaning, and the material of the expression. In Saussure this model consists of the marriage of signifier and signified in the linguistic sign. In Hjelmslev it consists of the dialectical relation between the form of meaning and the form of the material in the sign function. In structural linguistics the speaking/spectating subject remains "backstage" as it were, taken for granted as the transcendental origin of meaning.

Benveniste changed the direction of structural linguistics in the 1960s by introducing the philosophical question of the speaking subject into problems of language. In *Problems in General Linguistics,* he insists that language is not simply an abstract system of signs, but a means of communication between speakers.[10] The movement between these two faces of language in discourse, between "le sémiotique" and "le sémantique," respectively, is made possible by an act of predication in the speaking subject, the origin and condition of possibility of meaning. For communication to occur, the subject is bound to an interlocutor according to social contract, taken up in the endless shifting of positions between "I" and "you" in deixis.

Benveniste not only opened up the study of language to problems of the subject's performance in discourse, but provided means of advancing the state of the semiotics of theater and drama, which has not progressed very far since the 1930s. Theatrical representation cannot be reduced to a system of relations between the form and meaning of the dramatic text, consisting as it does of an intricate negotiation between the codes shaping discourse and the uncodifiable movement of the subject in the folds of representation. This explains why a structural approach fails to account for the complexity of the problem of theater. Theater is built entirely around deictic traces for reference and subject-address in dramatic dialogue which link the sense of speech to the space of spectacle in theatrical performance.[11]

Benveniste conceives of the speaking subject as a unity which transcends its implication in any given instance of discourse, indeed as the origin and condition of possibility of meaning. A close look at Benveniste reveals the difficulty inherent in this metaphysical assumption. In Benveniste, "I speak, therefore I am." However, when I speak I am *for* another, ruled by the social contract binding I and you in discourse. The division of the speaker into a subject for itself and a subject for others precedes its formation as a unity in discourse: I speak, therefore I am(not). This leads us to conclude that semiosis is inseparable from the question of how subjects become something for other subjects in performance.

The work of Jacques Derrida forms a frame of reference for the various essays in my book, since his critique of metaphysics aims specifically to shift the philosophical assumptions underlying theories of language and poetry. In *Of Grammatology*, for instance, Derrida points out that the claim to an original unity of the subject is but an ideologically determined construct, not a natural "essence" of being.[12] He argues that at the origin of being and meaning is a movement of doubling and division, an endless striving for unity across the medium of discourse.

In *Dissemination* Derrida addresses specifically the difficulty of classical poetics to account for trends in modern literature.[13] The ontological interpretation of mimesis fails to engage the question of the subject's production in literary discourse, focussing instead on the means of imitating transcendental reality. While Derrida does not discuss Artaud specifically in *Dissemination*, the theater of cruelty seems to shape his reading of Plato with Mallarmé.[14] Derrida discovers in the mime-play a figure for expanding Artaud's notion of pure mise-en-scène into an orientation of poetics which would transcend theater per se.

> The mime follows no pre-established script, no program obtained elsewhere. . . . His gestures, his gestural writing . . . are not dictated by any verbal discourse or imposed by any diction. (p. 195)

Moreover,

> in inserting a sort of spacing into interiority, it [the mimed operation] no longer allows the inside to close upon itself or be identified with itself. . . . This impossibility of closure, this dehiscence of the Mallarméan book as an "internal" theater, constitutes not a reduction but a *practice* of spacing. (p. 234)

Artaud's call for a "language of space,"[15] for the demise of imitation,[16] for the staging of passion in place of representation,[17] is echoed in Derrida's reading of a poetic revolution in Mallarmé. Thus by implication Derrida discovers the philosophical grounds for expanding Artaud's program for theater into a modern poetics of discourse, focussed on the subject's construction, deconstruction, and reconstruction in textual performance.

> The text is remarkable in that the reader . . . can never choose his own place in it, nor can the spectator. There is at any rate no tenable place for him opposite the text, no spot where he might get away with *not* writing what, in the reading, would seem to him to be given, past; no spot, in other words, where he would stand before an already *written* text. Because his job is to put things on stage. (*Dissemination*; p. 291)

I contend that Derrida's "deconstruction" of the metaphysical orientation of linguistics and poetics is not incompatible with semiotics per se. By placing the study of subjectivity in language in the framework of a critique of metaphysics, we discover means of accounting for those aspects of literature which elude the structural model while maintaining methodological tools such as distinctions between signifier and signified, enunciation and enounced, form and meaning.

The justification for this kind of approach stands with the creative works themselves. Genet and his contemporaries systematically challenge metaphysical notions of Man as an original, self-contained unity and demand a rethinking of poetics and semiotics from a philosophical standpoint. By studying those aspects of discourse which trace the subject's movement in textual performance, I am able to account for the evolution of Genet's famous "theater of the double"[18] out of his early work with subject-address and reference in narrative. Genet takes up the question of the subject in a problematic of narrative, dramatic, and cinematic voice, exposing the double at the origin of speech and the lie at the origin of meaning.

Given the theoretical scope of my book, I chose not to analyze all of Genet's works, but limited my corpus to texts which both characterize general trends in Genet and most clearly illustrate the theoretical issues at stake in a theory of performance. I will discuss in detail three novels, *Notre-Dame-des-fleurs* (1944), *Miracle de la rose* (1946), and *Pompes funèbres* (1947); Genet's only original film, *Un Chant d'amour* (1950); and three plays, *Les Bonnes* (first produced in 1947), *Le Balcon* (first produced in 1957), and *Les Nègres* (first produced in 1959).[19]

In the essays which follow, I discuss philosophical and theoretical issues surrounding the question of performance, while attempting to account for the role of the double in Genet's literary imagination. By reading Genet with his "others" in the the realm of theory, including Derrida, Benveniste, Bakhtin, Ricoeur, and Metz, I hope to come to grips with the overriding concerns of a man whose life in literature was never very far from his life as prisoner, as outcast, as self-proclaimed exile.[20]

JEAN GENET AND THE SEMIOTICS OF PERFORMANCE

ONE

███ ████

The Scene of Silence

L'auteur d'un beau poème est toujours
mort.
    Jean Genet, *Miracle de la rose*

Sartre has said that Genet lived the life of a dead man, whose personal will or self-hood had been absorbed into the idea of himself as a being-for-others.[1] Though Sartre wrote primarily of Genet the novelist, whose celebrated writings for theater had not yet reached fruition, Sartre understood the poetic implications of Genet's existential posture. To the extent that Genet confused his personal identity with his meaning for others, he played out the game of life and death like an actor on stage. Hence the title of Sartre's book *Saint Genet: Actor and Martyr*.

The threat of spiritual death or non-being not only underlies the existential relation of subject and other, but constitutes the driving force of the process by which subjects become something for other subjects in linguistic performance. Thus Derrida says that the threat of death or non-being is a condition of possibility of the speaking subject's relation to itself.[2] As soon as I utter the statement "I am," I am also for another, by virtue of the system of shared conventions which make possible the articulation of being and meaning in speech. The process of signification implies the necessary separation of the signifier "I" from both a transcendental identity, the "pure, original and unchangeable consciousness" of Kant's metaphysic, and an empirical or personal identity.[3] On this level, "I" is a trace of the subject traced in the production and circulation of signifiers among speakers.

> Whether or not perception accompanies the enounced of perception, whether or not life as self-presence accompanies the enounced of *I*, is perfectly indifferent to the functioning of intentionality. My death is structurally necessary to the pronouncing of *I*. (V.P.; 107–8, my translation)[4]

Since the word "I" signifies in the absence of an empirical or transcendental subject of discourse, since this absence is indeed a condition of possibility of signification, non-being or death underlies every act of predication. Inner experience is always and already inscribed with the possibility of an opening onto the stage of discourse with others. To the extent that the speaking subject is "spoken" by the social conventions which make discourse possible, the subject is threatened with the possibility of non-being, or death-by-representation.

By viewing subjectivity in the framework of the staging of difference between the self and its other in inner speech, we are able to place the self-reflexive and solitary discourse of first-person narrative within a problematic of identity played on the scene of silence. This problematic immediately and necessarily engages the problem of death in Genet, both as theme and as a structuring of relations between the subject and its others in textual performance.

We could say that while Sartre describes a *moment* in Genet's relation to others, one in which being-for-oneself is compromised by the experience of being-for-others, Genet is not simply or permanently a "dead man" in this figurative sense, but an author who has met death straight on. In his novels he plays out the drama of personal identity on the stage of literary representation, struggles with the problem of death along the lines of a problematic of performance shaping relations of intersubjectivity in literary discourse. This problematic would ultimately determine the meaning of Genet's style of theatrical performance.

Genet negotiates the question of personal identity in terms of an economy of difference underlying relations between proper names, characters named, and the one who names in narrative. While the philosophical question of the production of the subject underlies every aspect of discourse, it is nowhere quite as apparent as in the formation and utilization of proper names. Proper names transcribe the existential problem of identity as it is posed in the statement "I am" into a problematic of identification and representation. Since an act of predication in the subject underlies naming, and since names are the means by which others define and identify the person named, proper names reveal the original division of the speaking subject into a self and its other, a division which ordinary words obscure. Proper names are therefore central to the study of how subjects become something for other subjects in language.[5]

In *La Voix et le phénomène*, Derrida examines not only how the act of being something for someone else, which I define here as a general problematic of performance, shapes the very idea of the sign and, by extension, the subject of discourse, but also how the difference between being and being-for-others shapes the notion of subjectivity itself. He begins by discrediting Husserl's separation of speech into two moments: expression, which represents idealized impressions or perceptions to the mind as pure meanings, and indication, which situates these meanings in the empirical context of discourse and addresses them to other subjects.[6] He furthermore discredits the notion of an internal unity of the subject in self-representation.

In Husserl any problems arising from the interaction of expression and indication would occur within one's external representation for others, not within self-representation. Expression signifies idealized meanings; indication points to referents in the real world and implicates an interlocutor in discourse. In the communication of meanings to others through representation, the difference between expression and indication, between meaning and reference in purely linguistic terms, brings into play the problem of the speaker's intentions and the interlocutor's ability to read those intentions as they modify the standard meanings of the words. Self-representation would elude such differences, forming a unity of being which transcends external representation in speech.

Derrida claims that Husserl's separation of speech into expression and indication obscures their interaction in every instance of discourse. To the extent that speech represents the thoughts of the speaking subject to another subject through language, all discourse, including the simplest act of predication concerning an object, produces a subject divided between the interplay of meaning and reference.

> Everything which in my discourse is destined to manifest a lived experience to others must pass through the mediation of its physical side. This irreducible mediation engages every expression in an indicative operation. The manifestation function (*kundgebende Funktion*) is an indicative function. (V. P.; 41, my translation)[7]

The movement between indication and expression in discourse produces a life-death struggle shaping the subject's participation in textual performance. The personal pronoun "I," for example, is a trace for an absent subject, an index for the living consciousness which breathes life into discourse. On this level, "I" is a trace for the possibility of the presence of the subject to itself. "I" is also a sign for "the person who speaks in discourse," an idealization of the transcendental "I" which can be repeated indefinitely, shifting from one speaker to another. Derrida points out that the movement between expression and indication exemplifies the existential conflict underlying the predication of "I" in discourse.

Ironic discourse displays the complexity of this process. For example, in *Jokes and Their Relation to the Unconscious*, Freud mentions a play on the word "vol" (flight, theft) in the statement "C'est le premier vol de l'aigle," to describe Napoleon's seizure of royal property.[8] Here a contrast between the literal and figurative meanings of the word "aigle" produces a movement between the two possible meanings of the word "vol." The speaker's ironic intention is clear only if we know that the eagle refers to Napoleon through symbolic displacement, and that the speaker means to condemn Napoleon's takeover as an act of theft.

Irony exposes the vulnerability of signification, of the unity of being and meaning in expression, to the unpredictable course of indication shaping reference and subject-addresss in discourse. Irony betrays the fundamental division of the subject into a being-for-itself and a being-for-others, which logical discourse masks.

After proving an original intrication between expression and indication in the production of speech, Derrida moves on to disprove Husserl's notion of a transcendental subject whose unity prefigures, indeed makes possible, the production of discourse. In Husserl the solitary subject thinking to itself, in silence, escapes the threat of division and non-presence implied in performance by eluding the conflict of expression and indication altogether. Auto-affection constitutes the immediate presentation of meanings to consciousness without the mediation of the physical side of language. Auto-affection therefore lacks a moment of indication which divides the subject into the self and its other.

In Derrida auto-affection is a kind of inner speech, prey to the movement between indication and expression which divides the subject in communication with others. Derrida claims that the process of idealization, which permits the infinite representation of phenomena to consciousness as meanings, implies an original difference between things and their representation in expression, between identity and non-identity in signification. Moreover, the movement between perception and representation submits inner speech to the force of indication, to a movement between the self and its other or self-representation. Derrida claims that this movement constitutes the condition of possibility of thought and being.

Derrida posits a divided subject at the origin of speech in place of the transcendental subject of phenomenology. The movement of difference which divides the subject from its other in space and time defines a problematic of performance staged on the scene of silence, and is irreducible to a unity of meaning and being implied in the word "subject." Thus Derrida names the movement of difference and its effects on subject production by means of a play on the words *différer* and *différence*, "la différance".

> This movement of *différance* does not simply disturb a transcendental subject. It creates it. Auto-affection is not a modality of experience which characterizes a being who would be already himself (*autos*). It produces the same as a relation to self within the difference from the self, the same as non-identical. (V.P.; 92, my translation)[9]

Defining subjectivity in terms of a kind of spacing of the subject in relation to its other in inner speech, through time, we reveal the place of performance in the very constitution of subjectivity. Derrida himself employs a theatrical metaphor to describe this production.

> The concept of subjectivity belongs, *a priori* and in general, to the order of the *constituted*. That applies *a fortiori* to the analogical appresentation which constitutes intersubjectivity. The latter is inseparable from temporalization taken as the opening of the present onto an outside of itself, onto another absolute present. This being-outside-of-itself proper to time is its spacing: it is a proto-stage (*une archi-scène*). This stage, as the relation of one present to another present as such, that is as a non-derived representation (*Vergegenwärtigung*, or *Repräsentation*), produces the structure of signs in general as "reference," as being-for-something (*für etwas sein*), and radically prohibits their reduction. There is no constituting subjectivity. And the very concept of constitution itself must be deconstructed. (V.P.; 94, my translation)[10]

Derrida's theatrical metaphor for the movement of the subject between being for itself and being for others forms the philosophical ground on which I theorize about the divided subject of first person narrative. Neither transcendental "I" nor empirical identity, the narrating subject speaks from the scene of silence, engaging the reader in an act of performance shaping relations between "I" and "not-I", between subject and others in narrative. Nowhere is the force of these divisions quite as marked as in the process of naming.

Since the question of performance shapes Genet's work from beginning to end, and since naming is intimately related to this question, it comes as no surprise that a problematic of naming shapes relations between narrative discourse and story in his novels. It is less obvious why naming practices change from one novel to the next. The predominance of one type of name over others evolves from *Notre-Dame-des-fleurs* to *Miracle de la rose* and *Pompes funèbres*. For instance, the inclusion of baptismal names in *Pompes funèbres*, to the exclusion of sobriquets and the devalorization of patronyms, shapes an important contrast both with *Notre-Dame-des fleurs*, in which sobriquets predominate, and with *Miracle de la rose*, in which patronyms dominate. This pattern signals that naming has transcended its purely diegetic function of identifying characters, and shapes figures of narrative intervention into the story.

Naming practices in Genet trace an evolution of the problem of personal identity, including the question of the relation of Jean Genet, the author, to the narrator of the same name. In the early work, sobriquets name the other's, the character's, identity, by means of rhetorical reduction. Through naming, characters become figures for the narrator's alter ego, the other side of a single identity. In the later work, the gradual disappearance of sobriquets, plus the predominance of baptismal names and patronyms, symbolizes the narrator's gradual recognition of the other as that which he is not, and of himself as a double for another Jean Genet.

As I follow the problem of difference from one novel to the next, I show the close relation between the question of personal identity and the theme of death in Genet's work.

The staging of difference exposes the threat of death which the other represents. To the extent that I exist as an object for the other-as-another-subject, I cease to "be" for myself. I am a non-being. In his third novel, *Pompes funèbres*, Genet twists this problem into a grotesque masquerade destined to celebrate the death of the transcendental subject of the proper name.

In narrative the division of the subject can be represented in terms of differences between the subject of the enounced and the subject of the enunciation, or in the terms of Benveniste, between narrative voice and the voices of characters speaking in the narration. Benveniste distinguishes narration (*histoire*) from discourse on the basis of markings for the here and now of the speaking event.[11] The first-person voice and the imperfect and present tenses characterize the discourse, the instance of the narrator speaking in his own voice; the third person and past tense (the *passé simple* in French) characterize the narration. Adverbs referring to the "here" and "now" of the narrating event also trace narrative voice in narrative. To the extent that characters themselves utter "I" or perform acts of predication which imply their presence as subjects in the story, characters participate in a system of doublings between narrative voice and its other in narrative. Furthermore, to the extent that naming practices both identify a character in the story and trace the narrator's imbrication with characters, naming practices perpetuate a play of *différance* in narrative, thus submitting the present and presence, the "here" and "now" of narrative discourse, to a movement of division and absence.

From a linguistic standpoint, sobriquets are traditionally motivated by some property of the individual named, and formed by means of metonymical and metaphorical associations. For instance, the famous family name "Plantagenêt" was derived from a sobriquet for Geoffroy, the Count of Anjou, who used to "plant" a "genêt" in his hat.[12] Moreover, sobriquets are often ironic, entailing a reversal of an aspect of the individual into its opposite and a pejorative intention on the part of the namer. Dauzat gives the example "Bois l'eau" (Drink water) for "buveur de vin" (wine drinker).[13]

Sobriquets belong to a category of proper names which expose the difficulty inherent in calling names "proper" at all. Derrida speaks of "the unity of the proper as the nonpollution of the subject close to itself."[14] Names are "proper" to the extent that they indicate individual subjects in a given context, rather than express conventional meanings which can be interpreted by others. Since sobriquets both express conventional meanings (consisting as they do of common nouns) and indicate individual subjects in the framework of discourse, sobriquets expose the difference between expression and indication shaping the act of naming.

Sobriquets thus place in question the very notion of the "nonpollution of the subject close to itself" in proper names. The subject thus conceived would indeed be "unnamable," because irreducible to an original unity of being and meaning in language.[15]

In *Notre-Dame-des-fleurs*, Genet privileges the capacity of sobriquets to represent idealized meanings to the mind, over their indicative or referential function. He does this in order to blur the existential difference between namer and named. Sobriquets define characters in terms of their signification for an other, the narrating subject. When Genet describes characters as "des noms éclatés," he destroys their individual identities and makes them figures of narrative discourse.

> Dans la rue, sous l'auréole noire des parapluies minuscules et plats qu'elles tiennent d'une main comme des bouquets, Mimosa I, Mimosa II, Mimosa mi-IV, Première Communion, Angela, Monseigneur, Castagnette, Régine, une foule enfin, une litanie encore longue d'êtres qui sont des noms éclatés, attendent. . . . (N.D.F.; 11)

> In the street, beneath the black haloes of the tiny flat umbrellas which they are holding in one hand like bouquets, Mimosa I, Mimosa II, Mimosa the half-IV, First Communion, Angela, Milord, Castagnette, Régine—in short, a host, a still long litany of creatures who are glittering names—are waiting. (O.L.F.; 68)

In Genet, sobriquets say a great deal more about the narrator than about the diegetic or objective reality of the character named. Unlike ordinary sobriquets, whose irony or humor derives from the namer's associations around some property of the person named, Genet's sobriquets lead back to a figure of the divided subject of narrative discourse and signify properties of the narrator himself, such as moral and sexual ambivalence. In *Notre-Dame-des-fleurs*, sobriquets serve to mask the narrating subject's difference from others in the narration, so that characters represent extensions of the narrator's own struggle with the problem of personal identity.

In *Glas*, Derrida claims that when Genet borrows common nouns to create names for his characters, he forces language to conform to his personal ideolect by reducing the meanings of words to a single referent in the narration.[16] Genet thus appropriates language by "making proper" conventional signs.[17] From the point of view of textual performance, I argue that names based on common nouns allow Genet to appropriate the identities of others in the narration by reducing them to their meaning for him. "Mignon-les-Petits-Pieds," "Divine," and "Notre-Dame-des-fleurs" seem to lack diegetic motivation, that is, a relation of contiguity with the identities of the characters they refer to in the story.[18] "Mignon" refers to a tough brute of a thief, Paul Garcia. (Frechtman translates this sobriquet as Darling Daintyfoot. I prefer the literal translation, Cutey of the Little Feet, because Genet later weaves a chain of associations around the word "little," which have direct bearing on the development of this character.) "Divine" refers to Louis Culafroy, a drag queen and homosexual prostitute. "Notre-Dame-des-fleurs," Our Lady of the Flowers, names Adrien Baillon, a bisexual murderer. In Genet sobriquets not only generate oppositions between the identity of a character and his signification for the narrator, oppositions which are eventually resolved in a play of identification, but sobriquets do violence to the difference and autonomy of characters by reducing them to figures for Genet's own self-reflections.[19] Thus even the contradictory meanings generated by sobriquets are resolved with reference to the unity of narrative voice.

Naming in sobriquets represents a stage in Genet's struggle with the threat of death posed by the other. To the extent that I recognize the other as a subject, I also must recognize that I could become an object for him or her. The very act of speaking raises this possibility, the possibility of being something for another subject, a non-being. At this stage, Genet speaks in silence and produces a self-contained universe in which the other exists as an extension of the self.

In Genet's homosexual universe, characters are identified as feminine or masculine according not to their biological reality or even their sexual orientation, but to the role they perform for others. There are queens ("les tantes") and males ("les mâles"). Gender difference is based not upon physical differences between men and women as such, but between subjects and others in an economy of power and desire. Inasmuch as the "mâles" enter the narration by means of their signification for Divine, the main character, their sobriquets represent projections of her feminine orientation. To the extent that Divine herself represents the narrator's alter ego, Divine and her entourage represent the narrator's own sexual ambivalence.

The males do not use sobriquets among themselves in *Notre-Dame-des-fleurs*. The granting of sobriquets is an act of endearment and a symbol of the individual's initiation into the queens' world. Sobriquets can also be objects of shame or embarrassment, since the males resent the feminine identification. Divine's lover, Mignon, adjusts to Divine's world with some difficulty.

> Mignon a mis quelque temps à s'habituer à parler d'elle et de lui parler au féminin. Enfin il y parvint, mais ne toléra pas encore qu'elle lui causât comme à une copine. (N.D.F.; 21)

> It took Darling some time to get used to talking about her and to her in the feminine. He finally succeeded, but he still did not tolerate her talking to him as to a girl friend. (O.L.F.; 94)

In "Mignon-les-Petits-Pieds," the namer is thus inscribed in the name. That is, the sobriquet contains an opposition between the diegetic reality of the character, a tough thug ("Mignon le dur, le froid, l'irréfragable,"

[N.D.F.; 85]) and his meaning for Divine, cute or "mignon" (defined by Littré as "menue, gracieux, charmant; se dit en adressant la parole à des enfants, à de jeunes femmes").

Doubling and sexual ambivalence are inscribed in the inflections for masculine and feminine in standard French. "Mignon" is grammatically marked for masculine, and semantically marked for feminine. Here the conflict between grammar and meaning reiterates the conflict of masculine and feminine in the discourse.

Perhaps the most telling feature of Mignon's sobriquet is that it represents, by means of synecdoche, the total person by one of his properties, the property which is prized by the other, Divine. The complete name, "Mignon-les-Petits-Pieds," is formed by word-play having an erotic fixation, Mignon's genitals. The erotic meaning of "Petits Pieds" is camouflaged by a displacement of sexual interest from the genitals to the feet, the kind of displacement which characterizes the formation of fetishes.[20] The association of "Petits Pieds" with Mignon's genitals is developed later on in the narrative, when Divine recites a litany of names for Mignon's penis. These euphemisms contain the same marks of endearment expressed by the idea of smallness: "le Petit, le Bébé dans le berceau, le Jésus dans sa crèche, le Petit chaud, ton Petit frère" (N.D.F.; 30). Formal and semantic parallels created between these names and "Petits Pieds" motivate the erotic interpretation of Mignon's sobriquet.

The sobriquet contains yet another reversal of the character's diegetic reality. Judging from the narrator's description of Mignon's member, it is anything but "petit": "Longueur en érection o.m.24, circonférence o.m.11" (N.D.F.; 18). The sobriquet reduces the character to an "alias," an "other," whose identity equals his meaning for Divine.

> Pour Divine, Mignon n'est rien que la délégation sur terre, l'expression sensible, enfin le symbole d'un être (peut-être Dieu), d'une idée restée dans un ciel. (N.D.F.; 31)
> To Divine, Darling is only the magnificent delegation on earth, the physical expression, in short, the symbol of a being (perhaps God), of an idea that remains in heaven. (O.L.F.; 117)

To the extent that Mignon-les-Petits-Pieds is a projection of Divine's desire, Mignon exists as a reflection on the surface of her identity. Even when they make love, "Il plonge en Divine comme en un mirroir" (N.D.F.; 22). As Mignon buries his identity in Divine, he confronts the spectre of himself. This passage was totally tranformed in the Frechtman translation so as to miss the mirror figure completely (O.L.F.; 97).

> Mignon plonge en Divine comme en un miroir et la beauté un peu molle de son ami, lui raconte, sans qu'il le comprenne bien clairement, la nostalgie d'un Mignon mort, enterré en grand apparat et jamais pleuré. (N.D.F.; 22)

Mignon plunges into Divine as into a mirror, and the slightly flabby beauty of his friend tells him, without his understanding it very clearly, of the nostalgia of a dead Mignon, buried with great pomp, and never mourned. (my translation)

Eventually, it will be clear that Divine herself is a projection of the narrator's identity. A chain of rhetorical operations leads from Mignon-les-Petits-Pieds to Divine, from Divine to Genet in the discourse, reducing the other's identity to another face of Jean Genet.

Another character, Notre-Dame-des-fleurs, alias Adrien Baillon, enters the narration "par la porte du crime." He earns his sobriquet by murdering an old man.

Il sait que son destin s'accomplit et s'il sait (Notre-Dame le sait ou paraît le savoir) que son destin s'accomplit à chaque instant, il a le pur sentiment mystique que ce meurtre va faire de lui, par vertu du baptême du sang: Notre-Dame-des-fleurs. (N.D.F.; 35)

He knows that his destiny is being fulfilled, and although he knows (Our Lady knows or seems to know it better than anyone) that his destiny is being fulfilled at every moment, he has the pure mystic feeling that this murder is going to turn him, by virtue of the baptism of blood, into Our Lady of the Flowers. (O.L.F.; 127)

On the one hand, Notre-Dame is "queen" of the criminals ("des fleurs") and a queen in Divine's homosexual universe, just as, in Christian liturgy, Notre-Dame names the souveraine of Christians. Genet identifies "fleurs" with criminals in the very opening of the novel, thus motivating the second half of this sobriquet.

Cette merveilleuse éclosion de belles et sombres fleurs, je ne l'appris que par fragments. . . . *Ces assassins maintenants morts*. (N.D.F.; 9)

Les journaux arrivent mal jusqu'à ma cellule, et les plus belles pages sont pillées de leurs *plus belles fleurs (ces macs)*, comme jardins en mai. (N.D.F.; 10)

I learned only in bits and pieces of that wonderful *blossoming of dark and lovely flowers*. . . . These murderers, now dead, have nevertheless reached me. (O.L.F.; 62)

The newspapers are tattered by the time they reach my cell, and the finest pages have been looted of their finest *flowers, those pimps*, like gardens in May. (O.L.F.; 63)

The association of dead assassins and flowers appears absurd and unmotivated, since it identifies values such as life and beauty with their opposites. This figuration is motivated in a roundabout way: there is a cause and effect relation between death by execution (the crucifixion) and beauty (Man's redemption) in the discourse. Death by execution parallels the death of Christ by crucifixion, and constitutes a means of reparation for guilt through self-annihilation. The use of "fleurs" as a figure for eternal life gained through expiation reiterates the association of the sacred and the beautiful, the priest and the poet, in the discourse. Thus what originates as difference and oppostion is ultimately resolved in the narration.

"Notre-Dame-des-fleurs" also signifies the sexual ambivalence of the character named. Unlike Mignon, Notre-Dame-des-fleurs plays both the male and the queen in relation to others in the story. In the following scene, which was censored in the Gallimard edition of Genet's *Oeuvres complètes*, and consequently in the English translation, Notre-Dame plays these two roles in a single feat of sexual gymnastics. As he penetrates Divine, he is penetrated by the supermale, Gorgui.

> Gorgui chevauchait l'assassin blond et cherchait à le pénétrer. Déjà son membre intelligent était planté, son membre dur et gros, plus dur et plus gros que celui de Notre-Dame, et un désespoir terrible, profond, inégalable, la détacha du jeu des deux hommes. Notre-Dame recherchait encore la bouche de Divine pour y planter sa bite et trouvait les paupières, les cheveux . . . . Notre-Dame avait retrouvé sa bouche, et cette bouche s'ouvrit enfin, immense, terrible, pendant que s'y écoulait le chaud liquide de Notre-Dame, plus vigoureux encore parce que Gorgui le baisait. . . . (N.D.F.; 81)

> Gorgui mounted the blond murderer and tried to penetrate him. Despair—terrible, profound, unparalleled—detached her from the game of the two men. Our Lady was still seeking Divine's mouth and found the eyelids, the hair, ...(O.L.F.; 243) Our Lady had found her mouth again, and this mouth opened up finally, immense, terrible, while the hot liquid flowed in from Notre-Dame, more vigorous still because Gorgui was fucking him. . . .(my translation)

In Christian liturgy, Notre-Dame names not only the queen of the Christian realm but the mother of Christ. Since Christ's life is only meaningful with reference to his death on the cross, the Notre-Dame figure is implicated in the violence of her son's death. For Christ to perform his ultimate task of redeeming mankind, he must assume human dimensions, he must be born of woman. Since being born prefigures Christ's crucifixion, the liturgical Notre-Dame could be viewed as the author of Christ's death and suffering.

The implication of Notre-Dame in Christ's death and the association of this venerable mother figure with a bisexual criminal also betray Genet's usual irony and disdain toward women, especially mothers.[21] He reiterates this attitude in every representation of women in the novels, from the Medusa-like figures of Ernestine, Divine's mother in *Notre-Dame-des-fleurs*, and the nameless mother of John D. in *Pompes fu-*

nèbres, to the complete elimination of women from *Miracle de la rose*. Genet reduces sexual difference to the other side of the same, to a male figure posing as a woman.

The sobriquet "Notre-Dame-des-fleurs" thus generates metaphysical oppositions such as male/female, beauty/evil, etc., which are resolved with reference to logical relations in the discourse. Just as being born of woman prefigures Christ's death, so Christ's crucifixion prefigures Man's salvation. The author of Christ's death is also the author of man's eternal life. "Notre-Dame-des-fleurs" embraces this paradox. By committing a murder, Notre-Dame enters the divine realm of criminals who achieve saintliness on the guillotine. When Notre-Dame enters the narration "par la porte du crime," he prefigures his own death.

In the following figuration, the substitution of "assassins" by the names of flowers and the analogy between flowers and bells reiterate the relation of cause and effect between the act of murder and the execution/ redemption of the murderer, literally "announced" in the "ringing" of flowers:

> Notre-Dame l'a tué. Assassin. Il ne se dit pas le mot, mais plutôt j'écoute avec lui dans sa tête sonner un carillon qui doit être fait de toutes les clochettes du muguet, clochettes en porcelaine, en verre, en eau, en air. (N.D.F.; 35)

> Our Lady has killed him. A murderer. He doesn't say the word to himself, but rather I listen with him in his head to the ringing of chimes that must be made up of all the bells of lily-of-the-valley, the bells of spring flowers, bells made of porcelain, glass, water, air. (O.L.F.; 128)

Significantly, the narrator identifies with the murderer in the story, "hears" the reverberations of the murder, its implications for Notre-Dame. He *is* Notre-Dame-des-fleurs. Thus in an important way, "Notre-Dame-des-fleurs," a sobriquet inscribed with murder, self-sacrifice, and redemption, symbolizes the ultimate meaning of naming practices in *Notre-Dame-des-fleurs*. To the extent that naming in sobriquets destroys the other's identity, reduces difference to the opposite of the self in an economy of the "same," naming is tantamount to murder. Thus "ce meurtre va faire de lui, par vertu du baptême du sang, Notre-Dame-des-fleurs." Adrien Baillon becomes Notre-Dame-des-fleurs by sacrificing his personal identity on the altar of mimesis. This might explain why this name, rather than the name of the central character, Divine, became the title of the book.

Ironically, when Genet murders the other, the other as alter ego, he destroys a part of himself. As the image of Notre-Dame-des-fleurs merges with the identity of Divine, alias Louis Culafroy, and as Divine merges with Genet, murder and suicide become two faces of the same gesture.

(This figure would shape the ultimate meaning of murder in Genet's play *Les Bonnes*.)

The name "Divine" is a complicated figure for the adolescent trauma of homosexual rape, which caused Louis Culafroy to renounce his masculine identity and identify with women. Ironically, Culafroy's perversion also leads to his identification with the divine, but only after passing through the experience of death associated with violent sexual assault.

The story opens with the scene of Divine's death. The rest of the narration consists of a retrospection on a life viewed through its violent end. Genet describes Divine's death in a chain of far-fetched analogies which lead from sexual perversion to the divinity.

> Divine est morte hier au milieu d'une flaque si rouge de son sang vomi qu'en expirant elle eut l'illusion suprême que ce sang était l'équivalent visible du trou noir qu'un violon éventré, vu chez un juge à travers un bric à brac de pièces de conviction, désignait avec une insistance dramatique comme un Jésus le chancre doré où luit son Sacré-Coeur de flammes. Voilà donc le côté divin de sa mort. (N.D.F.; 11)

> Divine died yesterday in a pool of her vomited blood which was so red that, as she expired, she had the supreme illusion that this blood was the visible equivalent of the black hole which a gutted violin, seen in a judge's office in the midst of a hodge-podge of pieces of evidence, revealed with dramatic insistence, as does a Jesus the gilded chancre where gleams His flaming Sacred Heart. So much for the divine aspect of her death. (O.L.F.; 67)

The image of a gutted violin is central to the series of figures, "ce sang"—"le trou noir"—"le violon éventré"—"le chancre doré de Jésus," which leads to the association of Divine and the divinity. The term "violon" is also a condensation of several terms—*viol, violer,* and *voile*—which are formed by derivation and given specific meanings in other contexts in the narrative. These derivations also form a paradigm associating rape, castration, and death in the discourse.

The association of "violon" and the corpse of a child is implied later in a simile comparing a casket and a violin case. The argot term for casket, *étui à violon,* reinforces this association.

> Le village . . . où l'on enterrait des enfants mort-nés vers le soir, portés au cimetière par leurs soeurs dans les boîtes de sapin étroites et vernies comme des étuis à violon. (N.D.F.; 45)

> The village . . . where stillborn children were buried toward evening, carried to the cemetery by their sisters in pine boxes as narrow and varnished as violin cases. (O.L.F.; 154)

The comparison of two receptacles in the simile "boîtes comme des étuis," motivates the comparison of their contents, "enfants mort-nés"—"violons" by metonymical extension.

Culafroy understands the violence of language. Elsewhere in the novel he avoids naming his violin in the presence of his mother, because of its implication in the word "viol":

Culafroy fabriqua l'instrument mais devant Ernestine, plus il ne voulut dire le mot commençant par viol. (N.D.F.; 44)

The anagram "voile" is motivated by the idea of innocence and anticipates the seduction of young Culafroy by Alberto, the village rake ("veils were falling"):

Alberto mit posément, calmement, souverainement, sa main dans le fouillis de reptiles, et en ramena un, long et mince, dont la queue se plaqua, comme la corde d'un fouet, mais sans bruit, autour de son bras nu. 'Touche!', il dit, et en même temps amena la main de l'enfant sur le corps écaillé et glacé. . . . Le froid le surprit. Il lui entra dans la veine et l'initiation se poursuivit. *Des voiles tombaient.* (N.D.F.; 52, italics added)

The phallic imagery of the snakes overdetermines the sexual content of this scene of "initiation." The momentum and suspense created by the permutations of the word *violon* as one advances in the narrative culminate in the transformation of the noun form into the more aggressive verb form as Alberto "violates" Culafroy:

Alberto viola l'enfant de toutes parts. (N.D.F.; 53)

The act of rape reduces the victim to an object for another subject, robbing him of both his sexual identity and his being-for-himself in one violent action. Thus a complex figure of castration and death motivates the "divine" side of Louis Culafroy, who discovers that the road to saintliness is paved with self-renunciation.

Culafroy et Divine, aux goûts délicats, seront toujours contraints d'aimer ce qu'ils abhorrent, et cela constitue un peu leur sainteté, car c'est du renoncement. (N.D.F.; 52)

Culafroy and Divine, with their delicate tastes, will always be forced to love what they loathe, and this constitutes something of their saintliness, for that is renunciation. (O.L.F.; 170)

The figuration comes full circle as the dying Divine is compared to the Sacred Heart: "En expirant elle eut l'illusion suprême que ce sang était l'équivalent visible du trou noir qu'un violon éventré . . . désignait avec une insistance dramatique comme un Jésus le chancre doré où luit son Sacré-Coeur de flammes." The Sacred Heart symbolizes Christ's self-annihilation before a terrible God willing to sacrifice his son for an idea. The Sacred Heart figure also condenses the themes of guilt, love, and expiation in the single figure of the crucified Christ. This is a moving symbol for the tragedy of Divine's life, a life which she performed as a dead man.

When Culafroy renounces his identity to become an object for other men, he also buries his fear and hate of the other in a kind of passion play. Divine's lovers transform into godlike figures providing sexual union with God himself.

> Sa sainteté fut sa vue de Dieu et, plus haut encore, son union avec lui. (N.D.F.; 105)

> Saintliness was her vision of God and, higher still, her union with Him. (O.L.F.; 307)

The idea of homosexual rape is reiterated in word-play surrounding Divine's patronym, Culafroy. Homological derivations from "afroy" develop into variations on a theme beginning with "cul" (ass). These include *cul effroi* (fear), *cul à froid* (chilled), *(en)culé effroi* (fear of buggering), and so forth, and lead to the idea of fear with a homosexual fixation. The movement leading from Culafroy's sexual conversion to Divine's saintliness reminds one of Freud's famous case of Dr. Schreber, who hallucinated that he was having intercourse with God and being penetrated by sacred rays.[22] According to Freud, such hallucinations, and the extremes of idealization and degradation they represent, derive from extreme fear of the other or paranoia. For Schreber, as for Divine, fear of homosexual violence activates the drives of idealization and denial which twist the threat (of castration, of death) posed by the other into a blessing of divine origin. Thus Divine seeks to master his/her own victimization by reducing the other to an actor in his/her private drama.

Ironically, the movement of identification which assimilates otherness into a reflection of the subject fails to win for the subject any real mastery over the other and the threat of spiritual death which the other represents. Thus Culafroy/Divine repeatedly turns to suicide as a means of escape. The narrator's own drive to master the other by effacing difference parallels that of his character. Indeed, in the following passage, the narrator both destroys the difference between himself and the character, Culafroy, and plays at committing suicide:

> Le suicide fut sa grande préoccupation (le chant du gardénal). Certaines crises le mirent si près de la mort que je me demande comment il en réchappa, quel

choc imperceptible—et venant de qui?—le repoussa du bord. Mais un jour, *à portée de ma main*, se trouverait bien une fiole de poison qu'*il me suffirait* de porter *à ma bouche;* puis attendre. (N.D.F.; 25, italics added)

Suicide was his great preoccupation: the song of phenobarbital! Certain attacks brought him so close to death that I wonder how he escaped it, what imperceptible shock—coming from whom?—pushed him back from the brink. But one day there would be, within arm's reach, a phial of poison, and *I would have only to put it to my mouth;* and then to wait. (O.L.F.; 104, italics added)

In *Notre-Dame-des-fleurs*, sobriquets establish conflicts between the meaning of the name (the "expression") and the identity of the characters (the "indication"), a conflict which generates a series of paradigmatic oppositions such as good/evil, male/female, and so on. By tracing the path of associations leading from the name to the narrator, we discovered that rhetorical operations resolve such oppositions on the level of narrative discourse. Genet generates a synthesis of expression and indication by means of names, in order to force an illusion of the unity of narrative voice, a voice speaking in silence, immune to the threat of difference and death posed by the other. We discovered the futility of this strategy: the narrator directs the violence of metaphysical reduction in upon himself.

While in *Notre-Dame-des-fleurs* Genet speaks to himself in a kind of "inner speech," he nonetheless stages a problematic of identification and personal identity on the scene of silence, a problematic which would evolve into a deconstruction of narrative voice in the later novels.

Unlike sobriquets, highly indicative names such as patronyms, whose semantic motivation has been reduced through usage, open up the relation between namer and named to the spacing of two subjects in deixis.[23] To the extent that patronyms fail to create an image of the person named and point to the person named in the empirical context of discourse, patronyms expose more readily the difference between two autonomous subjects interacting in dialogue. By extension, this kind of naming practice looks death in the face rather than repressing it in an economy of identification.

Patronyms dominate naming practices in Genet's second novel, *Miracle de la rose*. Of all types of names, patronyms entail the greatest degree of reference to the code, since they involve the least amount of personal choice in the naming process and are not motivated by the idea of the person named. Since patronyms are inherited from the father and serve to register the individual in official records, patronyms symbolize the subject's existence for the state and society, rather than for specific individuals. Genet exploits this aspect of patronyms in *Miracle de la rose* in order to separate the narrator from the identities of characters in the story.

To some extent the setting of the narrative motivates the use of patronyms in this novel. At the central prison of Fontevrault, the prisoner has lost his personal identity and exists as a name on the registration books. It is noteworthy, however, that the characters use sobriquets and hypocoristics (names of endearment) with each other, and that only the narrator refers to them by their official names.

> Ils restaient une seconde saisis par l'horizon brusquement reculé, et se disaient bonsoir, de fenêtre à fenêtre. Ils connaissaient les diminutifs de leurs prénoms: 'Jeannot, Jo, Rico, Dédé, Polo' ou encore ces surnoms parfumés, légers et prêts à reprendre leur vol, posé sur les épaules des macs et qu'il me plaît de croire être des mots d'amour dont nous n'avions pas encore le secret à Mettray.... Alors flottaient, sous les étoiles, de la Centrale à Mettray: Princesse Milliard, La Corde au cou, Sous la dague, les Tarots de la bohémienne, La Sultane blonde. (M.R.; 110)

> They would stand there for a second, amazed at the suddenly withdrawn horizon, and they said good evening to each other from window to window. They knew the diminutives of each other's given name: 'Jeannot, Jo, Ricou, Dédé, Polo' and also those light, fragrant nicknames which were poised on the pimps' shoulders, ready to resume their flight, and which I like to think were words of love whose secret was still unknown to us at Mettray . . . Thus there floated beneath the stars, from Fontevrault to Mettray: Princess Billion, The Rope Around the Neck, Under the Dagger, The Gypsy's Tarots, the Blond Sultana. (M R.; 166)

The avoidance of sobriquets in *Miracle de la rose* is particularly noticeable, not only because the narrator says that sobriquets abound in the prison, but because this avoidance contrasts sharply with naming practices in the first novel, *Notre-Dame-des-fleurs*. The preference for patronyms symbolizes the narrator's disengagement from the feminine orientation of the earlier period, and a renunciation of his former infatuation with the *beaux voyous* who people the underworld.

> L'exacte vision qui faisait de moi un homme, c'est à dire un être vivant uniquement sur terre, correspondait à ceci que semblait cesser ma féminité ou l'ambiguïté de mes désirs mâles. (M.R.; 21)

Significantly, it is only to the extent that Genet has separated others from his personal fantasies that he can both become "a being living solely on earth" and realize his own masculine identity.

In *Miracle de la rose*, the kinds of rich rhetorical oppositions created by sobriquets in *Notre-Dame-des-fleurs* have been reduced to the single opposition of male and female. The males use patronyms, the effeminate types use sobriquets. Sobriquets, which served as tokens of passage in the queens' world, mark characters as targets of abuse in the virile world of this novel. The tough guys or "casseurs" dominate the narration and scorn the "cloches" or "females."

Genet recognizes differences between his and others' identities in the narration. The rare sobriquets in this novel describe some diegetic aspect of characters, an aspect recognized by other characters in the narration, rather than signify the narrator's projections. For example, "La Guêpe" refers to a thin, effeminate prisoner, Charlot. "Lou-du-Point-du-Jour" refers to a pederast. "Bijoux" names a jewel thief and "Bois-de-rose" names an effeminate guard. Genet nonetheless twists the meaning of sobriquets to conform to his own ideas about characters. In other words, he "re-motivates" names according to their function in narrative discourse.

When Genet uses "La Guêpe," The Wasp, to refer to Charlot, he develops not only the idea of a "fairy" having wings and "une taille de guêpe," but the idea of Charlot's sarcastic "sting," which provokes Genet to a fight.

Genet gives the name "Bijoux" to his friend Bulkaen when they first meet. Since he does not know the man's official name, Genet creates a name which identifies him with his crime. The granting of a sobriquet also symbolizes the character's sexual ambiguity ("Portait-il au fond de lui un pédé honteux et frétillant pareil au clodo piteux que tout le monde méprisait?" [M.R.; 19]). Genet elaborates upon an erotic meaning of "jewels": "Je vais t'en coller autant que tu voudras des bijoux" (M.R.; 89). Bulkaen pretends he likes this name only because it serves to disguise their clandestine correspondence from the guards. But in fact he enjoys the web of intimacy which the name creates with the namer, Genet.

"Bijoux" occurs only twice in the narrative, when the narrator explains its origin and when he explains he stopped using it for being "whorish": "Ça fait un peu catin" (M.R.; 48, 89). Thus on the level of discourse, Genet refuses the kind of intimacy that the name implies by referring to the character by his patronym.

Bulkaen gives himself another name, signing his love notes with "Illisible," Illegible. Genet in turn writes to Bulkaen as "Mon Illisible." While Bulkaen is referring to his own limitations as a writer, Genet pinpoints an aspect of his friend which describes their relationship. Since Bulkaen dies trying to escape from prison, his past life, his current allegiances, even his body remain a mystery to Genet. "Pierre Bulkaen restera pour moi l'indéchiffrable" (M.R.; 51).

Genet also targets an aspect of his friend which sums up the problem of naming in *Miracle de la rose*. Genet has discovered that others cannot be reduced to a meaning for the subject. While sobriquets permit the namer to appropriate the other by means of language, patronyms symbolize the distance between the namer and the person named. The "other," as subject-for-itself as well as for others, constitutes an unnamable movement of intersubjectivity. Thus Genet says he has no more names for Bulkaen: "Je ne le nomme plus."

The refusal of sobriquets in this novel parallels the more mature Genet's refusal to idealize the criminal world in poetic fantasy. Patronyms trace the pure difference separating subject and other along the lines of indication.

Je suis heureux d'avoir donné les plus beaux noms, les plus beaux titres (archange, enfant-soleil, ma nuit d'Espagne . . .) à tant de gosses admirables qu'il ne me reste plus rien pour magnifier Bulkaen. Peut-être pourrais-je le voir tel qu'il est, un voyou pâle et vif, si les mots ne s'en mêlaient pas trop, à moins que de rester solitaire, avec lui-même, innommable et innommé, le chargeait d'un pouvoir encore plus dangereux? (M.R.; 28)

I am glad to have given the loveliest names, the most beautiful titles (archangel, child-sun, my Spanish evening . . .) to so many youngsters that I have nothing left with which to magnify Bulkaen. Perhaps, if words do not get too much in the way, I shall be able to see him as he is, a pale, lively hoodlum, unless the fact of remaining solitary, alone with himself, unnamable and unnamed, charges him with an even more dangerous power. (M.R.; 36)

By refusing to appropriate the other in sobriquets, Genet exposes the the danger of the other for the subject. To the extent that Genet admits the subjectivity of the other, he must submit to the possibility of being an object for the other, a non-being. This explains the recurring identification of Genet with the fate of the *condamné à mort*, a character in the story and a symbol for the threat of death which the other represents.

The two other sobriquets "Lou-du Point-du Jour" and "Bois-de-rose" figure in this theme. "Lou Daybreak" is first of all a kind of feminine travesty veiling the character's thorny personality:

Le nom de Lou était une buée qui enveloppait toute sa personne, et, cette douceur franchie, quand on s'approchait de lui, quand on avait passé à travers son nom, on se déchirait à des ronces. (M.R.; 19)

Lou's name was a vapor that enveloped his entire person, and when you passed through his name, you scraped against the thorns, against the sharp, cunning branches with which he bristled. (M.F; 22)

This name also refers to the time of day when the condemned man, Harcamone, is executed. Genet gives the name this meaning after Lou disturbs the solemnity of Harcamone's death with a sarcastic remark.

Pour nous, pour Divers et moi, il était la personnification du moment fatidique, il était l'aube, le point du jour. Jamais jusqu'alors son nom n'avait une si exacte signification. (M.R.; 220)

To us, Divers and me, he was the personification of the fateful moment. He was dawn, daybreak. Never before had his name been so meaningful. (M.R.; 340)

"Bois-de-rose" exists, as a name and as a character, with reference to the destiny of the condemned man. Since the narrator mentions "cercueils de bois de rose" elsewhere in the novel (M.R.; 174), the association of rosewood with caskets suggests death and burial. Moreover, the guard who acquires this name exists in the narrative primarily as a vehicle for sealing Harcamone's fate. Harcamone kills "Bois-de-rose," "le gaffe insolent de douceur et de beauté qui l'avait fait le moins chier à Fontevrault" (M.R. 43) and so condemns himself to the guillotine. The name "Bois-de-rose" prefigures not only the death of the person named but the execution of his murderer.

The condemned man himself remains an untouchable symbol of pure difference. He has no sobriquet and no baptismal name. He is "Harcamone."

Traditionally, baptismal names symbolize the individual's inscription in the Christian faith and claim him or her as a child of God. The absence of baptismal names from *Miracle de la rose* symbolizes God's absence from the prison world. In Genet's reminiscences of childhood at the state institution of Mettray, the effacement of baptismal names symbolizes the utter depersonalization of the individual by the state. Boys are wards of the state, ignored by God and men. They are grouped together in artificial "families" according to the arbitrary order of the alphabet. The narrator argues that Mettray shaped the boys for lives of crime and destined them to perpetual incarceration at central prisons such as Fontevrault. Thus Genet mourns the absence of God from his adult world. "A Dieu je porte le deuil" (M.R.; 180).

As God is impossible in *Miracle*, so is love. Genet has ceased to people his world with gods and queens, has recognized the other as a dangerous reality. Thus desire takes the forms of cruelty and denial.

Je pressentais que mon amour était découvert. Je me vis en danger. Bulkaen se moquait de moi. J'étais joué. . . . Je tentais un dernier effort pour refermer sur moi une porte qui montrerait le secret de mon coeur. . . . Je répondis durement:
—Ton amitié? J'en ai rien à foutre, moi, de ton amitié. (M.R.; 50)

I had a feeling that my love had been discovered. I saw I was in danger. Bulkaen was kidding me. I was being made a fool of. . . . I made a final effort to lock myself in behind a door that might have revealed my heart's secret. . . . I therefore replied roughly: "Your friendship? Who the hell wants your friendship?" (M.R.; 70–71)

In reported speech, Genet calls Bulkaen "Pierrot," a hypocoristic implying intimacy and affection. Genet usually names him by his patronym, however, in narrative discourse. The substitution of the hypocoristic by the patronym calls attention to a change in the narrator's affections from the time of the story to the time of the narrating event.

When the narrator occasionally refers to Bulkaen as "Pierrot" in narrative discourse, such slips manifest a kind of Freudian return of the repressed and betray Genet's lingering yet denied attachment to his dead friend. Such slips and slides reflect the gradual breakdown of narrative voice into a being-for-itself and a being-for-others in the narration. The narrative no longer constitutes a mirror for the narrator's self-representation, but a play of reflections. As soon as we attempt to seize upon a profile of the narrator, the profile takes on the contours of another Jean Genet.

Ce livre est aussi traître que les systèmes de miroirs qui renvoient de vous l'image que vous n'aviez pas composée. (M.R.; 114)

This book . . . is as treacherous as the mirror systems that reflect the image of you which you did not compose. (M.R.; 172)

The difference between Genet's new identity and his identity for others in the narration, in prison, creates an insurmountable void between the here and now of narrative discourse and the non-present past of the narration. Genet is neither here nor there. He is "dead."

Ce nouveau visage du monde de la prison, j'eus le chagrin de le découvrir quand je m'aperçus que la prison était décidément l'endroit fermé, l'univers restreint, mesuré, où je devrais définitivement vivre . . . me sentant de si près participer à ce monde, le vôtre, au moment même que je conquérais les qualités grace auxquelles on peut y vivre. *Je suis donc mort.* (M.R.; 26, italics added)

And it grieved me to discover this new aspect of the prison world at a time when I was beginning to realize that prison was indeed the closed area, the confined, measured universe in which I ought to live permanently. . . . Since I feel so much a part of this world, it horrifies me to know that I am excluded from the other, yours, just when I was attaining the qualities by means of which one can live in it. *I am therefore dead.* (M.R.; 33–34, italics added)

Genet raises the question of death as a function of representation when he names the narrator of his novel "Jean Genet." Genet, the writer, is not the same as "Genet," the narrator, a semiotic function of narrative discourse. The identity of the names for author and narrator renders more acute the difference between these two sides of being, a difference masked by the traditional procedure of giving the narrator a fictional name.

The author of narrative is never equal to the "I" of the narrator.[24] Genet, the author, traces differences between the historical moment of writing the novels and "Genet's" experiences of narrating the action, in order to expose the difficulty inherent in self-representation. For example, while the narrator "Jean" produced the narration of Notre-Dame-des-fleurs in a single, continuous writing while awaiting his prison sentence, the author Jean Genet had to begin writing Notre-Dame-des-fleurs twice. The first fifty pages of the original writing were destroyed by a prison guard.[25] Moreover, Miracle de la rose was written at La Santé, Tourelles, if we are to believe the "author's" inscription at the end of the manuscript. The narration was produced, ostensibly, at Fontevrault. The narrator says he has just been transferred there from La Santé.[26] Pompes funèbres is narrated in the country, "auprès d'un monastère"; it was written in Paris. Is the autobiographical authority of the narrator thus a lie, or is the lie an essential ingredient of autobiography?

By using the autobiographical format within the narrative mode, by naming the narrator after himself and all the while leaving visible the artifices separating literature from biographical reality, Genet expands the figure of the divided subject beyond the limits of the doubled voice of narrative to a problematic of authorship. Just as the absence of the speaking subject is a condition of possibility of the utterance "I am," so the death or non-being of the author is necessary for the production of narrative discourse. ("My death is structurally necessary to the pronouncing of I.") Thus Genet describes the narrative as a hall of mirrors in which the subject speaks as a condemned man.

There are no sobriquets in Pompes funèbres, and most of the characters are named by their baptismal names or derivations of them, such as Paulo or Pierrot. Baptismal names are "empty signs," which signify nothing and merely point to their referents in the manner of indices. They resemble personal pronouns in this regard, and have a built-in reference to the subject and context of discourse. Moreover, unlike patronyms, which claim the individual for the state and the family, baptismal names trace a kind of pure intersubjectivity between individuals.

Since sobriquets are motivated by properties of the person named and shaped by the ideas of the person naming, it would appear as if sobriquets were more "poetic" than baptismal names or patronyms, and that naming therefore had a poetic function in Notre-Dame-des-fleurs, a novel dominated by sobriquets, but not in the other two novels. Though sobriquets may have a more obvious relation to poetry than other types of names, since they combine naming and meaning in a single rhetorical operation, sobriquets do not have an exclusive claim to the poetic function of naming in narrative. We saw that patronyms in Miracle de la rose opened up the question of authorial voice by exposing differences between the official identity of the writer and the semiotic function of the narrator. The poetic function of baptismal names and personal pronouns in *Pompes funèbres* will only be evident by first taking a new look at the very notion of "poetic function."

Structural theories concerning the literary uses of proper names focus on sobriquets and "motivated" patronyms, in which the name both indicates and signifies the person named. In critics such as Barthes, Genette, and others, names are poetic to the extent that they transcend their indexical function and mirror the signified.[27] Barthes calls this the "cratylean" character of names (and signs) in Proust.[28] It is noteworthy, moreover, that even Derrida, in his staging of Genet with Hegel in *Glas*, highlights names which signify meanings, in particular the sobriquets in *Notre-Dame-des-fleurs*.[29]

Structural poetics, modelled after the marriage of signifier and signified in the linguistic sign, privileges the closure of indication and expression in the poetic image, taking for granted the transcendental subject of poetic discourse.[30] As I show with regard to naming practices in *Pompes funèbres*, proper names, in conjunction with personal pronouns, have a poetic function by virtue of their very nature as indices. Genet's manipulation of proper names in this novel opens up the possibility of a new focus of poetics, a poetics built upon problems of subject-address and reference in deixis, a poetics of performance.

Jakobson situates baptismal names and personal pronouns in the group of duplex linguistic structures, because they not only serve to convey a message or "énoncé," but refer to the speech act or "énonciation."[31] Unlike the conventional signs which make up sobriquets (i.e., "fleurs") and which can usually conjure up some sort of mental image of a thing, baptismal names and personal pronouns are indices for the inscription of "person" in discourse. For instance, the referent for the name "John" is simply "the person named John" in the context. Personal pronouns are even more unstable since, within a given discourse, the referent can shift from one person to another. "He" might refer to John in one case and refer to some other character in another. The pronoun "I" defines the position of the speaker or subject of discourse and is defined by contrast with "you" the addressee of discourse. Since "I" and "you" are dialectically implicated in one another and can refer alternately to one or the other of two subjects engaged in communication, Jakobson calls them "shifters." While Jakobson excludes shifters from his discussion of the poetic function of language, a semiotics of performance would focus precisely on these aspects of discourse.[32]

In *Pompes funèbres* a system of baptismal names and personal pronouns moves the narrating subject through a series of masquerades, along the lines of deixis. Genet furthermore upsets the metaphysical assumptions of the present and presence of the subject to itself in deixis, by submitting subject-address and reference to the force of difference. Genet exploits the referential instability of indices in order to shift the position of the narrating subject from one identity to another in the narration. "I" becomes "he," "he" becomes "she," "she" becomes "I." Such shifts engender sexual, political, and existential conflicts in narrative discourse.

As soon as a referent for a name and its corresponding pronoun is established in the narration, it is undermined by a conscious shift in the referent from the objective position of a character to the subjective position of the narrator. "Je," the narrator Genet, trades places with "il," a character. For instance, "Erik" is the name of a German soldier sitting across from the narrator at the opening of the novel. Erik has murdered a boy, raped a militiaman, and lived with Hitler. The narrator at first clearly stages himself separately from the character in narrative space. Eventually, his fascination with Erik, the embodiment of evil, compels him to trade places with Erik in his imagination.

> Dès la première fois que je le vis, au sortir de l'appartement, je m'efforçai de remonter le courant de sa vie, et, pour plus d'efficacité, je rentrai dans son uniforme, dans ses bottes, dans sa peau. (P.F.; 27)

> When I left the apartment after our first meeting, I attempted to retrace the course of his life and, for greater efficiency, I got into his uniform, boots, and skin. (M.R.; 36)

The narrator suddenly becomes the referent for the name "Erik" and refers to Erik as "I" rather than "he." In other words, the referents for the name "Erik" and the personal pronouns "I" and "he" shift between two distinct identities in the narrative, the character and the narrator. This process becomes even more complicated as Genet proceeds to change places with first one and then another malevolent character in the narration.

The *movement* of the narrating subject *between* two identities, mapped by deictic indications in discourse (relations of reference and subject-address), contrasts sharply with the *identification* of the narrator *with* characters along the lines of rhetorical assimilation in *Notre-Dame-des-fleurs*. While the sobriquets in the earlier novel reduced characters to the other of the same, i.e., the narrator, baptismal names and personal pronouns in *Pompes funèbres* sustain the difference between subjects engaged in dialogue and permit the kind of role-playing so characteristic of Genet's theater. In the plays, characters are asked to assume the roles of others in the story while making clear the autonomy of their own identities. Thus the original duality produced by the autonomy of the actor from his role is doubled when the character him/herself adopts still another travesty.

The very notions of masquerade and travesty imply a doubling of identity into a subject for itself and its representation for others. To the extent that otherness is simply an extension of the "same," the work of artifice or masquerade disappears, leaving the figure of a unified, albeit ambiguous, subject of discourse. As I showed with regard to *Notre-Dame-des-fleurs*, ambiguity in and of itself does not constitute a divided subject, since ambiguity can be resolved by means of dialectical synthesis in narrative discourse. In *Pompes funèbres*, the articulation of difference between two subjects struggling for a place on the scene of silence anticipates Genet's unveiling of the masquerade forming theatrical performance.

Perhaps the distinction between *Notre-Dame-des-fleurs* and *Pompes funèbres* would be clearer with reference to Benveniste's categories for the tracing of "person" and "non-person" in narrative. The pronouns "I" and "you" belong to the first category and trace the movement of subject-address in discourse. "He" and "she" belong to the category "non-person" and refer to characters in the story. The movement between discourse and story is thus characterized by a movement between the categories of person and non-person, subject and other. In *Notre-Dame-des-fleurs*, sobriquets blurred distinctions between person and non-person in rhetorical figures. In the later novel, *Pompes funèbres*, Genet trades places with others in the narration, thus perverting the "normal" (dialectical) relation of subjects in discourse without reducing their difference.

In *Pompes funèbres*, the first person singular pronoun is situated in two time periods—in the discursive present, as the narrator refers to his experience of writing the story ("Je ne sais pas pourquoi il est nécessaire ici qu'Erik accomplisse un meurtre" [P.F.; 79]), and the historic past, as the narrator refers to his participation in the events of the narration. Shifts in the reference of "I" from the narrator to a character he names in the story are accompanied by shifts from the present tense of the discourse to the historic past of the narration. As Genet writes himself into scenes of crime, including murder, prostitution, and treason, he performs these actions as an other, acts "in the names of" characters in the narration. The theatricality of his masquerade helps him to conquer the fear of death which the other represents.

Take, for instance, the scene in which Erik shoots and kills an innocent boy. The narrator describes the action in the third-person objective voice; then he suddenly assumes the position of Erik by referring to him as "I" and, through Erik's persona, commits the murder himself.

Je ne sais pas encore pourquoi il est nécessaire ici qu'accomplisse un meurtre. . . . Pourtant si le meurtre de l'enfant n'est pas à sa place, c'est-à-dire placé selon un ordre logique justifiant sa présence dans le roman, je dois indiquer que *cet acte d'Erik* vient ici, à cet endroit même, parce qu'il s'impose à moi . . .

Un soir que *je me promenais* en dehors d'un petit village de France récemment conquis une pierre érafla le bas de mon pantalon. *Je crus à une attaque*

ou une insulte. . . . La peur d'abord et la colère d'avoir eu peur et un mouvement de peur, . . . et le fait d'avoir servi de cible à un Français, . . . me firent
arracher de l'étui mon revolver dont la main avait empoigné la crosse.
Je tirai. Je tirai trois coups. (P.F.; 79–81, italics added)

I still do not know why it is necessary for Erik to commit a murder at this
point. . . . However, if the murder of the child is out of place, that is, not in
accordance with a logical order that justifies its presence in the novel, I must
state that *this act of Erik's* comes in here, at this particular point, because it
forces itself on me. . . .

One evening, when *I was strolling* outside a small French village that had
recently been taken, a stone grazed the bottom of my trousers. *I thought* it
was an attack or an insult. . . . Fear and then anger at having been afraid and
reacting with fear in sight of a child's innocent eyes, and the fact of having
been a Frenchman's target . . . made me grab the grip of my revolver and tear
it from its holster. . . . (F.R.; 104–5, italics added)

I fired. I fired three shots. (F.R.; 104–5)

Just as abruptly, the position of the narrator shifts back to an objective
view of Erik leaving the scene of the murder:

Tenant, *dans ma main gauche immobile le long de mon corps,* mon calot
noir, et dans la droite, au bout du bras tendu, le revolver assez loin du corps,
lentement, dans mes bottes allemandes et mon pantalon noir gonflé d'effluves
de sueurs, de vapeurs bouclées, *je descendis dans la nuit,* vers la vie atroce
et consolant de tous les hommes. . . . Foulant des vaincus en sang, effrayé
non par le remords ni les sanctions possibles, mais par sa gloire, *Erik Seiler
rentra à la caserne.* (P.F.; 83, italics added)

Holding my black cap in my left hand, which hung motionless against my
body, and the revolver at the end of my outstretched right arm, rather far
from my body, I slowly went down into the night in my German boots and
my black trousers, which were swollen with sweaty effluvia and curly vapors,
and began moving toward the dreadful and comforting life of all men
. . . . Trampling on the bleeding vanquished, frightened not by remorse or
possible punishment but by his glory, *Erik Seiler returned to the barracks.*
(F.R.; 110, italics added)

The movement between "je" and "il," between I and he, generates a
movement between the subject of narrative discourse and the subject of
the narration, creating a paradigm of oppositions such as good/evil, male/
female, which is extended into the discourse. The figure je/il originates
early in the novel when the narrator renounces his hate of Erik, the symbolic murderer of Genet's friend, and relates to him on a first-name basis.

The scene occurs four days after the burial of Jean D., the narrator's
lover, whose death serves as a pretext for writing the novel. Jean D. was
a Resistance fighter killed during the Liberation of Paris. His mother has

invited Genet to pay a visit. Significantly, she is nameless and exists in the novel only as "la mère de Jean." In a discourse joining being and naming so intimately, the absence of a proper name signifies the narrator's supreme negation of this woman's existence, a negation of being more terrible than death. She is described as a mother who never loved her son. Moreover, she has the audacity to present to Genet her lover, Erik Seiler, a German soldier hiding from the liberating army. The narrator imagines him to be Hitler's lover as well. Jean D.'s mother forces an air of false *amitié* on the encounter by insisting that Genet drop the formal mode of address.

> Mais vous n'allez pas vous traiter de monsieur, dit la mère en riant. Voyons, vous êtes un ami. Et puis, c'est trop long. Ça oblige à des phrases interminables. (P.F.; 13)

> 'But you're not going to call each other Monsieur,' said the mother laughingly. 'After all, you're a friend. And besides, it's too long. It makes for endless formality.' (F.R.; 16)

The narrator agonizes over a situation which would force him to surrender his hate and accept the other, by means of the name.

> Etait-il possible que j'accepte sans déchirement dans ma vie intime un de ceux contre qui Jean avait combattu jusqu'à mourir? (P.F.; 13)

> Was it possible that in my personal life I was accepting without anguish one of those against whom Jean had fought to the death? (F.R.; 17)

Being on a first-name basis usually indicates a relation of familiarity, if not friendship, between namer and named in the France depicted in this story.[33] According to this convention, use of the first name, along with the devalorization of the patronym in discourse, should signal a rapport of intimacy between the narrator and the people he calls by name in the diegesis. This is indeed the case with Jean D. In this name the abbreviation of the patronym to a single initial is a deliberate effacement of the official identity of this character. The act of naming symbolizes Genet's intimacy with the person named.

As the use of baptismal names and their derivations is extended to include other characters in the narration, such as Erik and Paulo, Jean D.'s half-brother and a traitor, an ironic contrast is created between the narrator's (and the reader's) true appreciation of these characters and the intimacy implied in the use of first names. These characters are not friends of the narrator's, to say the least. Nor do they excite any sympathy in the reader. They personify the collective enemy who killed Jean D., a French patriot and the narrator's lover.

The polite masquerade which initiated the narrator's false intimacy with Erik generates a series of travesties in which Genet trades places with Erik, Paulo, and Hitler.

> Je m'enfonçai dans son passé, doucement d'abord, hésitant, cherchant la voie, quand, par hasard, une des ferrures de mon soulier buta contre le rebord du trottoir. Mon mollet vibra, puis tout mon corps. Je redressai la tête et sortis, les mains dans mes poches. *Je chaussai des bottes allemandes.* (P.F.; 27–28)

> I wormed my way into his past, gently and hesitantly at first, feeling my way, when the iron toe-plates of one of my shoes accidentally struck the curb. My calf vibrated, then my whole body. I raised my head and took my hands out of my pockets. I put on German boots. (F.R.; 36)

Ironically, Genet's determination to "s'enfoncer" into the pasts of Erik and Paulo has distinctly erotic motives which are clear in the double entendres in this passage (which escape the English translation) and in other descriptions of characters' erotic physiques. Experimenting with the masquerade, Genet enjoys imagining himself in sexual postures with the men that he hates (P.F.; 27).

Genet stages himself in erotic scenes involving Erik and a nameless "bourreau de Berlin," Erik and the *milicien* Riton, and Paulo and a pathetically comic figure of Hitler. These fantasies involve the narrator in even more complicated travesties, as he shifts positions between Erik and his partner, or between Paulo and his partners—between subject and object in an economy of desire. The movement between I and he also engenders oppositions between him and her. Homosexual desire submits the relation male/female to a dialectic of power in which the feminine constitutes the other of the "same", a castrated male. The narrator, who represents himself as the male in relations with Jean D., submits to this kind of castration as he projects himself into the lives of his characters. Erik is raped by the executioner of Berlin, Riton is raped by Erik, Paulo is raped by Hilter, and Hitler himself, forced into a "solitude glaciale et blanche," was literally castrated in the First World War (P.F.; 95).

While stepping into the shoes of another person usually symbolizes one's sympathy toward him or her, in this novel role-play allows the narrator to flirt with a kind of death or non-being. On the one hand, Genet claims to have realized the banality of crime and the necessity of virtue.

> On sait l'ordre contenu dans ma douleur: faire ce qui est bien. Mon goût de la solitude m'incitait à rechercher les terres les plus vierges, après ma déconvenue en vue des rivages fabuleux du mal ce goût m'oblige à faire marche en arrière et m'adonner au bien. (P.F.; 126)

> We know the command contained in my grief: do what is good. My taste for solitude impelled me to seek the most virgin lands. After my disappointing

setback in sight of the fabulous shores of evil this taste obliges me to turn back and devote myself to good. (F.R.; 169)

On the other hand, by trading places with Erik, Paulo, and other personifications of evil in the novel, Genet implicates himself in a moral and political stance contrary to his own. Such shifts cannot be reduced to a figure for the psychological ambivalence of the narrator, since they move the narrating subject between two separate identities in narrative performance. These shifts articulate the difference between I and other in terms of conflicting names and personal characteristics. In a similar fashion, costume, gesture, and voice help us to distinguish the various layers of travesty at work in Genet's theater.

In *Pompes funèbres* Genet has moved beyond the existential problem of death as the erasure of the author in narrative voice, and stages the game of life and death along the lines of a problematic of masquerade. By stepping into the shoes of his characters, Genet plays at being a dead man in order to celebrate death as a condition of possibility of life. By acting out the dangerous game of being and non-being on the stage of first-person narrative, Genet discovers a means of putting to rest his dead friend, of whom he says, "Je suis son tombeau" (P.F.; 24). But more importantly, he discovers means for engaging the spectre of death by means of performance.

When Genet transgresses the distance separating subject and object of discourse, when "I" suddenly becomes confused with "he," Genet exposes an original division of the speaking subject into a being-for-itself and a being-for-others, a division which precedes its identification by means of the name. By perverting deictic markings for subject into traces for the object of discourse, Genet stages the endless movement of difference between the self and its other which is, indeed, "unnamable."[34] He thus performs a kind of funeral rite on the transcendental subject of metaphysics.

In *Pompes funèbres* Genet also discovers the power of literature to implicate the reader in the narration.[35] Taking advantage of the intersubjective contract binding "I" and "you" in discourse, Genet implicates the reader in the masquerade. Early in the novel, Genet scorns the French for the righteousness of their outrage following the Liberation.

Les journaux qui parurent à la Libération de Paris, en août 1944, dirent assez ce que furent ces journées d'héroïsme puéril, quand le corps fumait de bravoure et d'audace. . . . Peu de temps après, ces journaux rappelleront les massacres hitlériens, les jeux que d'autres appellent sadiques, d'une police qui recrutait ses tortionnaires parmi les Français. (P.F.; 9)

The newspapers that appeared at the time of the Liberation of Paris, in August, 1944, give a fair idea of what those days of childish heroism, when the body

was steaming with bravura and boldness, were really like. . . . Shortly thereafter, these papers bring before us the Hitlerian massacres and the games,
which others call sadistic, of a police that recruited its torturers from among
the French. (F.R.; 11)

"Que d' autres appellent sadiques. . . . " Here Genet subverts the traditional opposition between good and evil in the discourse and questions
the historical distinction between the innocent and the guilty parties in
the atrocities of war. In the various references to "vous," the reader of
the narration, the reader is associated with the side of righteous bourgeois
morality and is placed in the position of judge before the events of the
narration. The narrator posits his own morality as something apart from
that of the reader, when he says, for instance,

Jusqu'à la dernière fraction de seconde il m'est cher qu'il continue par la
destruction, le meurtre—bref *le mal selon vous*. (P.F.; 120, italics added)

I'm keen on his continuing until the last fraction of a second, by destruction,
murder—in short, evil according to you. (F.R.; 160)

Ironically, as Genet says elsewhere, "The times have accustomed us
to such rapid transformations of gangsters into cops, and vice versa" (P.F.;
127), that the difference between judge and accused has been blurred.
Likewise, the reader is no longer in the position of judge reviewing the
events of the narration as the actions of others, but of the accused, implicated in those events by means of the intrication of "I" and "you" in
narrative discourse. When Genet points out the private acts of treason
performed by the French themselves, as he "pays homage" to the cham-
pions of evil and commits crimes in their names, he makes the reader
both a witness to the irony of the discourse and a target of that irony.
Genet addresses the reader in the second person in order to expose the
reader's complicity in his experiments with crime and his intercourse
with the devil.[36]

In his literary travesties, Genet both perverts normal relations between
"I" and "you" and suspends the presence and present, the "here" and
"now" of discourse, by placing the other there where "I" ought to be.
Genet thus stages the masquerade in first-person narrative by means of
a problematic of deixis. This kind of problematic would ultimately shape
relations between actors, their roles and the roles played by characters in
Genet's theater.

The question of deixis has received considerable attention in recent
semiotic research, mainly with reference to theories of theater and
drama.[37] Keir Elam, summarizing the prevailing scholarship, says,

Deixis is immensely important to the drama, . . . being the primary means whereby language gears itself to the speaker and receiver (through the personal pronouns 'I' and 'you') and to the time and place of the action (through the adverbs 'here' and 'now', etc.), as well as to the supposed physical environment at large and the objects that fill it (through the demonstratives 'this' and 'that', etc.). (*The Semiotics of Theater and Drama*, pp. 26–27)

In such statements, Elam and other scholars obscure something of the difficulty of deixis within a theory of performance, since performance challenges the very notion of the presence of the subject to itself in the immediacy of representation. Furthermore, when semiologists insist upon the particular importance of deixis for a semiotics of theater, they overlook the role of deixis in staging the subject of contemporary fiction.

This oversight stems from the philosophical assumption that a unity of "I" and "you" in the "here" and "now" of discourse transcends the spacing of deixis in poetic discourse—a metaphysical stance which underlies the seminal work of Emile Benveniste. When Benveniste charts current directions in semiotics by considering "Man's place in language," he privileges the moment in which the speaking subject is held as a unity in discourse. I speak, therefore I am. Benveniste also overlooks the problem of gender difference in the constitution of "I" in his discussion of the human dimension of discourse. Furthermore, this philosophical position shapes Benveniste's rapprochement of linguistics and poetics. Take, for instance, his interpretation of the poetic structure of difference in Rimbaud:

In effect, one characteristic of the persons 'I' and 'you' is their 'oneness': the 'I' who states, the 'you' to whom 'I' addresses himself are unique each time. But 'he' can be an infinite number of subjects—or none. That is why Rimbaud's 'je est un autre [I is another]' represents the typical expression of what is properly mental 'alienation', in which the 'I' is dispossessed of its constitutive identity.[38]

By reading Rimbaud's statement as a figure for mental alienation, Benveniste eliminates the spatial dimensions of the subject/other relation in favor of a single, albeit ambivalent meaning which transcends this relation. He thus reduces the movement of difference between I and what I is not to the dialectical synthesis of two sides of the "same."

By defining semiosis as an act which negotiates the division of the subject into a being-for-itself and a being-for others in discourse, we begin to understand both the meaning of Rimbaud's statement and its implications for poetic theory. When Rimbaud declared that "I is an other," he shook the metaphysical foundations of Romanticism and the cult of individual creativity by exposing a movement of performance in poetic discourse. I speak, therefore I am immediately taken up in a representation for others: I am-not. It is with reference to this original division of the speaking subject on the stage of silence that Rimbaud anticipated the place of performance in Genet's poetics, and signalled something of the importance of theater and drama for situating "Man" in language.

TWO

The Discourse of the Other

The contributions of Mikhail Mikhailovich Bakhtin to the theory of the novel take the notion of performance outside the strictly linguistic realm and situate it within the broader question of man's place in literary discourse. Bakhtin defines the "book", i.e., the text, as a "verbal performance in print, . . . calculated for active perception, involving attentive reading and inner responsiveness, and for organized, *printed reaction*" (*Marxism and the Philosophy of Language*; p. 95, Bakhtin's italics). For Bakhtin the narrative text constitutes a performance in the sense that it brings together multiple voices speaking in dialogue, thus implicating the speaking and reading subject in a play of difference with its "others."

Reading Genet with Bakhtin, we not only situate their discourses in a philosophical dialogue which transcends their historical and biographical differences, but discover means of accounting for the evolution of Genet's famous "theater of the double"[1] out of his work with narrative point of view. Structural theories of narrative, modelled after the closure of signifier and signified in the linguistic sign, preclude considerations of relations between the cinematic, the dramatic, and the narrative modes of representation, since such theories are based on the material and semiotic specificity of each mode as autonomous system. It was Hjelmslev who claimed that a "scientific" (i.e., semiotic) approach to the text must begin with the segmentation of discourse into minimal units structured according to the dialectical imbrication of the form of meaning and the form of the material of the expression.[2]

While Bakhtin was not to obtain the attentive reading and "organized printed reaction" of others in his lifetime, his ongoing debate with Russian Formalism, from the 1930s to the 1970s, has profound and urgent implications for contemporary theory and criticism. The problem of the subject's relation to others' discourse places literary theory within larger debates concerning the ideological and psychological effects of social structures, including narrative, on the constitution of the speaking subject. A dangerous project indeed, one which exposed Bakhtin and his circle to the cruel and blatant censorship of Soviet authorities under Stalin.[3]

The danger of Bakhtin's theory for totalitarian ideology lies in the subversive notion that discourse is the field of an ongoing struggle between subject and others in language, a struggle for personal freedom. While Russian Formalism and Socialist Realism negotiate relations between art and politics in terms of revolutionary form and socialist content, respectively, Bakhtin views literature in terms of the liberation of the subject of dominant discourse. Literature is revolutionary to the extent that it heightens awareness of the subject's binding inscription in cultural and ideological discourses.

> The tendency to assimilate others' discourse takes on an even deeper and more basic significance in an individual's ideological becoming, in the most fundamental sense. Another's discourse performs here no longer as information, directions, rules, models and so forth—but strives rather to determine the very bases of our ideological interrelations with the world, the very basis of our behaviour; it performs here as *authoritative discourse*, and an *internally persuasive discourse*. (*The Dialogic Imagination*; p. 342., Bakhtin's italics)[4]

Dostoevsky remained an important preoccupation of Bakhtin's throughout his career. Dostoevsky, according to Bakhtin, aimed to destabilize the authority of narrative voice over the narration by integrating the voices of characters, distinguished by contrasting speech styles, into narrative discourse. Dostoevsky, according to Bakhtin, invented the "polyphonic" novel, a new form in which the characters emerge as equal participants, as subjects, alongside the subjectivity of the author.[5] In this way, Dostoevsky replaces the monologic order of single-voiced discourse with the dialogic interaction of voices speaking in heteroglossia. Heteroglossia in narrative

> opens up the possibility of never having to define oneself in language, the possibility of translating one's own intentions from one linguistic system to another, of fusing 'the language of truth' with 'the language of everyday' . . . of saying 'I am me' in someone else's language, and in my own language, 'I am other'. (*The Dialogic Imagination*; p. 315)

Jean Genet carries out Bakhtin's project in the realm of literary creation. While Bakhtin wrote within the prison-house of political censorship, Genet wrote the early novels in prison, managing to publish them through friends on the outside. These novels, originally published by Marc Barbézat, were in turn censored by Gallimard in the later, standard edition of the (incomplete) *Oeuvres complètes* of Genet.

Furthermore, Genet is a kind of literary kin of Bakhtin's because he struggled throughout his life with the existential problem of freedom by engaging the question of others' discourse in the constitution of one's personal identity. In the novels, Genet addresses the issue of freedom in the form of a problematic of reported speech. In *Notre-Dame-des-fleurs*,

Miracle de la rose, and *Pompes funèbres,* Genet challenges the unifying authority of the author/narrator over the narration by replacing narrative voice with the doubled discourse of an actor playing narrator. Genet places the speaking subject on stage as the focus of literary discourse, destroying in turn a coherent representation of diegetic reality. Moreover, he threatens the linguistic authority of standard French by elevating subversive speech styles such as criminal argot and profane language to the level of poetry.

Bakhtin's debate with the means and ends of Russian Formalism has important implications for the study of writers such as Genet. Bakhtin criticizes the metaphysical orientation of formalism, which privileges the study of morphology at the expense of contextuality. The critic's task is to examine the production of the speaking subject in dialogic interaction with others' discourse, rather than to describe the work as a self-contained, closed system.[6]

Russian Formalists, including Shklovsky, Tomashevsky and Jakobson, built a poetics around those aspects of language, such as sound patterns and rhythms, which contribute to the internal closure of form and meaning in poetry.[7] Still other Formalists, such as Propp, strove for a scientific study of interrelations between the various levels of literary discourse, from the reiteration of sounds to the structure of plot to the global system of the work.[8] In this framework, discourse is poetic to the extent that the form mirrors the content of the message.

Jakobson led the development of Russian Formalism into the great formalist movements of the twentieth century, including the structuralism of the Prague School in the 1930s, and a particularly French version of structuralism in the 1950s and 60s. It is worth noting that the "structuralism" of the Prague School estheticians contains threads of a problematic of the speaking subject of discourse, and that this problematic was gradually erased as structuralism reached the Cartesian fields of French intellectual activity.[9] Structural poetics has come to be identified with French structuralism, whose debt to Jakobson cannot be overstated. Jakobson defined the "poetic function" of language with reference to structural linguistics, as the projection of the axis of similarity, the "paradigmatic" axis, onto the axis of contiguity or the "syntagmatic axis."

Bakhtin and his circle criticized the monologic order of the poetics of formalism, of language turned in upon itself in a closed system. He replaced the linguistic model with a problematic of the socially constituted subject of literary discourse.

> Language as a stable system of normatively identical forms is merely a scientific abstraction, productive only in connection with certain particular practical and theoretical goals. This abstraction is not adequate to the concrete reality of language. (*Marxism and the Philosophy of Language;* p. 98)

Moreover, Bakhtin shifted the focus of poetics and stylistics away from the structural system of the work to the interaction of voices speaking in narrative. Narrative, not poetry, becomes the model for a poetics which takes account of the speaking subject of discourse.

> Stylistics must be based not only, and *even not as much*, on linguistics as on *metalinguistics*, which studies the word not in a system of language and not in a 'text' excised from dialogic interaction, but precisely within the sphere of dialogic interaction itself, that is, in that sphere where discourse lives an authentic life. (*Problems of Dostoevsky's Poetics*; p. 202, Bakhtin's italics)

A major contribution of Bakhtin's was to distinguish narrative from the Aristotelian categories of poetic discourse, including drama and epic poetry. In this sense Bakhtin diverged from the Aristotelian slant of Formalists such as Propp, who focussed on plot structure as a perfect system of interrelated parts, the basis of mimesis.[10] Bakhtin focussed instead on the dialogical imbrication of the discourse of the narrator and the discourses of characters speaking in the story. "The novel can be defined as a diversity of social speech types (sometimes even a diversity of languages) and a diversity of individual voices, artistically organized" (*The Dialogic Imagination*; p. 262). Bakhtin not only differentiates narrative from the mixed form of the epic, the Aristotelian category characterized by the alternation of diegesis and mimesis, but also places in question the very opposition of mimesis and diegesis as means of defining poetic forms.

What characterizes the novel is neither the direct imitation of characters speaking in the story, nor the indirect narration of actions in the diegesis, but the dynamic of alterity produced by the interpenetration of multiple discourses. Thus narrative stages the performance of a divided subject engaged in the drama of self-representation. In his various works Bakhtin foregrounds the figure of the double as the major characteristic of the novel from its earliest forms.

> Heteroglossia, once incorporated into the novel . . . is another's speech in another's language, serving to express authorial intentions but in a refracted way. . . . Such speech constitutes a special kind of double-voiced discourse. In such discourse there are two voices, two meanings and two expressions. And all the while these voices are dialogically interrelated, they—as it were—know about each other . . . it is as if they actually hold a conversation with each other. (*The Dialogic Imagination*; p. 324)

The double is represented by means of heteroglossia, defining differences between speech styles of discourses brought together in narrative. Bakhtin distinguishes dialogism from dialogue per se, which, in everyday conversation or dramatic dialogue involves not the intrication of subject and other in a single, doubled discourse, but the interaction of two autonomous subjects in separate discourses.

> We are dealing with words reacting on words. However, this phenomenon is distinctly and fundamentally different from dialogue. In dialogue, the lines of the individual participants are grammatically disconnected; they are not integrated into one unified context. Indeed, how could they be? *There are no syntactic forms with which to build a unity of dialogue.* If, on the other hand, a dialogue is presented as embedded in an authorial context, then we have a case of direct discourse, one of the variants of the phenomenon with which we are dealing in this inquiry.
>
> (*Marxism and the Philosophy of Language;* p. 116, Bakhtin's italics)

The dialogic principle demonstrates the difficulty of situating narrative in the Aristotelian order of mimesis. Narrative discourse, inscribed in narration by means of figures of speech and markings for the first person and present tense of the verb, imitates the speech of the narrator. Narrative discourse, however, both imitates the narrator and includes traces of characters speaking in the story, either in the form of indirect discourse or reported speech. Likewise, reported speech and indirect discourse imitate character (speech), but also include traces of the narrator producing the narration. In this way direct discourse in the novel circumscribes mimetic closure between speech and speaker, and exposes a duality between the diegetic context of reported speech and the here and now of narrative discourse. The speaking subject of narrative, thus taken up in a movement between narrated space/time and narrating space/time, becomes a representation for another subject in narrative mise-en-scène. This movement constitutes a performative aspect of the novel which eludes classical poetics.

Bakhtin's disintrication of the novel from the monologic order of classical mimesis both anticipates and resolves certain problems facing structural poetics in the 1960s. Structuralist debates foreground the difficulty of situating the novel in the framework of classical poetics, citing the problematic relation between mimetic and diegetic functions of narrative. In "Frontières du récit," Gérard Genette examines the classical distinctions between narrative and dramatic poetry.[11] Genette points out that while Plato, in the *Republic*, and Aristotle, in the *Poetics*, diverge with regard to their classifications of diegesis and mimesis, they both oppose dramatic form to narrative and privilege drama with being more imitative than narrative. Plato defines mimesis and diegesis as two styles of discourse, the former consisting of the imitation of the discourses of characters in reported speech, the latter consisting of the narration of events by a narrator speaking in his own voice.[12] Aristotle defines diegesis as a form of imitation, the indirect imitation of nonverbal events in speech.

Direct imitation consists of the dramatic representation of speech on stage.

Genette does not mention that while Aristotle recognized the performances of actors as a form of direct imitation, he excluded performance per se from the realm of poetics, since performance does not belong to the strictly verbal realm of the poet. Thus in Aristotle, mimesis defines the direct representation of speeches of characters, diegesis defines the indirect representation of actions by means of words. In both Plato and Aristotle the distinction between mimesis and diegesis not only serves to distinguish drama from narrative but distinguishes between the two aspects of the "mixed" or epic form, in which the narrator periodically quotes the discourses of characters in the diegesis.

Genette argues that the classical definitions of mimesis and diegesis obscure the ontological unity between reported speech and its object, speech. For Genette, since reported speech does not actually *imitate* speech (in which case there would be a dialectical relation between signifier and signified), but simply *is* speech, reported speech does not belong to the order of mimesis. Narrative "representation" is presentation. Genette concludes that the only form of representation which escapes the circularity of reported speech is narrative discourse, the verbal representation of nonverbal events: "Mimésis, c'est diégésis."[13]

Thus Genette claims that speech transcends representation as such, by being ontologically bound to the voice of the speaker. In this and other essays in *Figures II* (such as "Proust et le langage indirect"), Genette's approach to poetics reflects the monologic turn of French structuralism. Authors such as Genette, Todorov,[14] and Barthes[15] posit an original closure between sound and meaning in single-voiced discourse by modelling poetic systems after the structure of meaning in the sentence.

Since structural theories of narrative foreclose considerations of an original duality of the speaking subject as it performs for others, they fail to account for the philosophical slant of authors such as Genet, who posit an alienated, divided subject in the position of narrator. In Genet's novels, narrative discourse not only creates an image of the narrator, but includes the discourse of characters. Reported speech not only produces an image of characters, but refers back to the narrator. Differences between speech styles of speakers in the narration represent the movement between the discourse of the narrating I and the discourse of the other, between the representation of the speaker and reference to the diegetic context. This disjunction systematically erodes any pretentions to narrative unity and reveals the masquerade at play in the reader's inscription in narrative. If the narrator wears a mask in order to represent character, for example, the mask intrudes into the reader's relation to the narrator. The doubled voice of the narrator is thus mirrored in the troubled identification of the reader with the narration. In this way Genet introduces the problem of the double into narrative.

In Genet, narrative is neither the representaton of nonverbal events by means of language, nor the direct imitation of living speech in direct discourse, but the staging of a dialogue between subject and others in narrative space. To the extent that representation constitutes the subject as something for another subject, representation, in the novel or in the theater, is a product of performance rather than simply a mirror for transcendent realities.

In *Notre-Dame-des-fleurs*, *Miracle de la rose*, and *Pompes funèbres*, the narrator calls himself Jean Genet, addresses the reader in the first person, and reflects upon his most intimate experiences in and out of prison, in the present and imperfect tenses of the verb. Such aspects are the most obvious instances of the narrator's self-representation, but not the only ones. Narrative discourse is also marked in figures of speech and personal commentary about the characters or events of the story.[16]

In Genet, reported speech incorporates traces of narrative discourse in the same way personal commentary and figures of speech inscribe narrative discourse into third-person narration. The narrator focusses attention on the speech of characters as verbal constructs, as both traces of his creative hand in the production of character and seeds for the production of narrative discourse. In this way Genet defines narrative representation as a problematic of identification and imbrication between discourses, thereby challenging the Aristotelian ideal of mimetic closure between discourse and the speaking subject.

Genet takes advantage of differences between argot, standard French, foreign languages, and personal idiolects in order to show the participation of reported speech in narrative discourse. Contrasts between argot and standard French prevail. In *Notre-Dame-des-fleurs* and *Miracle de la rose* in particular, the world seems to be divided between speakers and nonspeakers of the *argot des malfaiteurs*. Though criminal argot no longer constitutes an impenetrable linguistic "cover," it remains an unmistakable indicator of social identity. The perversion of standard French through prefixing, suffixing, and semantic inversion and derivation follows rules available only to the initiate.[17] Unlike French novelists of the nineteenth century such as Balzac, Hugo, and Sue, who used argot in reported speech mainly to add local color and plausibility to the representation of character,[18] Genet exploits contrasts between the speech styles of characters in order to represent a struggle between the speaking subject and the discourse of authority. In Genet the quest for personal freedom is first and foremost a question of the power of language to form the individual as social subject. For this reason, very little happens in his novels. The drama of the subject is played out directly by means of a focus on the dialogic aspect of discourse, on discourse as action rather than as bearer of meaning.[19]

The relation between the narrator's discourse and discourses of characters evolves from one novel to the next. In the early work, *Notre-Dame-*

des-fleurs, the narrator regularly integrates the speech styles of characters into his speech. In *Miracle de la rose* the narrator addresses the question of his autonomy from his characters, submitting his discourse less and less to the influence of other speech styles. By *Pompes funèbres*, the narrator has not only eliminated others' speech from his own discourse, but periodically replaces character speech with his own speech style. In this way Genet reveals the play of masks underlying mimesis in the novel, just as he would later expose the double at the origin of theatrical representation.

In *Notre-Dame-des-fleurs* criminal argot characterizes the initiate of the fraternity of thugs (*les mecs*) and pimps (*les macs*). Far from marking the speaker as a social outcast, in the criminal milieu of this novel, argot constitutes an enviable linguistic gift, an ideal which the narrator, looking in on this world, hopes to attain. In the following passage, the narrator reports with awe the discourse of a prisoner describing his seduction by another man. The violence done to standard French in the argot passages has disappeared in the English translation. As Genet has said, the *argot des mâles* cannot be properly translated:

> Comment qu'j'ai commencé d'l'avoir à la bonne? C't en tôle. Le soir on devait se défringuer, enlever même la liquette devant l'gaffe pour lui faire voir qu'on ne passait rien en loucedé (ni cordelettes, limes ou lames). Alors, avec le p'tit mec on était tous les deux à poil. J'ai zieuté de son côté pour voir si l'était aussi musclé qui l'dit. J'ai pas eu le temps de bien voir, on gelait. L'a fait presto pour s'rhabiller. Juste j'ai eu le temps de viser qu'il était bath! Ah! qu'est-ce que j'ai pris dans l'oeil (une douche de roses!) Alors mes amis j'ai été jalmince. Parole! J'ai eu mon compte. . . . Ç'a duré un moment, quatre ou cinq jours. . . . (N. D. F.; 23)

> How I started getting a crush on him? We were in the jug. At night we had to undress, even take off our shirts in front of the guard to show him we weren't hiding any thing (ropes, files, or blades). So the little guy and me were both naked. So I took a squint at him to see if he had muscles like he said. I didn't have time to get a good look because it was freezing. He got dressed again quick. I just had time to see he was pretty great. Man, did I get an eyeful (a shower of roses!). I was hooked. I swear! I got mine (here one expects, inescapably: I knocked myself out). It lasted a while, four or five days. (O. L. F.; 98)

Argot is an extension of the virile dress and physical posture expected of a true *mac*, such as Mignon-les-Petits-Pieds. Contemplating his reflection in a department store window, Mignon sees the embodiment of an underworld hero.

> Il vit ce Mignon vêtu d'un costume Prince de Galles, chapeau mou sur l'oeil, épaules immobiles (qu'il garde ainsi en marchant pour ressembler à Polo-la-Vache et Polo pour ressembler à Tioui et ainsi de suite; une théorie de macs

purs, sévèrement irréprochables aboutit à Mignon-les-Petits-Pieds, faux-jeton, et il semble que de s'être frotté à eux, de leur avoir dérobé l'allure, il les ait— vous diriez souillés de sa propre abjection, je le veux ainsi pour ma joie), gourmette au poignet, cravate souple comme une langue de feu, et ces extraordinaires chaussures qui ne sont qu'aux macs, jaune très clair, fines, pointues. (N. D. F.; 20)

He saw this Darling wearing a glen plaid suit, a felt hat over one eye, his shoulders stiff, and when he walks he holds them like that so as to resemble Sebastopol Pete, and Pete holds them like that so as to resemble Pauley the Rat, and Pauley to resemble Teewee, and so on; a procession of pure, irreproachable pimps leads to Darling Daintyfoot, the double crosser, and it seems that as a result of having rubbed against them and stolen their bearing, he has, you might say, soiled them with his own abjection; that's how I want him to be, for my delight, with a chain on his wrist, a tie as fluid as a tongue of flame, and those extraordinary shoes which are meant only for pimps— very light tan, narrow and pointed. (O. L. F.; 92)

Genet's cast of male characters divides according to specific codes governing male and female role-playing. More than any of his physical trappings, argot in Mignon's speech determines his virility. Argot is "la langue mâle" and a secondary sex trait.

Ainsi que chez les Caraïbes la langue des hommes [l'argot] devenait un attribut sexuel secondaire.... Tout le monde pouvait le comprendre, mais seule le pouvait parler les hommes qui, à leur naissance, ont reçu en donne les gestes, le port des hanches, les jambes, et les bras, les yeux, la poitrine, avec lesquels on peut le parler. (N. D. F.; 24)

Slang was for men. It was the male tongue. Like the language of men among the Caribees, it became a secondary sexual attribute. It was like the colored plumage of male birds, like the multicolored silk garments which are the prerogative of the warriors of the tribe. It was a crest and spurs. Everyone could understand it, but the only ones who could speak it were the men who at birth received as a gift the gestures, the carriage of the hips, legs and arms, the eyes, the chest, with which one can speak it. (O. L. F.; 100)

Louis Culafroy, alias Divine, would not dare to speak like the macs, any more than Mignon would speak like the queens, "les tantes." The virility of argot shakes Divine's sensitive nature. She would not speak the male tongue any more than she would assume any of the other visible trappings of the pimps: "L'argot, pas plus que les autres filles ses copines, Divine ne le parlait. Cela l'eût bouleversée autant que pousser avec sa langue et ses dents un coup de sifflet voyou.... " (N. D. F.; 23). The identification of argot with the male sex also excites her. Unravelling Mignon's speech, Divine seems already to be making love to him. "Il lui semblait qu'elle déboutonnait une braguette, que sa main introduite soulevait la chemise" (N. D. F.; 24):

The queens have their own speech style, which contributes to their travesties as surely as the costumes they wear and the poses they assume. In a typical conversation between queens, words are extensions of physical gestures, indeed substitutes for movement:

> Quand elles avaient à exprimer un sentiment qui risquait d'amener l'exubérance du geste ou de la voix, les tantes se contentaient de dire: 'Je suis la Toute Toute', sur un ton confidentiel, presque de murmure, souligné d'un petit mouvement de leur main baguée qui apaisait une tempête invisible. (N. D. F.; 32)

> When they had to express a feeling that risked involving an exuberance of gesture or voice, the queens contented themselves with saying: 'I'm the Quite-Quite,' in a confidential tone, almost a murmur, heightened by a slight movement of their ringed hand which calms an invisible storm. (O. L. F.; 121)

> —Je suis bien sûr, sûr, sûr, la Toute Dévergondée!
> —Ah! Mesdames, quelle gourgandine je fais.
> —Tu sais (le *us* filait si longtemps qu'on ne percevait que lui), *tussé*, je suis la Consumée-d'Affliction.
> —Voici, voici, regardez la Toute-Frou-frouteuse.
> . . . Puis, peu à peu, elles s'étaient comprises en se disant: 'Je suis la Toute Toute', et enfin: 'Je suis la T' T'. (N. D. F.; 32–33)

> 'I really am, sure sure sure, the Quite-Profligate.'
> 'Oh Ladies, I'm acting like such a harlot.'
> 'You know (the *ou* was so drawn out that that was all one noticed), *yoou-know*, I'm the Consumed-with-Affliction.'
> 'Here here, behold the Quite-Fluff-Fluff.'
> . . . Then, little by little, they understood each other by saying, 'I'm the Quite-Quite,' and finally: 'I'm the Q'-Q'.'(O. L. F.; 122)

The constative function of such discourses is minimal.[20] Like religious litanies, whose cathartic function derives from a formula for redundancy which reduces the information of a given utterance to the barest minimum, so Divine's "litanies" achieve orgasmic intensity as the words are reduced to a sort of chirping, ending only as Divine collapses in a state of divine exhaustion.

When Genet focusses on stylistic differences between discourses in the novel, he highlights the performative function of discourse, the speech act as such, rather than the message. As Bakhtin points out, this kind of focus constitutes the dramatic element of narrative, in that it replaces the monologic order of lyrical expression with the dialectical order of voices speaking in dialogue (*The Dialogic Imagination*; p. 266).

Once the difference between masculine and feminine speech styles has been established, Genet plays with these distinctions in order to represent the perversity of his only female character, Ernestine, Divine's mother. Masculine argot in Ernestine's speech symbolizes the virility

Genet projects into his female characters, making them as sexually ambivalent as the homosexual men. Ernestine is tough, heartless, and capable of cruelty. Her doubled discourse symbolizes a deeper ambivalence in her character, as illustrated in the following passage:

> Elle alla chercher le revolver chargé depuis longtemps par une Providence pleine d'égards, et quand elle le tint dans sa main, pesant comme un phallus en action, elle se comprit grosse du meurtre, enceinte d'un mort. (N. D. F.; 14)

> She went to get the revolver, which had long since been loaded by a most considerate Providence, and when she held it in her hand, weighty as a phallus in action, she realized she was big with murder, pregnant with a corpse. (O. L. F.; 75)

Ernestine strikes one as a man in female travesty whose speech style betrays his true identity. Differences between sexual identity and gender identification shape the doubled figure of an actor playing a role. This figure originates in the novels and is fully developed in Genet's plays. For instance, Genet requested an all-male cast for the staging of *Les Bonnes*, a play with only female characters.[21]

Ernestine's doubled discourse symbolizes an ongoing struggle between two faces of her personality. The masculine side seeks to destroy the child of her feminine side. Ernestine brings to mind the Medusa figure of a female head coiffed with snakes. The Medusa does not simply symbolize a castrating mother, but combines symbols of the father and mother in a circle of Oedipal desire. This figure returns to the spectator a reflection of his own fear of reprisals by the father. Hence any man who looks directly at the Medusa is rendered impotent or "petrified."[22] Ernestine performs a kind of verbal castration on her imaginary lover by uttering repeatedly, "une prise de couilles à la Tartare," a phrase suggesting both a grasp and a conquest of the male genitals which leaves them in the state of raw, ground-up meat.

Genet endows language with the materiality of flesh. Thus argot not only symbolizes Ernestine's masculine side, but is a displacement of the man she dreams of devouring. In a narrative style which equates speaking with acting, the interpenetration of Ernestine's speech and male argot constitutes a heterosexual act occurring in the dramatic present of the narrative. Savouring argot behind locked doors, Ernestine performs illicit acts with her mother tongue.

> Elle se disait à elle-mème, 'Une Gauloise, une tatouée, une cousue'. Elle s'affalait dans son fauteuil, murmurait ces mots en avalant la fumée lourde comme sperme de sa cigarette. (N. D. F.; 24)

She would say to herself: 'A Gauloise, a butt, a drag.' She would sprawl in her chair and murmur these words as she inhaled the thick [like sperm] smoke of her cigarette. (O. L. F.; 101, My translation in brackets)

The narrator's commentary, including the comparison between smoke and sperm, highlights the ironic contrast between Ernestine's social and sexual identity and her virile speech style, a contrast directly related to her verbal performance. Current theories of irony focus on a performative aspect of discourse which accounts for the role of the referent in determining the meaning of an utterance.[23] For instance, if a speaker says, "What a beautiful day!" to refer to a blizzard, irony is produced by a contrast between the meaning of the statement ("a beautiful day") and reference to the context (a blizzard). The irony of Ernestine's speech also derives from a performative focus of narrative discourse. Unlike the irony of "What a beautiful day!", however, the irony of Ernestine's speech is shaped by a dialogic interaction between subject and other in a single, doubled discourse. This type of irony in Genet derives precisely from a grotesque game of dissimulation which undermines the mimetic function of reported speech.

Though the very structure of irony poses the philosophical question of the unity of the speaking subject, the irony of double-voiced discourse in the novel poses this question as the problem par excellence of narrative representation. Bakhtin traces this problem back to the ancient Menippean satire, structured as a dialogue which integrates the comic and tragic faces of man in grotesque role-play. The satire mocks the claims of official ideology to an ideal unity between word and voice, the ideal of monologic discourse.

This destruction of the wholeness and finalized quality of a man is facilitated by the appearance, in the menippea, of a dialogic relation to one's own self (fraught with the possibility of split personality). (*Problems of Dostoevsky's Poetics*; p. 117)

The irony of double-voiced discourse in the modern novel both introduces the grotesque into narrative and exposes the difference between subject and other as a condition of possibility of speech. While the figure of the mask appears in *Notre-Dame-des-fleurs*, Genet would not develop this figure into a general problematic of reported speech until *Pompes funèbres*, in which characters freely alternate speech styles in order to perform for others.

In Genet the double shapes not only reported speech but spills over into the narrator's self-representation. If performance defines the act of being something for someone else, then Genet is indeed an actor, if not a comedian, since he borrows the discourses of others in the narration in order to chide the seriousness of official discourse. Such verbal performances are also means of coming to grips with his own ambivalent relation to the discourse of authority. Genet writes from prison. He occupies a kind of no-man's-land between the discourse of proper society and the discourse of the underworld. As Jean-Paul Sartre points out in *Saint Genet* (p. 425), Genet has stolen the language of proper society to write his novel. In the criminal milieu he borrows the language of the underworld. Genet not only imitates criminal argot in reported speech and indirect discourse, in which case he would simply mirror the discourse of the other, but he copies the means of formation of argot, including suffixing, prefixing, and semantic derivation, in order to produce a hybrid speech style, the speech of a double-voiced narrator.

In the following example, the reported speech of Mignon generates the narrator's comments about language and fashions the narrator's own linguistic elaborations:

S'il dit: 'Je lâche une perle' ou 'Une perlouse a tombé', il veut dire qu'il a peté d'une certaine façon très doucement, que le pet s'est coulé sans éclat. Admirons qu'en effet il évoque une perle à l'orient mât: cet écoulement, cette fuite en sourdine nous semblent laiteux autant que la pâleur d'une perle, c'est-à-dire un peu sourds. Mignon nous en apparait comme une sorte de gigolo précieux, hindoue, princesse, buveuse de perles. (N. D. F.; 20)

If he says, 'I'm dropping a pearl,' or 'A pearl slipped,' he means that he has farted in a certain way, very softly, that the fart has flowed out very quietly. Let us wonder at the fact that it does suggest a pearl of dull sheen: the flowing, the muted leak, seems to us as milky as the paleness of a pearl, that is, slightly cloudy. It makes Darling seem to us a kind of precious gigolo, a Hindu, a princess, a drinker of pearls. (O. L. F.; 90)

The focus on Mignon's speech as a verbal construct, as material for creative interpretation by the narrator, erodes the mimetic function of reported speech and makes narrative the scene of textual performance.

Unlike Divine, who is seduced by the "argot des mâles," the narrator feels himself "virilized" by manipulating argot. Inventing an erotic meaning for "making the beds [les pages]," an expression uttered by two pimps in prison, Genet imagines himself in the virile stance of a medieval guard, "making" the boys (the pages) of the palace.

Dans ma cellule, tout à l'heure, les deux marlous n'ont-ils pas dit: 'On fait les pages.' Ils voulaient dire qu'ils allaient faire les lits, mais moi une sorte de lumineuse idée me transforma là, mes jambes écartées, en un garde costaud ou palefrenier du palais qui, comme certains jeunes hommes font les poules, font les pages du palais. (N. D. F.; 24)

A while ago, in my cell, the two pimps said: 'We're making the pages.' They meant they were going to make the beds, but a kind of luminous idea transformed me there, with my legs spread apart, into a husky guard or a palace groom who "makes" a palace page just as a young man makes his chick. (O. L. F.; 101)

Argot is "la langue mâle." In perverting argot by the same means that the thugs and pimps pervert standard French, the narrator participates in others' discourse, he feels like a man among men. This initiation into the underworld is, of course, an illusion, a charade. Ever an outsider, Genet borrows the discourse of others only to twist it into literature.

When Genet introduces the discourse of the underworld into standard French, he perverts the proper (the conventional and the respectable) meaning of words into sexual transgressions of language. In this final example from *Notre-Dame-des-fleurs*, the discourse of the other generates a homosexual fantasy built upon the expression "être envergué" (to get fucked). Here narration is not primarily the verbal representation of nonverbal events, as Gérard Genette claims, but a verbal event performed at the expense of a coherent representation of action. As a result, Genet's perversity must be viewed primarily as a stance toward official discourse. Unfortunately most of the word play on the words "verge" "vergue" has been lost in the English translation.

Ici, je ne puis—c'est plus fort que moi—m'empêcher de revenir sur ces mots d'argot qui fusent des lèvres de macs comme ses pets (perles) fusent du derrière douillet de Mignon. C'est que l'un d'eux, qui plus peut-être que tous me retourne—ou, comme dit toujours Mignon, me travaille, car il est cruel—fut prononcé dans une des cellules de la Souricière. . . . D'un solide garde, j'entendis qu'on murmurait: 'l'encaldossé', puis, peu après: 'l'envergué'. Or, il se trouvait que l'homme prononçant cela nous avait dit avoir navigué sept ans. La magnificence d'une telle oeuvre—le pal par une vergue—me fit trembler du haut en bas. . . . (N. D. F.; 84)

Here I cannot refrain from coming back to those words of argot which stream from pimps' lips as his farts (pearls) stream from Darling's downy behind. The reason is that one of them, which, more perhaps than all the others, turns me inside out or, as Darling always says, gnaws at me, for he is cruel—was uttered in one of the cells in the Mousetrap. . . . About a husky guard, I heard someone mutter: 'the lock-sucker'; then a moment later: 'the yard-on.' Now, it so happened that the man who said that had told us that he had been at sea for seven years. The magnificence of such an achievement—impalement by a boom—made me tremble from head to foot.(O. L. F.; 252)

"Vergue" is a nautical term referring to the horizontal bar on the ship's mast which supports the sail. The sailors change "vergue" into a sexual term, "envergué," by shifting attention from the nautical meaning of "vergue" to its argot meaning, motivated by similarity with "verge" (= an erect member), and by prefixing and suffixing "en" and "é." The narrator, excited by the erotic possibilities of "vergue," adds his own analysis of the formation of "envergué." He interprets the word as a condensation of "empalé" and "vergue," which associates sexual penetration with the violence of an impalement.

This figure occurs again in *Miracle de la rose*, Genet's second novel, where it develops into a full-length sexual scenario. Here reported speech transcends the diegetic context of one novel and generates narrative discourse in another novel.

> J'ai besoin de calme, du grande calme évocateur du soir où, la galère voguant sur une mer chaude et plate, l'équipage m'obligea à grimper à la grande vergue. Les matelots m'avaient mis à poil en enlevant mon froc. Je n'osais même pas me débattre pour me dépêtrer de leurs rires et de leurs insultes. Tout geste n'eût fait que m'entortiller un peu plus dans leurs hurlements. (M. R.; 117)

> I need calm, the great calm that recalls the night when the galley sailed on a warm, smooth sea and the crew made me climb to the main yard. The sailors had stripped me by taking off my pants. I dared not even struggle to free myself from their laughter and insults. Any gesture would only have entangled me more in their shouts. (M. R.; 178)

The passage develops into the following paradoxical figuration, in which the narrator is both immobilized and climbing the mast, completing the idea of violent sexual assault. Here the association of *monter* and *pénétrer* is motivated by the inversion of the active and passive sides of a gang rape in which the narrator is victim. As he proceeds to "monter," he is "monté":

> Je restais aussi immobile que possible, mais j'étais déjà sûr que je monterais au mât. . . . Les larmes dans les yeux, je l'entourai de mes bras maigres, puis de mes jambes, en croisant l'un sur l'autre mes pieds. La frénésie des hommes fut à son comble. Leurs cris n'étaient plus des injures, mais des râles de cruauté déchirante. Et je montai. . . . Les hommes ne râlaient même plus. Ils haletaient ou, peut-être, de si haut où j'avais atteint, leur râle ne me paraissait qu'un halètement. J'arrivais au sommet. (M. R.; 117–18)

> I remained as still as possible, but I was already sure I would reach the top of the mast. . . . With tears in my eyes, I put my thin arms around it and then my legs, folding one foot over the other. The frenzy of the men was at its height. Their cries were no longer insults but excruciatingly cruel growls. And up I went. . . . The men were no longer even growling. They were panting, or perhaps their growling seemed to me, from the height I had reached, to be only a panting. I got to the top. (O. L. F.; 178)

The erotic meaning of this passage becomes explicit as the crew pull out their "verges." This line is missing from both the Gallimard edition and from the English translation.

De toutes les verges sorties des braguettes, est-ce le foutre qui gicla jusqu'à moi et me fit croire que la vergue avait enfin joui? (M. R.; 118)

Was it the semen which spurted up at me from all the members (*verges*) taken out of flies that made me think that the mastpole (*vergue*) had finally "come"? (my translation)

Furthermore, just as we begin to seize upon a coherent diegetic action, a gang rape in which the narrator is held captive, the narrator shifts the focus of the passage from the reference of the discourse to the creative power of the words themselves. Drawing attention to the homological attraction of "vergue" and "verge," Genet creates the outrageous image of a ship's mastpole, "la vergue," in the act of coming.

As Sartre argues so persuasively in *Saint Genet*, Genet was not a thief by inclination but by existential choice. Crime was an act of liberation from the rules of a society to which he could not belong (pp. 402–23). Genet's pornographic treatment of language is also a crime of liberation, a perversion of the discourse of authority. By pushing standard French to the limits of semantic polyvalence, by forcing it into perverse (speech) acts with others' discourses, Genet not only aims to shock his reader, but to test the limits of his own declaration of independence from proper literary tradition. As Pierre de Boisdeffre has said, not without a certain scorn, "Pour décrire son abjection il use du langage de Racine."[24]

When Bakhtin shifts the focus of poetics from the formal unity of the poetic text to the polyphony of voices speaking in dialogue (in *Problems of Dostoevsky's Poetics*; pp. 78–100), he suggests a political ideal of literature: to improve communication among subjects in spite of their linguistic or ideological differences. In Dostoevsky, for example, speakers interact according to a balanced give and take between subjects, rather than a monologic relation of the subject to its reflection or "other":

At the center of Dostoevsky's work there stands, in place of the relationship of a single cognizant and judging "I" to the world, the problem of the inter-relationship of all these cognizant and judging "I's" to one another. (p. 100)

Bakhtin clearly describes a utopian state of discourse. As Todorov explains in a recent book inspired by Bakhtin, communication is usually achieved at the expense of one voice or another, as the discourse of power assimilates the discourse of the weak.[25] Thus what speakers gain in communication they lose in heteroglossia. Communication requires that speakers agree on the meaning and reference of discourse. Communication thus improves as the process of standardization increases. However, standardization reduces differences between the languages of speakers and risks containing difference in the monologic order of the "same."

For Genet communication is impossible between society and the outlaw, be it a thief or a political dissident. Communication, implying standardization, would symbolize a kind of abdication, in the realm of language, of the other's subjectivity. Differences between speech styles in *Miracle de la rose* perpetually destroy communication between prisoners and figures of authority such as priests and prison guards, creating a permanent state of violent confrontation.

In *Miracle de la rose*, the production of narrative discourse with reference to character speech is even more evident than in *Notre-Dame-des-fleurs*. The novel unfolds in the virile world of Fontevrault prison. Even characters who are suspected of a feminine posture "play tough." The narrator's reflections and extrapolations on the language of prisoners are shaped by creative oppositions between the narrator Genet's literary style, described by de Boisdeffre as "le langage de Racine," the argot of the toughs, and the speech of the law (including clergy and guards). These contrasts lead to breakdowns in communication which provoke the characters to violence, shape the narrator's irony, and represent Genet's isolation from his entourage. As in *Notre-Dame-des-fleurs*, reported speech in this novel contributes to the representation of the narrator as well as the characters. This dialogic function of reported speech is more important than communication between characters.

The narrator's commentary on the impossibility of communication is also represented in the clash of speech styles between characters, which leads to violent misunderstanding. The narrator's commentary is colored with irony, a discursive operation nourished by the incompatibilities between what is said and what is understood by the characters.

Irony can be shared by the speaker and receiver (encoder and decoder) of a message or can be enjoyed by an outside observer at their expense. If irony is shared, it means that the interlocutors agree about the code used and the context referred to in the speech act. Communication occurs even if "communication" is restricted to the expression of an ironic mood. For instance, if the speaker and receiver agree that a blizzard is raging out of doors (agreement about the context), the statement "What a beautiful day!" commmunicates the speakers' indirect derision of the weather. However, disagreement about the code or the context results in an ambiguous message and a breakdown in communication.[26] The consequences may be a source of confusion for the observer who is unaware of the dual codes and contexts included in the speech act. For instance, if the speaker, referring to the blizzard outside, says, "What a beautiful day!" and if the receiver is unaware of the storm, the latter will "read" a different message, and may even act upon the misinformation (leave the house without an overcoat). Consider the following confusion about the code. If a speaker says, "This tea is bitter," and the receiver hears "better," the latter might proceed to fill his interlocutor's cup with the undesirable brew.

In everyday discourse, in which the emphasis is on communication, the goal is to clear up the ambiguity and restore communication. In *Miracle de la rose*, a novel about the impossibility of comunication, ambiguity in reported speech is an end in itself. While characters themselves are unaware of the source of misunderstanding, the narrator reports their discourse in order to underscore the irony of a speaking situation in which speakers seem to be performing two distinct texts at the same time. In the following passage, the Bishop of Tours speaks to the boys in the reformatory at Mettray:

> Dudule fit un discours pour accueillir l'évêque qui répondit en s'adressant surtout aux colons qu'il appelait ses agneaux égarés. Au début de la guerre, les vielles dames en coeur bleu pâle s'abordaient en parlant de 'nos petits soldats . . . nos petits pioupious'! Eux, dans la tranchée à pleines mains boueuses, la nuit, ils chopaient leur bite. Ainsi faisaient dans les bancs, de poche en poche, les petits agneux de Dieu. (M. R.; 122)

> Dudule made a speech welcoming the bishop, who replied by addressing the colonists in particular, whom he called stray lambs. In the early days of the war, old ladies with pale-blue hearts entered into conversation by talking about 'our little soldiers . . . our little doughboys'! They, in the trenches, jerked off at night with their mud-caked hands. God's little lambs, sitting in the pews with their hands in their pockets, did likewise. (O. L. F.; 186)

The irony of this passage derives from a focus on the puerile speech style of the speaker. Both "petits pioupious" and "petits agneaux" refer to the boys who are anything but childlike, cute, and innocent. The "little soldiers" spend the night masturbating in the trenches, while the "little lambs" do the same in their pews at Mettray. As the Bishop continues, the utter failure of his speech to convert these poor lost souls is painfully obvious. The boys turn from thoughts of salvation and turn to violent action.

> Je suis profondément touché par cet acceuil qui indique, en effet, la fidélité aux principes de votre sainte Religion. C'est un réconfort puissant pour moi, venant des villes où l'agitation perverse veut faire oublier Dieu, d'entrer dans cette oasis d'un calme religieux. . . . Monsieur le Directeur et Monsieur le Sous-Directeur, dans un domaine que nous savons différent et pourtant semblable, collaborent avec une même âme intéressée seulement au succès de cette entreprise sacrée: relever l'enfance déchue. (M. R.; 124)

> I am deeply moved by this welcome, which is indeed an indication of fidelity to the principles of your holy religion. It is a very deep comfort to me, coming from cities where perverse unrest tries to make men forget God, to enter this oasis of religious calm. . . . The Director and Assistant Director are collaborating, with a single-hearted will, in a sphere which we know is different and yet similar to, the success of that sacred undertaking: the rehabilitation of wayward children. (M. R.; 187–88)

If Mettray reformatory is "an oasis of religious calm," it is a Mettray which eludes the inmates, who know only depravation, loneliness, and violence. The sad irony of this passage derives from a focus on the dialogic structure of discourse. Unlike the irony of Ernestine's speech in *Notre-Dame-des-fleurs*, the irony of the Bishop's statement derives from conflicts between the frames of reference of speakers and interlocutors in the speaking situation. The ideological framework of the speaker has nothing in common with that of his interlocutors. He clearly does not "speak their language." Lacking any voice in the Bishop's monologic discourse, the boys respond with physical violence, making it impossible for the Bishop to continue speaking.

Bakhtin describes linguistic standardization as an act of violence perpetrated on the individual by discourses of authority:

> It is not a free appropriation and assimilation of the word itself that authoritative discourse seeks to elicit from us; rather, it demands our unconditional allegiance. Therefore authoritative discourse permits no play with the context framing it, no play with its borders, no gradual and flexible transitions, no spontaneously creative stylizing variants on it. . . . It is indissolubly fused with its authority—with political power, an institution, a person—and it stands and falls together with that person. (*The Dialogic Imagination*; p. 343)

The speaking situation at Mettray is a fit model for social revolt provoked by the utter incapacity (unwillingness) of authority to acknowledge the discourse of others, to recognize the other as a subject. Throughout *Miracle de la rose* the failure of priests and guards to speak the discourse of others, and the refusal of prisoners to speak the discourse of authority, lead to violent misunderstandings.

For example, the guards at Mettray fail to understand the codes forming erotic meanings in the discourse of inmates. The narrator describes the evolution of an *argotism*, "faire un doigté," as it passes from inmate to inmate. "Faire un doigté," as the narrator defines it, means to be poked in the derriere by one of the tough guys or "marles." Though the verb "faire" is in the active form, it actually means, according to the narrator, "*se laisser* faire," meaning that the verb "faire" in this expression marks the subject as the receiver of the gesture. The active form of the expression, referring to the man who performs the finger job, is "prendre un doigté."

> Voici l'expression transformée par un marle: 'J'ai pris un doigté', c'était comme on dit: 'Je lui dérobai un baiser'. (M. R.; 140)

> The following is the expression as transformed by a big shot: 'I took a finger job.' It was as if one said: 'I stole a kiss.' (M. R.; 213)

The active and passive forms of this expression are marked for gender identification; thus a "marle's" virility would be insulted if someone accused him of "faire un doigté." The problem is that only the initiates are privy to the codes determining the active and passive markings. A well-meaning guard, attempting to penetrate the prisoner's world by speaking their language, improperly uses the expression "faire un doigté" and incurs the wrath of a "marle." Thinking it means "s'être branlé" (masturbate), the guard jokes with Villeroy, a tough brute.

—T'es encore fait un doigté la nuit passée. (M. R.; 140)

His masculinity insulted, Villeroy responds quickly and terribly: he jumps on the guard, knocks him to the floor and beats the life out of him. The narrator explains, in a passage which was cut from the Gallimard edition and the translation,

Les gaffes ont des yeux et des oreilles. Ces organes ne collaborent jamais. Autrement dit, les gaffes sont des cons. (M. R.; 140)

The guards have eyes and ears. These organs never collaborate with each other. In other words, the guards are cunts. (my translation)

For the narrator, argot represents a secondary male sex trait since it symbolizes the eroticization of language on an individual, idiosyncratic level which escapes standardization.[27] The speech of clergy and guards in *Miracle de la rose* lacks this sexual, virile dimension. These characters either speak like old ladies or misread the sexual expressions uttered by the prisoners.

The erotic code governing the encoding and decoding of argot symbolizes linguistic creativity. Ignorance of the sexual code symbolizes the castration to which standardization submits language. Genet typically describes clergy, prison guards, lawmakers, and other speakers of official language in effeminate terms. For example, the chaplain at Mettray has a feminine verbal tic, the habitual use of "si," "expression of a sigh and common in feminine conversation and literature" (M. R.; 230). " 'On se sentait si heureux," 'Je fus si loin de tout' " (M. R.; 150).

It goes without saying that argot terms normally fall into conventional usage as they pass from person to person, generation to generation. As Guiraud points out, however, secret codes governing the formation of argot cause the lexicon to undergo constant renewal, playing with the context, as Bakhtin would say, the "borders" of language, submitting language to "spontaneously creative stylizing variants."[28] The narrator of *Miracle de la rose* is interested in the parallels between argot and poetry, between the criminal and the poet as militant renovators of language.

For Genet argot and standard French are at odds because of the different priorities determining their formation. The goal of standardization is communication—among the greatest number of speakers, with greatest efficiency of effort. Standardization reduces the natural polyvalence of words and limits personal creativity according to codes. Argot shapes language to fit the needs of the speaking subject by exploiting the polyvalence of words and the plasticity of their sounds. As a result,

Ce que nous disions et pensions, je le sens maintenant, ne pourra jamais être traduit par la langue française. (M. R.; 140)

But I now feel that the French language will never be able to render what we said and thought. (M. R.; 213)

For Sartre speakers of argot are indeed criminals, since they transgress the official code governing linguistic homogeneity in order to sustain a subculture which thrives on the systematic corruption of society:

Argot is, in its words and syntax and by virtue of its whole semantic content, the permanent practice of rape (*Saint Genet*; pp. 288–89)

Parasitic and destructive, argot is the very image of Evil which borrows the Being of Good only to corrode it with its acids. (*Saint Genet*; pp. 289)

Sartre does not point out that speakers of argot in Genet do not succeed in communicating among themselves any better than with the lawmakers. The plasticity of the words and the instability of their meanings cause endless misinterpretation of discourse among prisoners. Even a special inflection or intonation of the voice can twist the meaning of words. The narrator shows how an innocent exclamation, "Oh, dis!" can be interpreted as an invective. Spoken by the prisoner Beauvais, the expression incites Villeroy to violence.

A Villeroy il dit simplement: 'Oh, dis!' Mais les mots ont le sens qu'on leur donne et, à vrai dire, tout notre langage était chiffré, car les exclamations les plus simples signifiaient quelquefois des insultes compliquées. Ce 'Oh, dis!' ici voulait dire: 'Tu n'es pas tout à toi seul'. Villeroy bondit. (M. R.; 114–15)

All he said to Villeroy was: 'Oh, say!' but words have the meaning one gives them, and the fact is that our entire language was a code, for the simplest exclamations sometimes signified complicated insults. (M. R.; 174)

In the next passage, the narrator not only illustrates Villeroy's propensity for violence, but points to the power of another *argotism*, "Il lui vola dans les plumes" ("He tore into him" or literally, "flew into his feathers"), to move the character to action.

Il l'esquinta, hanté par son âme terrible, emporté par la fougueuse allure de cette expression. (M. R.; 94)

He beat him up as if carried away by the spirited drive of this expresssion. (M. R.; 139)

Genet then expands this same expression into his own discourse and is similarly moved to violence. Using "il lui vola dans les plumes" to describe the action of Villeroy, the narrator remembers another incident when he himself engaged in a fight with a fag, Charlot. The fight was incited by a verbal challenge, a play of wit leading to the narrator's own statement, "I'm going to tear into him." Word-play on the words "voler" (to fly) and "plumes" (feathers), which engenders this passage, is lost in the English translation. Referring to his sexual prowess with women, Charlot declares,

—De ce côté là j'suis surnaturel. (M. R.; 95)

'When it comes to that, I'm supernatural.' (M. R.; 140)

The narrator free-associates on "surnaturel" with the quip,

—T'es surnaturel? Ah, je saisis, tu te fais aider par les anges. (M. R.; 95)

'You're supernatural? Ah, I get it. You get the angels to help you.' (M. R.; 141)

A metonymical chain of semantic derivations, surnaturel—anges— [ailes]—plumes, leads to the battle cry, "J'vais lui voler dans les plumes!" Repeating this expresion in a sort of incantation moves the narrator to violence.

Mais dès le début de la phrase: 'De ce côté-là j'suis surnaturel' . . . je me répétais: 'J'vais lui voler dans les plumes! P'tit con! J'vais lui voler dans les plumes!' Je me répétai la phrase mentalement, deux fois. Envivré par elle, qui me soulevait, . . . je bondis. (M. R.; 95)

But as soon as he started the sentence, 'When it comes to that, I'm super-natual,' I repeated to myself, 'I'm going to tear into him! The little prick! I'm going to tear into him!' I repeated the phrase mentally, twice. Excited and buoyed by it, I didn't wait for him to hit first. I lunged at him. (M. R.; 141)

The free-associations generated by Charlot's speech not only produce the narrator's discourse but shape the direction of the action. Charlot meant by "surnaturel" his greater-than-average sexual prowess with women, literally, supernatural. The word makes the narrator think of celestial, winged beings, a likely image for Charlot's true sexual ambivalence. Associating Charlot with the idea of a fairy, Genet in turn remotivates the expression "voler dans les plumes." To the extent that Charlot has "wings," so will his flight be curtailed as the fight ensues.

Reported speech not only forms a semiotic model for the narrator's transformations of another's discourse through derivation, condensation, prefixing and so on. The remotivation of "voler dans les plumes" and its expansion into the narrative demonstrate the power of dialogic interaction to produce actions as well as verbal performances.

In *Miracle de la rose* the slippery movement of the narration between a focus on the speech act and reference to a diegetic context reveals a disjuncture between speaking and being in narrative discourse and allows the narrator to elude representation as such. While standard French and criminal argot define the speaker according to his social milieu and his gender identification, the dialogic interaction of these speech styles in Genet constitutes a mise-en-scène of the existential problem of freedom. Genet struggles to escape the prison-house of language which holds the subject in a dialectic relation to the discourse of authority.[29] A re-formed prisoner (not "reformed" according to society's laws, but his own), the narrator speaks neither the language of prisoners nor the language of the law. Genet has ceased his former complicity with the other's discourse, traced in *Notre-Dame-des-fleurs* by the fragile boundaries separating his discourse from the discourses of his underworld characters. In *Miracle de la rose* the narrator's growing separation from the criminal milieu is traced by quotation marks which distinguish argot from his own speech style.

Quoted argot usually occurs within the narrator's descriptions of himself as a participant in the narration. In these cases the narrator seems to be quoting his former self rather than highlighting someone else's speech style.

S'il ne fût agi que d'une tante, j'aurai su tout de suite quel personnage me composer; je l'eusse fait 'à la brutale', mais Pierrot était un casseur preste, un gamin peut-être profondément désolé. (M. R.; 60)

If he had been simply a queer, I would have immediately known what act to put on: I would have 'played tough,' but Pierrot was a smart crasher, a kid who was perhaps sore at heart. (M. R.; 86)

Il ne se rangea pas assez vite dans l'escalier que je dévalais à toutes pompes et je le bousculai. Il me le fit remarquer gentiment, mais je 'montais'. (M. R.; 94)

He didn't get out of the way fast enough as I hotfooted it down the stairs, and I jostled him. He simply made a mild comment, but I "worked myself up." (M. R.; 139)

Here the quotation marks separating narrative discourse from reported speech lack the ironic distance which characterized the narrator's earlier commentaries upon characters' speech. They are traces, rather, of the narrator's rejection of his underworld heroes, a renunciation of his former self. The discourse of the other in these passages is the discourse of another Jean Genet.

The disintrication of the narrator's speech from the speech of others in *Miracle de la rose* marks a stage in the realization of his personal identity.

> Je ne désirais plus ressembler aux voyous. J'avais le sentiment d'avoir réalisé la plénitude de moi-même. (M. R.; 21)

> I no longer yearned to resemble the hoodlums. I felt I had achieved self-fulfillment. (M. R.; 26)

Genet even takes advantage of his distinct, literary style to keep others at a distance.

> J'allais reprendre le ton littéraire qui m'écarterait de lui, couperait le contact trop immédiat car il ne pouvait pas me suivre. (M. R.; 60)

> I was about to resume the slightly literary tone that would alienate me from him, that would cut the too immediate contact, for he would be unable to follow me. (M. R.; 86)

Genet concludes *Miracle de la rose* with a somewhat pessimistic solution to the dialogic problem of personal freedom. Refusing both the discourse of authority and the discourse of the outlaw, the narrator condemns himself to silence.

> Il faut se taire. Et je marche les pieds nus. (M. R.; 233)

> I say no more and walk barefoot. (M. R.; 344)

In this passage, Genet brings to mind his namesake, San Juan de la Cruz, who founded, with Santa Teresa d'Avila, the Carmelite order of the *frères déchaussés*. Like Genet, San Juan de la Cruz was poor, was imprisoned, and was led to merge mysticism and eroticism in his poetry. Robert Graves points out a homosexual component to his mysticism: the ideal, sexual union of Man with God the Father.[30]

Marguerite Duras has said that to write is to be no one, to be "dead"; "Ecrire, c'est n'être personne. 'Mort', disait Thomas Mann."[31] Unlike San Juan de la Cruz, Genet did not ultimately pursue literary mysticism as a way out of his silence, but chose writing as a means of being "no one."

In his future work he wrestled with the problem of speaking one's mind while eluding identification with one discourse or another. In *Pompes funèbres* Genet discovered the mask.

Bakhtin describes the mask as the most important element of medieval folk culture, since it permits the subject to draw a line between his official, serious life and his carnival, instinctively humorous life.

> The mask is connected with the joy of change and reincarnation, with gay relativity and with the merry negation of uniformity and similarity; it rejects conformity to oneself . . . it reveals the essence of the grotesque. (*Rabelais and His World*; pp. 39–40).

The mask constitutes a social convention signalling the suspension of social sanctions and the free play of creative, transforming laughter. Bakhtin insists on the constructive function of laughter in folk culture.

> True ambivalent and universal laughter does not deny seriousness but purifies and completes it. Laughter purifies from dogmatism, from the intolerant and the petrified; it liberates from fanataicism and pedantry, from fear and intimidation, from didacticism, naïveté and illusion, from the single level, from sentimentality. Laughter does not permit seriousness to atrophy and to be torn away from the one being, forever incomplete. It restores this ambivalent wholeness. (*Rabelais and His World*; p. 123)

Carnival laughter is intimately related to the subject's scorn of censorship, including internal restraints such as fear (of death, of evil), and is inseparable from grotesque imagery which integrates the extreme oppositions of human existence, such as male and female, the spiritual and the physical, beauty and evil, comedy and tragedy. The mask symbolizes man's fundamental cleavage into a subject for itself and a subject for someone else. The mask also permits the human subject to face the terror of death (of hell?) behind an assumed identity.

The figure of the mask originates in Genet's novels and ultimately shapes his style of theatrical performance. As I mentioned ealier, Bakhtin excludes theatrical dialogue from the realm of dialogism per se, since the latter is characterized by the doubling of narrative voice with reference to other voices in the narration, rather than by the one-dimensional speech of characters engaged in dialogue on stage. Though Bakhtin himself does not theorize about the place of folk culture in contemporary theater, his study of medieval carnival suggests means of locating a dialogic movement of discourse in Genet's theater, which resurrects the mask of medieval carnival. It is along these lines that Genet's novels and theater overlap.

While the narrator and characters in Genet's third novel, *Pompes funèbres*, lack the droll aspect of medieval fools and clowns, and while the masks they wear consist of linguistic impersonations rather than theatrical disguises, their use of the mask resembles carnival laughter by giving free play to the contadictions within being. Genet twists reported speech into grotesque disguises which permit him to confront the pain and horror of death in a personal and literary form of funeral rite.

> Mes précédents livres je les écrivais en prison. Pour me reposer, en imagination j'entourais de mon bras le cou de Jean et lui parlais des chapitres les plus récents. Pour ce livre, dès que j'arrête d'écrire, je me vois seul au pied de son cercueil ouvert dans la salle de l'amphithéâtre et je lui propose sévèrement mon récit. (P. F.; 75)

> My earlier books were written in prison. In order to rest, I put my arm around Jean's neck in my imagination and spoke to him quietly about the latest chapters. As for the present book, whenever I stop writing I see myself along at the foot of his open coffin in the amphitheater and I relate my tale to him sternly. (F. R.; 99)

In *Pompes funèbres* Genet has not really abandoned the prison motif but displaced it onto society at large. The novel is narrated in Paris during the German occupation of World War II and the Liberation of France. While this novel contains elements of the previous novels, the dialogic participation between reported speech and narrative discourse is traced not so much by differences between argot and standard French as between a multiplicity of speech styles, representing a plurality of voices clamoring to be heard. Thus, in one sense, Genet escapes the dialectic of power which opposes the discourse of authority and the discourse of the outlaw by blurring distinctions between the prison and normal society, between the law and the outlaw, between the judges and the accused in the story.

The narrator, Jean Genet, is mourning the death of Jean D., a Resistance fighter killed on the eve of the Liberation. Other characters, who seem to enter the story only to contribute their speech styles to the polyphony of voices, include Erik Seiler, a German soldier who is also the lover of Jean D's mother, and Hitler. Both Erik and Hitler speak French as well as their native tongue. Only Riton and his pals, recruited into the Milice, or secret police, from the Parisian underworld, speak argot.

The narrator has less occasion to free-associate on argot spoken by characters in *Pompes funèbres* than in the other two novels, but when he does so he uses reported speech to pull together the major threads of the novel. In this novel Genet seems to have discovered the political meaning of others' discourse and the relations among sex, death, and representation which the dialogic structure puts into play.

Early in the novel, Genet visits the mother of his dead friend, only to be greeted by Erik, a German officer. Though Erik is a personification of the enemy that killed Jean D., and though he might even have pulled the trigger himself, his virilty excites Genet. Faced with the difficult irony of this situation, the narrator Genet borrows another's discourse to speak about his desire. Once again, the narrator's transformations of reported speech are the moving force of narrative discourse. Looking at Erik planted uncomfortably in his chair, the narrator fantasizes about buggering him up his "oeil de Gabès." Then he remembers hearing this expression spoken by a soldier in the street, boasting about his sexual exploits in Tunisia. This word-play is lost in the English translation.

—. . . et moi j'demandais pas mieux, alors, j'y ai foutu le doigt dans l'eil deug Habès! Et toc! (P. F.; 16)

'. . . that was all I wanted, so I stuck my finger in his eye.' (F. R.; 19)

"Oeil de Gabès" ("eil deug Habès") condenses a sexual *argotism*, *oeil*, and a place-name, *oued Gabès*, a waterway in Tunisia which is too shallow for large ships to enter. Exploiting the ambivalence of this expression, the narrator, still speaking inwardly, discusses the exotic world of North Africa and the various synonyms in argot for the homosexual aim.

Il n'est pas indifférent que parte mon livre peuplé des soldats les plus vrais, sur l'expression la plus rare qui marque le soldat puni, l'être le plus travaillé confondant le guerrier avec le voleur, la guerre et le vol. Les Joyeux appellent encore 'oeil de bronze' ce que l'on nomme aussi 'la pastille', 'l'oignon', 'le derche', 'le derjeau', 'la lune', 'son panier à crottes'. (P. F.; 16)

It is not a matter of indifference that my book, which is peopled with the truest of soldiers, should start with the rarest expression that brands the punished soldier, that most prudent being confusing the warrior with the thief, war with theft. The *Joyeux* likewise gave the name 'bronze eye' to what is also called the 'jujube,' the 'plug,' the 'onion,' the 'meanie,' the 'tokas,' the 'moon,' the 'crap basket.' (F. R.; 21)

Contemplating the profane discourse of others in the narration leads Genet to thoughts of love-making with Jean D. and to his "oeil de bronze." Though he is still seated in front of Erik, this linguistic and erotic fixation is the vehicle for moving in time and space from the street scene to the scene of Jean D.'s funeral. Genet recalls still another man's discourse to describe the interior of the church, "noir comme dans le trou du cul d'un nègre." His memory of the funeral ends and the narrator returns to the diegetic present and his erotic fixation on Erik's "oeil de bronze."

Genet, like Bakhtin, recognized that monologic discourse subjects the individual to institutionalized terrorism by silencing, overtly or covertly, others' discourse.[32] Thus Genet blurs distinctions between war and theft, the warrior and the thief. It is not a matter of indifference that the novel begins with a long digression on the various argot terms for the homosexual aim, a digression which ties together the themes of politics, death and desire along the lines of a (mis)-representation of the discourse of others. By weaving the narration around a pornographic fixation of language, Genet not only establishes the grotesque as a model for the narration; he plants a bomb in the French literary pantheon.

If argot constitutes the permanent "rape" of standard French, this act is normally rendered impotent by the fact that bourgeois society marginalizes speakers of argot, assimilating their discourse into dominant culture as the opposite of the "same," as the dark side of monologic discourse. Genet, an author/narrator standing on the border between both worlds, an author both recognized for his literary prowess and scorned for his "abjection," uses others' discourse as a political weapon. In Genet, the dialogic structure of discourse represents the complicity between the discourse of authority and the discourse of the outlaw, exposing a permanent movement of perversion in the construction of official discourse.

In *Notre-Dame-des-fleurs* and *Miracle de la rose*, double-voiced discourse serves mainly to represent the author/narrator's struggle to learn his own identity. In *Pompes funèbres*, Genet poses the question of other's discourse in terms of a politics of representation. Representation is political in the sense that it constitutes a moment in the production of (historical, ideological) truth, not simply a means of mirroring universal truths. While Socialist Realism avoids the question of the ideological production of the subject by masking the means of this production, and while Russian Formalism eludes this question by highlighting the technical and material structure of literary discourse, Bakhtin asks us to examine the lie at the origin of representation. Jean Genet seems to fulfill this project when he exposes an act of dissimulation underlying narrative discourse, producing a subject always and already divided in language. The political setting of *Pompes funèbres* allows Genet to project this problematic onto the representation of history.

The German occupation of France did not dismantle the monologic order of bourgeois society but placed it within the political hierarchy of a police state. Difference, in this order, is less a function of linguistic contrasts between the speech of one, dominant group and its "other," than of structural oppositions between subject and other in a dialectic of power. Thus, for example, Riton speaks argot with other militiamen, German with the occupying army, and occasionally falls into a speech style which suspiciously resembles the narrator's. Throughout *Pompes funèbres* this kind of performance undermines the claim of any one social group to the discourse of authority.

Jean D.'s mother usually whines in an inflected version of standard French, but occasionally slips into argot. Putting argot into her mouth, the narrator takes a typical stab at motherhood. The sexual symbolism of argot is not as important here as in the other novels. Argot in Madam

D.'s speech is not a figure for her virility as it was for Ernestine, but a means of humbling her aristocratic pretensions.

> —Une bonne! Une bonne! murmurait-elle. Au fond, qu'elle se soit fait bourrer par Jean, qu'est-ce que j'ai à en foutre? Moi, je suis "Madame." (P. F.; 128)

> 'A maid! A maid!' she muttered. 'After all, damn it, what's it to me if Jean knocked her up? I'm Madame.' (F. R.; 171)

In such speech, "Madame" resembles her maid. Genet would later develop the irony of this speaking situation in his play *Les Bonnes*. In the play, Madam's speech betrays her inferior social origins, while the maids speak like poets.

Contrasts between German and French, as well as those between standard French and argot in reported speech, are the primary means for tracing the dialogic participation between character and narrator in *Pompes funèbres*. Erik's foreign nationality figures in his spoken French in the pronunciation, syntax, and vocabulary he uses in this scene with Genet:

> —Jean était très jeune. . . .
> Il prononçait 'Djan', en laissant tomber sèchement le 'an'.
> Je ne répondit pas. Il dit:
> —Aber, vous aussi vous Jean.
> Oui. (P. F.; 27)

> 'Jean was very young.' . . . He said 'Djan,' pronouncing the 'an' very curtly.
> I did not reply. He said:
> '*Aber, you too, you Jean.*'
> 'Yes.' (F. R.; 35)

The representation of Erik's speech changes with respect to the different characters with whom he speaks. With Riton he commands discourse and speaks German more than French.

> —Komm schlafen, Ritône. . . .
> —Komm mein Ritône. . . . (P. F.; 88, 90)

These changes in Erik's speech represent changes in the power structure of the various speaking situations. In other words, characters speak for other characters in their entourage according to a political "economy." French is the language of authority in the apartment of Jean D.'s mother. Since the liberating army has occupied Paris, Erik relies on Madam D. for his very life. Thus, with her, Erik speaks French to the best of his ability.

For Riton, speaking argot symbolizes a basic refusal of bourgeois values and allegiances, and therefore precipitates his recruitment into the Militia, whose password is betrayal.

Le recruitement de la Milice se fit surtout parmi les voyous puisqu'il fallait oser braver le mépris de l'opinion générale qu'un bourgeois eût craint. (P. R.; 59)

Members of the Militia were recruited mainly from among hoodlums, since they had to brave the contempt of public opinion, which a bourgeois would have feared. (F. R.; 77–78)

Equally symbolic is the fact that in this novel members of the Resistance speak flawless French.[33] They represent proper bourgeois society.

In Erik, Riton recognizes his master's voice. From this moment on there is no turning back, no means of escape from this web of enmeshed discourses.

—Komm schlafen, Ritône.
On lui saisit doucement le bras. Il se retourne, épouvanté. Le navire avait sombré. Sans le savoir, Riton venait de couler au fond de la mer et déjà il entendait la langue qu'on y parle. Il ne pouvait plus se dégager. (P. F.; 88)

'Komm schlafen, Ritône.' Someone gently took hold of his right arm. He turned around in terror. The ship had gone down. Without realizing it, he had just sunk to the bottom of the sea and was already hearing the language that is spoken there. (F. R.; 117)

Soon Riton himself speaks the enemy tongue, thereby betraying his mother tongue while sealing his pact with the devil.

Dans l'obscurité la main qui cherchait découvrait une main d'Erik et la serra. Riton murmura avec une douceur qui devenait de plus en plus le ton de sa voix, en se penchant jusqu'à effleurer de son haleine le cou du Frisé:
—Gute nacht, Erik. (P. F.; 109)

The hand seeking in the darkness found one of Erik's and squeezed it. As Riton bent forward until his breath lightly stroked the Fritz's neck, he murmured with a gentleness that more and more became his tone of voice, 'Gute nacht, Erik.' (F. R.; 145)

Ironically, the very qualities which serve Riton in the Militia—ruthlessness, unscrupulousness, eagerness for a weapon—render him suspicious in the eyes of the occupying army. Moreover, his ability to serve the French government separates him from the "pure crook," by nature an anarchist (P. F.; 158). Hated by patriots, alienated from the underworld, suspected by the Germans, Riton adjusts his speech to conform to others' discourse, losing his own voice in the process. Riton thus embodies the theme of social and psychological alienation which figures so prominently in Genet's treatment of speech acts.

Differences in speech styles distinguish the narrator from characters in the narration. These same differences permit Genet to represent the narrator speaking from the mouths of his characters. From time to time characters drop their habitual speech styles and speak in the narrator's literary style. These changes correspond to the shifts in position of the narrating subject, the "I" of the discourse, from the narrator to one of his characters, discussed in chapter 1 of the present book.

We first read the narrator Genet's voice in Erik's speech in a scene where Erik grants sexual favors to the executioner of Berlin. Rather than speak with his usual German inflection and syntax, Erik speaks flawless French. Finally, the narrator reveals himself by inserting narrative "I" into the scene. The executioner asks Erik,

> —Alors? Non, tu ne vois pas?
> Je l'avais reconnu. Je n'osais pas le dire. Je répondis:
> —C'est l'heure que je rentre à la caserne.
> —Tu as peur parce que je suis le bourreau? (. . .)
> —Non. (. . .)
> —Non? C'est sûr?
> —Mais oui, pourquoi?
> Et pour attendrir le bourreau *j'ajoutai*: 'Je ne t'ai rien fait de mal'. (P. F.; 30, italics added)

> 'Well? Can't you see?'
> I had recognized him. I dared not say so. I replied: 'It's time for me to be getting back to the barracks.'
> 'Are you scared because I'm the executioner?' (. . .)
> 'No.' (. . .)
> 'No? Are you sure?'
> 'Of course I am, why?'
> And to mollify the executioner, *I added*: 'I haven't done any harm.'
> (F. R.; 40)

Likewise, Riton's use of standard French in several brief dialogues with Erik, rather than *argot* or German as usual, reveals the presence of the narrator speaking through this character.

> —Maintenant j'ai l'impression que je t'aime plus qu'avant. (P. F.; 190)

and

—Aide-moi à mourir. (P. F.; 191)

'I now have the impression that I love you more than before.' (F. R.; 254)

'Help me die.' (F. R.; 255)

Notice the contrast with Riton's usual speech. Here again the grammatical and semantic transgressions of standard French by argot are not as marked in the English translation.

—C'est de la connerie, mais faut que je voie quel jour qu'on est. (P. F.; 177)

and

—Heureusement que je m'suis un peu nettoyé l'oignon. (P. F.; 179)

'It's ass-headed, but I've got to see what day it is.' (F. R.; 236)

'Good thing I cleaned my hole a little.' (F. R.; 239)

The dialogic interaction of voices in *Pompes funèbres* culminates in a kind of role-playing which anticipates Genet's theater, where the speaking and spectating subject is staged in a play of reflections between the actor, his character, and his character's role. The narrator of *Pompes funèbres* even refers to theatrical performance as an ideal mode of creative transformation.

> J'assume un rôle très grave. Une âme est en peine à qui j'offre mon corps. Avec la même émotion le comédien aborde le personnage qu'il rendra visible. Mon épouse peut être moins désolée. Une âme endormie espère un corps; qu'il soit beau, celui qu'apporte pour un soir le comédien. Ce n'est pas une petite affaire. Nous exigeons la plus rare beauté et l'élégance pour ce corps chargé d'un soin terrible, pour ces gestes détrisant la mort et ce n'est pas trop que demander aux acteurs d'armer leurs personnages jusqu'à la crainte. L'opération magique qu'ils accomplissent c'est le mystère de l'Incarnation. (P. F.; 57)

> I am taking on a very grave role. A soul is in purgatory and I am offering it my body. It is with the same emotion that an actor approaches the character whom he will make visible. My spouse may be less wretched. A sleeping soul hopes for a body; may the one that the actor assumes for an evening be beautiful. This is no small matter. We require the rarest beauty and elegance for that body which is charged with a terrible trust, for those gestures which destroy death, and it is not too much to ask the actors to arm their characters to the point that they inspire fear. The magical operation they perform is the mystery of the Incarnation. (F. R.; 75)

Like an actor in search of a character,[34] the narrator breathes life into Hitler. Only now can Hitler in turn play the role of actor perversely embodying another Jean Genet.

> Et même d'ici, le regard fixe, le corps immobile ou presque, je parvenais à déléguer à Nuremberg cet acteur célèbre où de ma place auprès du cerceuil de Jean je lui soufflais. Il paradait, il gesticulait et hurlait devant une foule de S. S. médusés, délirants, ivres de se sentir les figurants nécessaires d'un théâtre qui se jouait dans la rue ... on peut comprendre la beauté de ces représentations devant cent mille spectateurs-acteurs quand on sait que l'officiant sublime était Hitler, jouant le rôle d'Hitler. *Il me représentait.* (P. F.; 58, italics added)

> And even from here, I was able, by fixing my gaze and remaining motionless, or almost, to delegate my powers to the famous actor in Nuremberg who was playing the role in which I was prompting him from my room or from my place beside the coffin. He was strutting, he was gesticulating and roaring before a crowd of spellbound, raving Storm Troopers who were thrilled to feel that they were the necessary extras in a performance that was taking place in the street.... One can realize the beauty of those performances before a hundred thousand spectator-actors when one knows that the sublime officiant was Hitler playing the role of Hitler. *He was representing me.* (F. R.; 76, italics added)

By substituting his own speech for the speech of characters, the narrator places a mask there where the subject appears to speak. Reported speech, traditionally a means of representing character, becomes a vehicle for representing the narrator in disguise. The imbrication of reported speech and narrative discourse in Genet evolves from *Notre-Dame-des-fleurs* to *Pompes funèbres* into a doubled figure of the narrator-actor playing the roles of his characters.[35]

It might be asked why the narrator goes to the trouble of replacing character speech with his own discourse, rather than speaking directly to the reader without disguise. By developing an esthetic of dissimulation, Genet seeks to create a tension within narrative representation which transforms the narrative into a kind of mise-en-scène. Neither a mirror of transcendental reality—the signified of Kantian metaphysics, nor an image of universal truth—the object of Aristotelian poetics, narrative representation shapes a hall of mirrors in which reality itself is redefined as an illusive imitation of an imitation.[36]

When Genet exposes the mask underlying the production of narrative discourse and reported speech, he shifts the focus of poetics from mimetic relations between speech and being to dialectical relations between subject and other in textual performance. This kind of performance marks both the erasure of individual identity (such as the identity of the author) and places in question the notion of an original unity of the speaking subject of poetic discourse (the identity of the narrator), by defining the subject as something for someone else. Thus being is endlessly doubled in textual performance, threatened with death in the moment of its externalization in representation. The "funeral rites" of Genet's novel not only refer to the narrator's mourning for a dead friend, but celebrate the death of the transcendental subject and signified of narrative discourse.

The work of contemporary authors, including Genet, Duras, Beckett and Robbe-Grillet, demands a rethinking of poetry and poetics to account for passages between text, theater, and film in any given work. To the extent that poetic theories focus on semiotic performance rather than on the closure between the form, the substance, and the material of discourse, they free representations from their ontological destinies and focus instead on the movements between modes and genres. Bakhtin himself saw the relation between performance and the merging of genres in his study of medieval carnival.[37] Carnival performance mediated humankind's temporary liberation from the social constraints of monologic authority and transcended the boundaries between the arts of song, dance, and theater.

The figure of the mask originates in Genet's novels and ultimately shapes his style of theatrical performance. Genet could more fully realize his ideal of the double in theatrical representation because theater includes a vast repertory of semiotic systems, including gestures, voice, and movement, as well as language. In the plays, role-playing occurs not only along the lines of borrowed discourse, but by means of borrowed costumes, vocal intonation, and decor. No doubt the theater's greater possibilities for the representation of difference and doubling influenced Genet's decision to turn to the theater. After publishing a fourth novel, *Querelle de Brest* (1948), which is considerably more "diegetic" or focussed on the story than the other three novels, Genet would quit the narrative form as such.[38]

In a letter to Pauvert, the publisher of *Les Bonnes*, Genet writes:

> ... déjà ému par la morne tristesse d'un théâtre qui reflète trop exactement le monde visible, les actions des hommes, et non les Dieux, je tâchai d'obtenir un décalage qui, permettant un ton déclamatoire porterait le théâtre sur le théâtre. J'esperais obtenir ainsi *l'abolition des personnages*—qui ne tiennent d'habitude que par convention psychologique—au profit de signes aussi éloignés que possible de ce qu'ils doivent d'abord signifier, mais s'y rattachant tout de même afin d'unir, par ce seul lien l'auteur au spectateur. Bref, obtenir que les personnages ne fussent plus sur la scène que la métaphore de ce qu'ils devaient représenter. (italics added)[39]

> ... already moved by the dismal sadness of a theater which reflects too exactly the visible world, the actions of men, I tried to obtain a distancing which, permitting a declamatory tone, would refer the theater back to theater. I hoped

to obtain thus *the abolition of characters*—which usually only hold by means of psychological convention—in favor of signs as far-removed as possible from that which they should signify at first, but connecting with it [the conventional meaning] all the same in order to unite, by this single link, author and spectator. In short, to obtain characters on stage which are no longer but a metaphor for what they were supposed to represent. (my translation)

As I discuss in chapter 5 of the present book, Genet's theatrical characters are fictional creations, but might also be means for representing the "author," a sort of narrator playing the role of another Jean Genet. Characters seem to speak "out of character": maids speak like poets, prostitutes like bankers, blacks like aristocrats. Though an ideal of theatrical performance shapes narrative representation in Genet's novels, the opposite is also true. The dialogic interaction between narrative voice and the discourses of characters in the novels shapes Genet's ideal of theatrical performance. The figure of the mask opens up critical differences between the actor, the fictional role, and the roles characters themselves play in Genet's theater, reinforcing a doubling of dramatic "voice." This process both "destroys" character in the traditional sense and points to the reader and spectator as participants in the performance.

Genet's work, like Bakhtin's, is nourished by the discovery that discourses of authority do violence to the individual by containing racial, social, and sexual difference in an order of the "same." By exposing representation to the dangers of performance, Genet, a homosexual and a thief, not only challenges the Aristotelian tradition in poetry and poetics, he commits acts of terrorism against the French literary establishment.

THREE

Semiosis as Performance

In one of the rare attempts to situate Genet's writing style in a modern tradition, Joseph MacMahon has said that the generation of Genet's narrative proceeds, like Proust's *A la recherche du temps perdu*, according to a process of memory and the reconstruction of a narrative past.[1] He also claims that Genet's homosexuality shapes the synthesis of opposites, such as beauty and evil, in coherent symbols. To say, however, that in Genet "literary memory" actually recaptures the past by means of a chain of metaphorical associations is to miss the deliberately disjunctive style of Genet's writing and his radical departure from the esthetics of synthesis which Proust, in *some ways*, represents.[2] Moreover, I contend that the overtly homosexual meaning of the *form* of metaphor in Genet's work derives precisely from a movement of irreconcilable difference between elements of literary discourse.

Genet, whose sexual practices separate him from dominant, heterosexual society and the discourse of homogeneity, deploys metaphors in a way which works against the creation of a "proper sense" through which semantic difference can be contained. By this means, Genet focusses on the movement of the subject in narrative space, a kind of performance which metaphorical difference puts into play.

Paul Ricoeur suggests means of accounting for the performative dimension of metaphor in Genet, in terms of a general theory of semiosis modelled after the movement of the speaking subject in metaphorical discourse. In *La Métaphore vive*, Ricoeur shifts the focus of poetics from relations between words in tropes to relations between figures and the discourses producing them.[3]

> This vast domain of analogy could only be held together if one gave up confining metaphor to single-word tropes and followed to its limit the movement which detaches it [metaphor] from the word-play of nomination in order to attach it to the central act of discourse, predication. (M. V.; 83, my translation)

In the same gesture Ricoeur challenges the primacy of the image fostered by the Aristotelian tradition. In the theory of tropes the proper sense is not a concept per se, but an image which hovers somewhere between the literal and figurative usages of a word, while moving the speaking subject from the logical plane of discourse to the realm of the senses.[4] The image creates an illusion of the immediate presence of meaning to perception, masking the irreconcilable conflict between meaning and reference to the context.[5]

Ricoeur claims that theories which privilege the closure of form and meaning, including Roman Jakobson's notion of the poetic function of language and Gérard Genette's notion of the "signe poétique," fail to account for the problem of the human being's place in figurative discourse, a problem which can only be addressed with reference to an act of predication in the speaking subject. By circumscribing the relation of the figure to the discourse in which it occurs, trope theories avoid the difficulty posed by the disjuncture between the meaning and reference of metaphor, thereby ignoring philosophical differences between logic and rhetoric. This kind of disjuncture constitutes the metaphorical "force" of discourse, and originates in the paradoxical nature of the copula "to be" underlying metaphorical statements.

> The 'locus' of metaphor is neither the name, nor the sentence, nor even discourse, but the copula of the verb to be. The metaphorical 'is' signifies at once 'is not' and 'is like'. (M. V.; 11, my translation)

By locating metaphor in the verb producing metaphorical meaning, Ricoeur introduces the philosophical question of the place of the speaking subject in metaphorical discourse, a subject produced by an act of predication divided in its very function.

Before discussing Ricoeur in detail, I would like to point out that when Genette examines the metonymical "motivation" of metaphors in Proust ("Métonymie chez Proust"), shaped by the contiguity of two terms in the diegesis or fictional context, he does not theorize about the *act* underlying the formation of metaphors, but describes formal relations leading up to and justifying the final comparison between two terms in the figure. Genette concludes that the interaction of metaphorical and metonymical associations assure the " 'necessary' cohesion of the *text*,"[6] while Ricoeur emphasizes the inherently conflictual structure of poetic discourse.

In Ricoeur the speaking subject creates a new level of semantic "pertinence" on which to negotiate relations of difference and similarity joining/separating the literal meaning and the figurative use of a word. This process implies a shift between the structure of meaning and reference to the context. For example, the reference to Achilles in the statement "A lion walked into battle" constitutes the figurative *use* of "lion." The "proper sense" or metaphorical meaning of the statement results from the isolation of those semantic traits common to both the idea of the lion and the idea of Achilles, such as courage and leadership. Ricoeur argues that the "proper sense" of metaphor resists assimilation into a coherent image or final concept, because the act of predication which produces metaphorical meaning is contradictory. Achilles both is and is not a lion.

Next, by showing that the movement between the structure of meaning and reference to the context is at the origin of all meaning production, Ricoeur is able to claim that the movement of metaphor can be generalized into a model for semiosis or sign production. In other words, the "to be or not to be" of metaphorical naming characterizes the very process by which the literal meaning of words comes into being in the first place. In this move Ricoeur both discredits the notion of a final interpretation of metaphorical discourse and places in question the assumption of an original, literal meaning of words from which figures seem to digress. Ricoeur echoes the point of view of Bakhtin, for whom

> there can be neither a first nor a last meaning; [anything that can be understood] always exists among other meanings as a link in the chain of meaning. . . . In historical life this chain continues infinitely, and therefore each individual link in it is renewed again and again, as though it were being reborn.[7]

Metaphor would be a special case of the general movement of semiosis generated by the subject's performance in discourse. The subject constantly negotiates differences between the semiotic plane of discourse, defining the relation between signifier and signified in conventional signs, and the semantic plane, defining the relation of signs to the context.[8]

Ricoeur clarifies distinctions between indexation (shaping logical relations of reference and subject-address in discourse), metonymy (shaping relations of contiguity between the lexical terms of a figure), and syntagmatic alignment (shaping relations between words in the sentence). Such distinctions allow us to move beyond semiotic questions as to the *structure* of discourse toward philosophical issues surrounding the construction of being and meaning through discourse.

Ricoeur reacts in part to Jakobson's famous reduction of differences between grammar and rhetoric to a single binary opposition between associations by similarity and associations by contiguity, under the rubric metaphor/metonymy.[9] While Jakobson made this move in the hope of defining a general semiotic of discourse which would transcend linguistics per se, he effaced ontological and epistemological distinctions between logic and rhetoric, pushing aside an entire category of association by contiguity formed by indexation. Indices, including, in the most rigorous sense of the term, personal and demonstrative pronouns, govern not so much the structure as the force of discourse, consisting as they do in the inscription of subject-address and reference in language. The question of semiosis as performance engages neither the structure nor the force of metaphor taken separately, but the interaction of the two in poetic discourse. By tracing the movement of indexation within metaphor, we can begin to approach poetics in terms of a staging of the subject in the literary text.[10]

When Ricoeur disintricates the structure of metaphorical meaning from the movement of subject-address and reference in metaphorical discourse, he also responds to debates fostered by speech act theorists concerning relations between rhetoric and performance. While structural theories privilege the form of meaning over the contract shaping communication between subjects in an empirical situation, speech act theorists, including Austin, Searle, and Strawson, privilege questions of reference and subject-address, at the expense of strictly semiotic concerns. When Austin first defines a new category of utterances, "performatives," with reference to the meaning of the speech act itself, when he ultimately declares all utterances to be in some sense "performative" because of their implicit reference to the contract binding subjects in discourse, he excludes sentences whose meaning, i.e., the conventional signification of the words, might be at odds with the speaker's intentions and the situation of the speaking event. For instance, a promise to wed uttered during a wedding rehearsal or a theatrical performance cannot be upheld in a court of law. Such statements are not lies, they are simply "unfelicitous": they cannot be included in Austin's category of everyday verbal contracts.

Performatives focus on the "here" and "now" of the speaking event and exclude the problem of signification per se, the realm of "locutionary acts." Rhetoric would belong in the realm of locutionary acts and would seem to have nothing to do with performatives. When Austin delimits the category of performatives in terms of the sincerity of the speaker and the appropriateness of the pragmatic situation of discourse, he takes for granted a unified subject of everyday, logical discourse, a subject whose intentions transcend those accidents inscribed in language itself, including the force of irony, role-play, and word-play.

What is at stake here is not whether Austin correctly or consistently defines the form or function of performative utterances, or even the performative function of all utterances, but whether his taxonomy helps to address the question of the fundamentally "unhappy" situation of man in language, namely, that saying is fundamentally at odds with meaning. If, for example, someone says, "I'll bet it rains today," we do not necessarily expect him to pay up if he is wrong. The verb "to bet" can be intended literally or figuratively, depending on the context.

Thus while performative utterances seem at first to have nothing in common with the problem of metaphor, they both involve a conflict between saying and "meaning" (including the intentions of the speaker).[11] The "intended" meaning and metaphorical meaning (the proper sense of poetic discourse) intersect along the lines of a movement between the conventional meaning of words and the reference of discourse, the "semiotic" and "semantic" levels of language defined by Benveniste.

For example, if the speaker says, "I'll bet," in the course of a card game, his intention to stake money or some other property on his move is expressed in the literal meaning of the verb. Reference to the context helps to clarify the meaning of discourse, and the meaning of the speech act in turn, but does not provide a fool-proof guard against ambiguity. The gambler might be using the expression figuratively, and be held to his words by a strict enforcement of the verbal contract implied by the relation of "I'll bet" to the speaking situation. Though this ambiguity could lead to a fight over the responsibilities of the speaker, communication can continue once the ambiguity is resolved.

Metaphor, on the other hand, produces a movement in the imagination between the figurative use and the literal sense of an expression, a movement which produces the "force" of metaphor and which gradually diminishes as metaphors are assimilated into conventional usage. If an author writes, "was this the face that launched a thousand ships," reference to the historical events motivating the figures "face" and "launched ships" (i.e., the beauty of Helen provoked the Trojan War) helps to clarify the meaning of the statement without reducing the meaning to a concept. In this statement the movement between the figure and reference to the discourse remains lively, resisting assimilation into a logical, one-dimensional meaning. As Ricoeur says,

> Metaphor opens up a space defining the play of difference and similarity which cannot be reduced to a concept. (M. V.; 252, my translation)

To some extent, metaphors cease to be "metaphors" as they lose their force through disambiguation, as the proper sense replaces the literal sense in common usage.

From the standpoint of interpretation, metaphorical meaning differs from the intended meaning of literal statements in that metaphors derive their force from the interaction of difference and similarity between two meanings, while the force of a verbal contract derives from the ultimate clarification of the speaker's intentions. If however, following Austin, we distinguish between the *effects* of speech acts on the interpreter of the message, the "perlocutionary effects," from the *production* of the intended meaning, we discover important parallels between the "metaphorical meaning" of poetics and the "intended meaning" of speech act theory.[12] On the level of their production, the notions of metaphorical meaning and intended meaning share a common origin in an act of predication in the speaking subject, who must negotiate differences between the conventional meaning of words and the reference of discourse. Thus Ricoeur claims that a movement of metaphor shapes the subject's performance of all kinds of statements, including the meaning of verbal contracts, statements or dimensions of statements which focus on the "here" and "now" of the speaking event.

When Ricoeur uncovers a movement of metaphor generating speech acts, he states something of the difficulty of formulating a fail-safe category of statements defined by the verifiability of the contract binding subjects in discourse.[13] Ricoeur places in question the very notions of the "here" and "now" of discourse, the immediate present and presence of the speaking event, by exposing the inevitable division of the subject in that space, that time. "The literal 'is' accompanies the metaphorical 'is not' " (M. V.; 271, my translation). Thus Austin's "performative function," which calls into play the sincerity of the speaker and the felicity of the speaking situation, is always and already troubled by the not-here, the not-now of the subject to itself in metaphor.

By including both performatives and metaphorical statements in a general semiotics of performance, we not only isolate the act of predication shaping man's place in language, but are able to discuss how subjects become something for other subjects in metaphorical discourse. It is at this juncture that we can examine how relations between poetics and performance shape the rhetorical space of Jean Genet's novels.

In Genet analogical figures join terms which are either discontiguous in the diegesis, or so semantically incompatible or far-fetched as to resist assimilation into an image or "proper sense." There is an indexical dimension to such figures which leads the narrating and reading subject between the time of the narration and the time of the narrating event, in the same way that it shapes interrelations between on- and off-stage space in Genet's plays, which I discuss at length in chapter 5. Suffice it to say here that in the plays this kind of movement disturbs the mimetic closure of text and performance, holding the spectator in suspense as he tries to find himself (his projections) in the representation.

By accounting for the indexical function of metaphors in Genet, we are able to describe the implication of the speaking subject in the production of metaphorical meaning, since the indexical function, by definition, introduces questions of reference and subject-address into problems of semiosis. In this context, "reference" does not name relations between words and empirical reality as it does in Austin's speech act theory, but between words and the context or world shaped by literary discourse.[14] The problem of subject-address is inscribed in the reference of discourse, since reference is produced by an act of predication in the speaking subject.

For instance, in the following figure from *Pompes funèbres*, the semantic disparity between a matchbox and a casket conceals a transference of desire from one object to the other in the narrator's imagination, while tracing a movement in time and space between the present of the narration and the narrator's memories. Sitting in the apartment of Jean D.'s mother, Genet remembers how he came to associate the matchbox with the casket of his dead friend during the funeral. We move from the narration of the funeral scene back to the present along a trajectory traced by a displacement of the matchbox:

> Le regard fixe je suivis le cercueil de Jean. Dans la poche de ma veste, ma main joua quelques secondes avec une petite boîte d'allumettes suédoises. *Cette même boîte que mes doigts trituraient quand la mère de Jean me dit:* —Erik est Berlinois. (P. F.; 17, italics added)

> My staring eyes followed Jean's coffin. My hand played for a few seconds with a small matchbox in the pocket of my jacket, the same box that my fingers were kneading when Jean's mother said to me: —Erik's from Berlin. (F. R.; 22–23)

The displacement of the matchbox between the funeral and the scene with Erik ultimately generates the substitution of "matchbox" by "casket." The figure toward the end of the passage, "j'ai un petit cercueil dans ma poche" ("I have a little casket in my pocket"), results from a series of associations beginning with the somewhat fortuitous comparison of the matchbox with a package or "colis":

> —C'est une petite boîte d'allumettes que j'ai dans ma poche.
> Il était assez naturel que me revînt à ce moment la comparaison, qu'un jour, avait faite un gars en prison, me parlant des colis permis aux prisonniers:
> —T'as droit à un colis par semaine. Qu'ça soye un cercueil ou une boîte d'allumettes, c'est pareil, c'est un colis.
> Sans doute. Une boîte d'allumettes ou un cercueil, c'est pareil, me dis-je. J'ai un petit cercueil dans ma poche. (P. F.; 23)

> —There's a little matchbox in my pocket.
> It was quite natural for me to recall at that moment the comparison a fellow prisoner once made while telling me about the packages which the inmates were allowed to receive.
> —You're allowed one package a week. Whether it's a coffin or a box of matches, it's the same thing, it's a package.
> No doubt. A matchbox or a coffin, it's the same thing, I said to myself. I have a little coffin in my pocket. (F. R.; 30)

"Colis" serves as a semantic transition between the two more disparate terms, matchbox and casket. It also diverts attention from the psychological importance of this substitution by focussing on the physical similarity of the two terms. As the association of casket and matchbox is repeated, the superficial point of comparison, "colis," disappears and the matchbox takes on the funereal meaning of the casket.

Je portais son cercueil dans ma poche. Il n'était pas nécessaire que cette bière, aux proportions réduites, fût vraie. Sur ce petit objet le cercueil des funérailles avait imposé sa puissance. (P. F.; 25)

I was carrying his coffin in my pocket. There was no need for the small-scale bier to be a true one. The coffin of the formal funeral had imposed its potency on that little object. (F. R.; 33)

Thus, "coffin" is not merely a metaphor for "matchbox," but also an index for the transference of desire from one object to another. As the casket is closed over the body of Genet's friend, the transference follows the movement of the narrator's look, from the body to its receptacle. The metaphorical substitution of the casket for the matchbox brings the lost love object into the symbolic possession of the narrator: if the casket contains the body of Jean D., and if the casket is identical to the matchbox, then the matchbox contains the body of Jean D.:

Ma boîte était sacrée. . . . Elle contenait Jean tout entier. . . . Toute la gravité de la cérémonie était amassée dans ma poche où venait d'avoir lieu le transfert. (P. F.; 25–26)

My box was sacred. It did not contain a particle merely of Jean's body but Jean in his entirety. . . . The whole gravity of the ceremony was gathered in my pocket, to which the transfer had just taken place. (F. R.; 33)

Then follows a kind of montage sequence moving between the funeral and Genet's encounter of the German officer, the lover of Jean D.'s mother. Genet lets go of the matchbox as his eyes take in the aura of Erik's sexuality. Desire has moved from Jean D., to the casket, to the matchbox, to Erik, carrying death in its train.

While such figures anchor the relation between narrative past and present, they place in question the unity of narrative voice by submitting the proper sense of metaphor to the pull of indexation.

I must insist that by "indexical function," I do not mean the "metonymical motivation" of metaphor described by Genette.[15] Genette's use of "metonymy" to describe the spatial proximity of the two terms of metaphors in Proust, derives from Jakobson's reduction of all associations by contiguity to "metonymy."[16] Genette, like Jakobson, confuses the discursive and rhetorical levels of language. Metonymy, and for that matter, synecdoche, are defined structurally in terms of the replacement of one word by another. Metonymical contiguity defines a relationship inherent in the signifieds themselves. In the statement "Sails appeared on the horizon," the word "sails" evokes the idea of a ship because sails constitute highly visible parts of sailing ships. No such "natural" contiguity exists between a casket and a matchbox. This relationship depends entirely on spatial and psychological associations established by the context of discourse.[17]

Eco suggests something of the effects of indexation on the production of metaphor when he discusses the movement of the trace in iconic signs.[18] He reformulates Peirce's semiotic to show the complexity of the notions of iconic and indexical sign functions, claiming that these types of sign function interact in every instance of discourse. He names the relation of the trace to its content *ratio difficilis*, since "the form of the expression is motivated by the form of the content one gives it: it has the same visual and tactile marks as the sememe corresponding to it, even if the trace does not represent them identically." Eco gives the example of the trace left by horses' hoofs on the ground: the hoof marks are both similar to the hoofs they represent, though not identical to them, and are indices for the event that left them on the ground. The trace "digitalizes" iconic signs by means of reference. Though the relation of hoofprints to hoof is metonymical and derives from the conventional meaning of the word, the relation of hoofprints to the event which produced them is indexical. Its meaning requires a reference to the discourse: "Horses passed by here in x direction x number of hours ago."

The indexical aspect of metaphor is not dictated by linguistic code, as it is for conventional indices such as proper names and personal pronouns. Whereas the name "John," for instance, signifies nothing, pointing rather to "the person named John" in the context, digitalized metaphors both struggle with the meaning of words and point to referents in the context. As a result we cannot reduce this kind of metaphor to a category of linguistically coded indices, but can describe a "pointing function" of metaphor created by the speech act in which it occurs.

In Genet, the indexical pull of metaphor joins two locations and two levels of narration, the diegetic event and the narrating event. Take the following example from *Pompes funèbres*:

Les fleuves rapides et sans rives de la verte colère coulaient en moi, du nord au sud. (P. F.; 79)

The swift, shoreless rivers of green anger were flowing within me, from north to south. (F. R.; 105)

Isolated from the context, the association of "fleuves" and "colère" can be justified semantically: the idea of a violently flowing river reminds one of the violent pulse of an angry man. Moreover the word "fleuves," by means of similarity with "torrents," acquires something of the conventionalized meaning of that fluvial metaphor for forceful agitation. The agitation wells up in the narrator acting the part of one of his characters, Erik. The geographical indications, "du nord au sud," could refer to the circulation of the blood through the body (in an unscientific way), but they also concretize the idea of the river as a real location in the narration:

> J'écris ce livre auprès d'un monastère élevé tout droit au milieu des forêts, dans les roches et les ronces. Le long du torrent, j'aime revivre les angoisses d'Erik. (P. F.; 10)

> I am writing this book near a monastery that stands deep in the woods, among rocks and thorns. As I walk by the torrent, I enjoy reliving the anguish of Erik. (F. R.; 13)

Metaphors are supposed to allow the reader to apprehend meaning immediately by painting a mental image.[19] The indexical function of metaphor in Genet causes the reader to see double by pointing to the prismatic intrication of different moments of the narration in the uncertain present of the narrating event. Thus, rather than simply creating an image of anger in terms of a torrent, the "fleuves"/"colère" figure shifts the reader between two locations in narrative space.

This aspect of Genet's style cannot be explained by structural theories of narrative. While structural poetics, modelled after the Saussurian sign, focusses on relations between poetic signifier and signified,[20] a theory of performance would highlight an act of predication in the speaking subject, an act which negotiates metaphorical difference and similarity, creating a new level of semantic pertinence. When Ricoeur insists on the contradictory structure of the verb "to be" producing metaphorical meaning, he leads us to an understanding of metaphorical discourse as an act of dissimulation or disguise, a performance shaping the subject's (mis)representation for other subjects through language.

The effects of this performance can only be described with reference to the rhetorical style or philosophical slant of a given author or esthetic movement. Genet not only understands the importance of disguise for the outsider to perform on the inside of dominant culture, but discovers an act of dissimulation at the origin of dominant, heterosexual culture as well. Refusing the plenitude of the poetic image, Genet deploys metaphors which display the underlying cleavage of the subject in language, introducing the violence of his "difference," his homosexuality, into narrative representation.

In Genet's spatial metaphors, those which articulate dynamic relations between moments of the narrative, reference to the context does not permanently resolve the disparity between the literal meaning and the figurative usage of a word according to a truer sense of things. Paradoxically, the reference reinforces a disparity between the two by anchoring them in the physical reality of the fiction. For example, in the sentence "J'ai un cercueil dans ma poche," the casket and matchbox stubbornly resist assimilation into a third meaning, the proper sense of metaphor, because they insistently refer to the events in which Genet found them.

Ordinary metaphors usually combine a concrete, diegetic term with a signifier of something else, motivated or not by their contiguity in the diegesis.[21] The assimilation of the two terms into a poetic meaning or image is facilitated by the very abstract nature of the signifier. (Saussure, after all, defined the signifier as an "image acoustique.") In Genet, metaphors trace the intersection of two moments of the narrative. The referential pull of the two terms toward opposite directions in the narration subordinates the poetic image to the force of difference. In Genet, analogical figures are characterized by a dialectical movement between the outside and inside of metaphorical meaning, between the spacing of disparity and the melding of a juncture.

Likewise, the comparing agents *comme* and *pareil* in the following figuration from *Notre-Dame-des-fleurs* function primarily to trace the dynamic interaction among the narration, the narrating event, and the narrator's memory, by means of a displacement of the word "perles." This movement is more important than similarities between the various terms of the association. The story of this novel takes place in Paris; the speaker narrates it from a prison workshop, while his memory refers to the provincial cemetery of his childhood.

> La couronne de perles tombe à terre et se brise. . . . Les petites perles roulent dans la sciure semée sur le plancher où elles sont semblables aux perles de verre que les colporteurs vendent peu de chose aux enfants, et celles-ci sont pareilles aux perles de verre que nous enfilons chaque jour dans des kilomètres de fil de laiton, avec quoi, en d'autres cellules, on tresse des couronnes mortuaires, pareilles à celles qui jonchaient le cimetière de mon enfance. (N.D.F.; 65)

> The crown of pearls falls to the floor and breaks. . . . The little pearls roll about the sawdust-covered floor, and they are like the glass pearls that peddlers sell to children for a penny or two, and these are like the glass pearls that we thread every day on miles of brass wire, with which, in other cells, they weave funeral wreaths like those that bestrewed the cemetery of my childhood. (O.L.F.; 203–204)

The traditionally analogical function of *comme* and *pareil* thus serves to trace dynamical relations between the various moments of the narrative, rather than to assimilate the various terms of the comparison into a new meaning of "pearls."[22] In Genet the indexical function of metaphors and similes reveals the division of the speaking subject in the not here and not now of narrative discourse, exposing a game of dissimulation at work in the art of imitation. For this reason, metaphorical figures in Genet do not generate a synthetic, analogical, "Impressionist" or Proustian vision of the world, but a kinesthetic, geometric, almost "Cubist" vision, shaped by the force of difference separating things in time and space.[23] This stylistic tendency in Genet reflects, even more than Gérard Genette imagined, "contemporary man's preference for space, after the Bergsonian inflation of duration."[24]

Sometimes the resistance of "difficult" metaphors to semantic resolution contributes to the indexical focus of the figure. Take the association of "head" with the (implied) metaphorical term "airplane" in this passage from *Miracle de la rose*, in which the narrator describes a vision of the condemned man, Harcamone:

> Il n'avait pas de chaussettes. De sa tête—ou de la mienne—sortait un bruit de moteur d'avion. Je sentais, dans toutes mes veines, que le miracle était en marche. (M.R.; 14)

> From his head—or from mine—came the roar of an airplane engine. I felt in all my veins that the miracle was under way. (M.R.; 15)

The absurd association of the diegetic term, "tête," with the source of the airplane noise, "moteur d'avion," shapes a relation of participation between two events occurring simultaneously in the narration. *Miracle de la rose* is a chronicle of the narrator Jean Genet's incarceration in Fontevrault prison during the German occupation. The prisoners experience the reality outside the prison indirectly, in metonymical fragments. We know, for instance, that "Genet" works in a prison shop making camouflage nets for the German army occupying France, and that the war outside caused a reduction in the food supply (M. R.; 10, 27). The fortuitous passage of an airplane over the prison furnishes another trace of the war outside on the prison scene inside and provides sound effects for the narrator's erotic hallucination about Harcamone, the "miracle" of the rose. Whereas the relation of airplane noise to airplane motor is metonymical, the relation of a head to an airplane motor is indexical. It can only be understood in terms of the movement between two events, including the private drama of the narrator's desire and the public drama of World War II, in a single moment of the narrative. This kind of figure resembles a piece of evidence left at the scene of a crime or an *objet trouvé* in a contemporary painting.[25] It transcends its metaphorical function (i.e., to enrich the meaning of "head" by means of comparison with an airplane motor) in order to point to the participation of one event in another in the narrative. Unlike the traces mentioned earlier, this figure is not "motivated" by simple analogy, but by coincidence. In the same way, Eco's example of the denture found at the scene of a crime is not a metaphor for the agent that left it there, but a pure index for his or her implication in the scene.[26]

In *Miracle de la rose*, analogical figures impress the feudal history of Fontevrault abbey on the present of the narration, when Fontevrault is used as a prison. Upon arriving at Fontevrault after his arrest, the narrator evokes the distant past by means of analogy:

Huit gaffes nous attendaient comme des valets de pied. (M.R.; 7)

Eight guards, lined up like footmen, were waiting for us on the lighted steps. (M.R.; 5)

The prisoners themselves have a no less noble allure:

Cet assassin avait la fragilité d'un duc de Guise ou d'un chevalier de Lorraine. (M.R.; 15)

This murderer was as delicate as a Duke of Guise or a Knight of Lorraine. (M.R.; 16)

Like the traces of Baroque and Renaissance renovations still visible on the prison walls, such figures are traces for the past. While they are "motivated" by similarity (valets, like guards, hail the guests at the gate; criminals and knights both have inhabited the buildings of Fontevrault), they function within the narrative to point to the former presence of valets and knights in the current location. "We used to cross through courtyards with infinite sadness, sad because of the neglect which condemns to death the facades of an admirable Renaissance" (my translation). "Nous traversions des cours d'une tristesse infinie, tristes par le fait déjà de l'abandon qui voue à la mort des façades d'une Renaissance admirable" (M.R.; 13).

The digitalization of metaphors in this manner fulfills the narrator's fantasy of participating physically in the pomp and virility of the *cheval-rèsque* world by staging an experience of continuity between an imaginary past and the present. In the following figuration, the narrator establishes a new order of knighthood whose members are thugs and assassins:

Le coude posé contre le mur, Bulkaen s'appuyait de telle façon que sa tête passait sous son bras qui paraissait le couronner. . . . Sa main gauche était posée sur l'os de sa hanche comme sur la poignée d'une dague. (M.R.; 18)

Bulkaen was leaning against the wall with his elbow, in such a way that his head was under his arm, which looked as if it were a crown. . . . His left hand was placed on his hip bone as on the handle of a dagger. (My translation. M.R.; 21)

J'ai vu des gars tatoués de l'Aigle, de la Frégate, de l'Ancre de Marine, du Serpent, de la Pensée, des Etoiles, de la Lune et du Soleil. . . . Ces figures ornaient les torses d'une chevalerie nouvelle. (M.R.; 116)

I saw guys tattooed with the Eagle, the Frigate, the Navy Anchor, the Snake, the Thinker, Stars, the Moon and the Sun. . . . These figures adorned torsos with a new order of knighthood. (My translation. Most of the passage is missing from Frechtman, M.R.; 173)

Il ne semble pas que les noblesses romaines, hindoues ou franques d'avant environ l'an mille, aient bénéficié d'un prestige religieux, plus que religieux, et autre que religieux, comparable à celui dont bénéficie la noblesse écroulée et j'en vois la raison dans l'établissement des armoiries. . . . Ainsi les tatouages sacrèrent les marles. (M.R.; 146)

It does not seem that the Roman, Hindu, and Frankish nobilities of about the year 1000 or earlier enjoyed a religious prestige, a prestige more and other than religious, like that enjoyed by the crumbling nobility, and the reason for this, as I see it, lies in the creation of armorial bearings. . . . In like manner, the tattoos consecrated the big shots. (M.R.; 222)

The power of metaphor to shape the movement between past and present also shapes the interference of the narrator's hallucinations into the reality of the diegesis. Caught up in the magic of metaphor, the narrator sees his prison cell transform with the wave of a magic wand and finds himself holding a knight instead of his friend, Bulkaen.

Comme dans les illustrés d'autrefois, une chaumière en palais et la servante en fée, ma cellule est changée d'un coup dont je vois encore la baguette qui va disparaître, en une chambre de parade éclairée de cent flambeaux, et ma paillasse, suivant cette transformation, est devenue un lit paré de rideaux attachés par des guirlandes de perles fines. Tout chancelle sous les rubis, les émeraudes; tout est d'or, de nacre et de soie et, dans mes bras, je tiens un chevalier dévêtu, qui n'est pas Bulkaen. (M.R.; 83–84)

Just as the cottage is changed into a palace and the servant girl into a fairy in the illustrations of old magazines, so my cell is transformed by a stroke, of which I still see the wand about to disappear, into a stately chamber lit up by a hundred torches, and my straw mattress, continuing this transformation, has become a bed adorned with curtains that are attached by garlands of true pearls. Everything wavers beneath the rubies and emeralds; everything is made of gold, silk, mother of pearl; and in my arms I hold an unclothed knight, who is not Bulkaen. (M.R.; 125)

This kind of "poetic hallucination" in Genet,[27] is created by metaphors which do not simply make images or make meaning visible, but refer to an act of performance shaping the interpenetration of diegetic and extra-diegetic events. Unlike Nerval's visions in *Aurélia* or Proust's description of Swann's dream in *La Recherche*, which appear as parenthetical departures from the immediacy of the narration, Genet's hallucinations occur on a continuum with diegetic reality: now you see it, now you don't. Describing a hallucination in *Pompes funèbres*, Genet says:

> Ma ferveur transformait en une machine infernale. Elle explosa. Le plus beau soleil d'artifice, par l'âme de Jean développé, dispersait une gerbe de verre, de tifs, de trognons, d'épluchures, de plumes, de côtelettes rongées, de fleurs fanées et de délicates coquilles d'oeufs. Le temps d'un battement de paupières et tout était pourtant dans l'ordre terrestre. (P.F.; 164)

> My fervor transformed into an infernal machine. It exploded. The most beautiful pyrotechnical sun, developed by the soul of Jean, scattered a spray of glass, hair, stumps, peels, feathers, gnawed cutlets, faded flowers, and delicate eggshells. And yet in the twinkling of an eye everything was in earthly order. (F.R.; 218)

The metaphor I discussed earlier from *Pompes funèbres* comparing anger and a torrent recurs later in the narrative, again with reference to the double figure of the narrator playing Erik. It is used as an index not only for the participation of the narrating event in the narration, but as a trace for the participation of both the narrating event and the narration in a poetic hallucination. Here Genet is the chief participant in a cannibalistic feast:

> Il était à nouveau parcouru par les fleuves de la verte colère. Ils roulaient la nuit, sous un ciel sillonné d'éclairs de chaleur, une eau pleine d'alligators. Sur leurs bords où croissaient des fougères, les sauvages adorateurs de la lune, dans les forêts, dansaient autour d'un feu. La tribu conviée au festin s'enivrait de la danse et du régal que serait ce jeune mort cuisant dans un chaudron. Il m'est doux et consolant, parmi les hommes d'un continent noir et bouleversé dont les tribus mangent leurs rois morts, de me retrouver avec les naturels de cette contrée d'Erik, afin de pouvoir, sans danger, sans remords, manger la chair du mort le plus tendre, de pouvoir l'assimiler à la mienne. (P.F.; 185)

> He was again traversed by rivers of green anger. They were sailing at night, beneath a sky streaked with heat lightening, down a river full of alligators. On the shore where ferns grew, the savage moon-worshipers were dancing around a fire in the forest. The tribe that had been invited to the feast was reveling in the dance and in anticipation of the young body that was cooking in a caldron. It is nice and comforting to me, among the men of a black, disrupted continent whose tribes eat their dead kings, to find myself again with the natives of that country of Erik's so that I can eat the flesh of the tenderest body without danger or remorse, so that I can assimilate it to mine. (F.R.; 247)

The image of a river refers to three locations in narrative space: the place of the narrating event (next to a "torrent"), the place of the narration in which the metaphor occurs, and the place of the narrator's cannibalistic hallucination. The movement of reference here destabilizes the unity of narrative voice in the immediacy of narrative discourse. While this figure leads to the comparison of Hitler's Germany to a country of cannibals, the construction of these parallel scenes turns the movement of metaphor in opposite directions.

In *Miracle de la rose* the commonplace association of melancholy with an autumn day shapes the participation between the outside and the inside of the narrator's prison cell.

> La tristesse de son départ [devenait] une espèce de mélancholie chronique pareille à un automne embrumé. . . . Après les coups de soleil, pour que mon coeur, blessé par tant d'éclats, se repose, je me recroqueville en moi-même afin de retrouver les bois mouillés, les feuilles mortes, les brumes, et je rentre dans un manoir où flambe un feu de bois dans une haute cheminée. Le vent que j'écoute est plus berceur que celui qui geint dans les vrais sapins d'un vrai parc. . . . Cet automne est plus intense que l'automne vrai, l'automne extérieur car, pour en jouir, je dois à chaque seconde inventer un détail, un signe, et m'attarder sur lui. Je le crée à chaque instant. Je reste des minutes sur l'idée d'une grille rouillée, ou de la mousse pourrie, des champignons, d'une cape gonflée par le vent. (M.R.; 98)

> The sadness of his leaving soon . . . became a kind of chronic melancholy, like a misty autumn. . . . After the sunshine, in order that my heart, which is hurt by such brilliance, may rest, I curl up within myself in order to return to the wet forest, the dead leaves, the mists, and I enter a mansion where a log fire is blazing in a high fireplace. The wind to which I listen is more lulling than the one which moans in the real firs of a real park. . . . This autumn is more intense and insidious than real autumn, external autumn, for in order to enjoy it I must invent a detail or a sign every second and must linger over it. I create it every instant. I dwell for minutes on the idea of rain, on the idea of a rusty gate, or of damp moss, of mushrooms, of a cape puffed out by the wind. (M.R.; 146)

Here, use of a commonplace metaphor in lieu of a fresh association is the site of the indexical, spatial movement of the figure. Though "autumn" has not replaced "melancholy" in the lexicon, this association has been virtually codified by lyric poets. Statements such as "Those years were the autumn of his life" excite little in the way of an image. The reduction of the visual force of this figure allows it to function as a juncture between reality, fantasy, and memory in the narrative, submitting the metaphorical meaning of "automne" to the staging of difference. Moreover, just as the metaphor takes the narrator outside the prison to a country scene, so the indexical pull of the figure establishes a play between the inside and outside of language, between language turned in upon itself in the poetic sign, and language opened up to the movement of reference in narrative discourse. The prison motif thus becomes itself a metaphor for the prison of linguistic convention which the poet-criminal dares to escape.[28]

Genet uses metaphorical figures to expand the space of narrative, while submitting the present and presence of narrative discourse to the disturbing effects of difference. While critics who comment on the disjunctive nature of Genet's style tend to place him among the surrealists, they fail to distinguish between the role of difference in Genet's metaphors and its role in surrealist metaphors.[29] Surrealist poets destroy conventional associations between things and ideas in order to construct fresh meanings around familiar objects. Surrealist discourse produces a new level of semantic pertinence on which the proper sense of metaphor can be located.[30] When André Breton calls for the creation of a new world order by means of automatic writing, he counts on the unifying force of analogy to build that order.[31] Genet, on the other hand, uses metaphor in ways which expose the very difficulty of producing a "proper" sense of homosexual discourse, a discourse muttered on the margins defining the "improper" of dominant, heterosexual discourse. In an important way, the movement of difference in metaphorical figures is itself a metaphor or a model for the movement of homosexual desire in Genet's discourse.

In heterosexual discourse, relations of difference demarcate first and foremost the sexual opposition between male and female from which all other differences are derived, including relations between subject and object, master and slave, active and passive. Inasmuch as the "female subject" defines the "other" of the male subject, the feminine is always and already shaped within an economy of the "same," a being whose ontological difference has been reduced to a figure of negation defining "that which the male is not." This ontology is derived from a biological model defining woman as a man lacking a penis, as the lack itself, which can be recuperated in an image of Man which transcends sexual difference.[32] In heterosexual discourse, the movement of desire translates into a move toward the reduction of difference, toward the unifying coherence of the "proper" sense. In other words, heterosexual discourse, including surrealism, reduces difference to the dialectical opposition of I and not-I, rather than recognizing the relation between male and female as one of irreconcilable difference. Hence the importance of the image in surrealist poetry, which masks semantic conflict in a synthesis of the senses, thus linking surrealism with Romanticism. Moreover, surrealist artists and poets translate the violence of metaphorical reduction into images of women being blinded, dismembered, raped, and otherwise subjected to the violence of dominant discourse. Buñuel's and Dali's film, *Un Chien Andalou*, illustrates my point.[33]

The subject of metaphorical discourse in Genet cannot be conceived as a fixed identity but as a trace for the movement of difference destroying/producing relations of intersubjectivity in discourse. This means that the categories of masculine and feminine, master and slave, active and passive, are not properties stemming from natural, biological differences between the sexes, but positions determined by the psychological stance the characters, all men, assume in Genet's fantasies. For example, the passive male is "feminized" by the virility of the more dominant male.

Romantic literature profits from a certain degree of blindness to problems of sexual difference, in order to celebrate an ideal of spiritual unity between men and women in romantic love. Genet both displaces difference from the biological realm to the realm of the subject's performance of/in erotic discourse and lifts the veil of censorship masking difference in Romantic literature. Furthermore, Genet rejects the reductive coherence of Romanticism by replacing the unity of the subject to itself in the poetic image with an endless play of reflections between subjects in masquerade.

In the following "hallucination" from *Notre-Dame-des-fleurs*, a metaphorical play between masculine and feminine symbols produces the doubled figure of the female impostor. Here, Notre-Dame, alias Adrien Baillon, confesses his crime to Mignon, who turns out to be his father. By revealing his feminine sobriquet, Notre-Dame also exposes his bisexuality.

Pendant que le nom mystérieux sortait, c'était si angoissant de regarder la grande beauté de l'assassin se tordre, les boucles immobiles et immondes des serpents de son visage endormi s'émouvoir et bouger, que Mignon perçut la gravité d'un tel aveu, à tel point, si profondément, qu'il se demanda si Notre-Dame n'allait pas dégueuler des pafs gluants de foutre. (N.D.F.; 38)

As the mysterious name emerged, it was so agonizing to watch the murderer's great beauty writhing, the motionless and unclean coils [foul curls] of the marble serpents of his drowsy face moving and stirring, that Darling realized the gravity of such a confession, felt it so deeply that he wondered whether Our Lady was going to puke pricks [sticky with semen]. (O.L.F.; 137, my translation in brackets)

The sexual symbolism of the Medusa's head coiffed with snakes, a condensation of male and female figures in a single image, is translated into literal terms as Genet compares the snakes to phalluses sticky with semen.

As the scene progresses, Notre-Dame's body transforms into a religious reposary revealing an apparition both human and celestial, Our Lady of the Flowers:

Quand le nom fut dans la chambre, il se produisit que l'assassin, confus, s'ouvrit, laissant jaillir comme une gloire, de ses pitoyables morceaux, un reposoir où était couchée dans les roses une femme de lumière et de chair. (N.D.F.; 39)

When the name was in the room, it came to pass that the murderer, abashed, opened up, and there sprang forth, like a Glory, from his pitiable fragments, an altar on which [a reposary where] there lay, in the roses, a woman of light and flesh. (O.L.F.; 138, my translation in brackets)

The paradoxical substitution of "Notre-Dame-des-fleurs" for the male name Adrien Baillon, plus the comparison of the male body to a receptacle containing a female body, represents the implication of masculine and feminine in the figure of the *beau mâle*, Genet's anti-hero. As the vision comes to a close, we move from the realm of the subject's performance of metaphorical discourse to the sexual performances of Mignon and his son in the narration.

Le reposoir ondulait sur une infâme boue dans laquelle il sombra: l'assassin. Mignon l'attira à lui et, pour le mieux étreindre, fit avec lui une courte lutte. Il me plairait de les rêver tous les deux dans bien d'autres postures, si, dès que je ferme les yeux, mon rêve obéissait encore à ma volonté. (N.D.F.; 39)

The altar [reposary] undulated on a foul mud into which it sank: the murderer. Darling drew Our Lady toward him, and, the better to embrace him, struggled with him briefly. I would like to dream them both in many other positions if, when I closed my eyes, my dream still obeyed my will. (O.L.F.; 138)

In Aristotle, the art of imitation comes naturally to Man, indeed distinguishes Man from animals.[34] Genet forces us to ask who is this man, and how does the metaphysical claim to the unity of Man exclude differences separating outsiders from the insiders of dominant culture? Aristotelian poetics fails to account for voices speaking from the margins of dominant discourse by reducing difference to the ontological order of "the same." Genet, whose difference excludes him from the Aristotelian category of Man, has mastered the art of imitation only to use it against the violence of metaphysical reduction.

The political dimension of Genet's art is especially clear in a type of figure which twists symbols borrowed from liturgical and literary tradition into metaphors for crime and sexual perversion. Conventional symbols are signs which present meanings to the mind by way of concrete images. For instance, the cross refers to Christianity without the help of long explanations about the relation of the crucifixion to Christian theology. Genet typically constructs analogies between contradictory terms which, taken by themselves, are conventional symbols for beauty or evil, sacred or profane. Analogies comparing flowers to murderers, for instance, upset normal relations between the symbol and its referent. In the process, Genet exposes the power of representation to reduce the difficulty of moral and social questions by fostering an illusion of the "natural" relation between signs and culturally determined meanings.

The distinction between metaphor and symbol is crucial for under-

standing relations between rhetoric and philosophy and for clarifying relations between symbol and metaphor in Genet. In "White Mythology:
Metaphor in the Text of Philosophy," Derrida sheds light on the place of
metaphor in symbolic discourse, while creating new problems over the
meaning of the word "metaphor" in his own argument.[35] Derrida claims
to examine the problem of conventionalized metaphors, while returning
time and again to the nature of symbols as tools of metaphysical philosophy. The confusion of metaphor with symbol not only presents technical difficulties, but threatens to undermine the very philosophical issue
at stake in Derrida's argument. He states that "metaphors" (symbols) do
not expose the difference underlying their formation, thereby claiming a
natural affinity with the meanings they embody. Derrida's claim about
"metaphors" clearly would seem to go against the grain of Ricoeur's argument, which highlights the movement of negativity producing metaphorical statements, until we realize that Derrida is not debating the
status of metaphor per se, but the rhetorical function of symbols in philosophical discourse.

On the one hand, Derrida refers to Aristotle's definition of metaphor
as " 'giving the thing a name that belongs to something else, the transference being either from genus to species, from species to genus, from
species to species, or on grounds of analogy' " (W.M.; 31). On the other
hand, Derrida supports his own claim about the place of "metaphor" in
philosophical discourse with reference to *symbols*, which by definition
assign sensorial qualities to abstractions. Thus Derrida can state that
"abstract notions always conceal a sensible figure" (W.M.; 7). Symbols
produce a natural or "motivated" link between the sign and its referent
which masks the dichotomy between signifier and signified in ordinary
signs, the material of metaphors. While the structure of signs leaves room
for the possibility that truth is a function of meaning production, and
that meaning is a product of culturally codified discourse, symbols function rhetorically to represent the "truth," meanings which appear to transcend culture and discourse.

Metaphors play on the relations of signs to each other, while symbols
involve the relation of signs to universal meanings. The difference between metaphor and symbol is not simply a question of the formal structure of the two. This difference implies profound distinctions between
the truth value of discourses shaped by each kind of figure. While metaphors produce meanings by way of dissimulation, "giving a thing a name
that belongs to something else," symbols claim to bear witness to the
absolute, to truths which transcend the very act of giving names.

When Derrida states, in line with Ricoeur, that "metaphor is the moment of possible sense as a possibility of non-sense" (W.M.; 42), he raises
the possibility that a movement of metaphor *within* symbolic discourse
could place in question the natural affinity between symbols and their
conventional meanings, undermining the very substance of metaphysical

discourse. However, by confusing symbol and metaphor throughout the essay, Derrida presents something of a tautology, claiming that the movement of metaphor deconstructs metaphor. While this kind of "deconstruction" might be of interest in describing the rhetorical style of a given poet, it does not aim directly at the larger question of the truth value of the signs of philosophical discourse. Since symbols have a stronger claim to the truth than metaphors to begin with, presenting, as they do, meanings in the immediate present and presence of a thing, it seems that the main interest would be to show how a movement of metaphor shaping all discourse can place in question the epistemological weight of symbols, not metaphors themselves.

Derrida's reference to the text of Anatole France has direct bearing on my discussion of the philosophical status of symbols in Genet. He quotes a passage between Polyphilos and Aristo on the question of symbols:

'Wherefore I was on the right road when I investigated the meanings inherent in the words spirit, God, absolute, which are symbols and not signs.
'The spirit possesses God in proportion as it participates in the absolute'. (W.M.; 10)

The symbols in question are not those which might be produced in the train of the production of individual discourses (such as the association of Proust's madeleine with the narrator's spontaneous memories), but conventional symbols such as the cross for Christianity, whose meanings transcend both the discourse in which they occur and the material in which they are represented. (The cross has the same meaning whether it is represented in the form of language, pictures, or sculpture.) Such symbols provide metaphysical philosophers means to construct epistemological categories for naming and ultimately mastering the unknown or unknowable. Symbols are the means by which ordinary men master each other by building ethical and moral systems of inclusion and exclusion, the inside and outside of dominant discourse. "The spirit possesses God in proportion as it participates in the absolute."

We might say that ordinary men have access to the absolute, to knowledge and the power which knowledge confers, in proportion as they participate in the symbols of dominant culture. Genet, a homosexual and a thief, participates in these symbols, but participates in a manner necessarily different from that of ordinary men. This difference shapes, in turn, Genet's relation to God, to truth, to the categories of good and evil which guide the lives of ordinary men. Genet participates in the dominant orders of beauty, morality, and sanctity as an outsider, as a man whose voice has already been divided by his difference from other men.

While the metaphysical identification of Man with the idea of consciousness masks the difficulty posed by the forces of desire and history in the constitution of the subject, the identification of homosexual men with the movement of their desire for other men immediately takes one out of the realm of ontology and into the realms of psychology and ideology. Homosexual discourse raises the question of personal identity as a conflict between being for society and being for oneself—as a performance—and poses a threat to the transcendental subject and meaning of dominant discourse. When Genet submits the conventional meaning of religious and poetic symbols to the effects of homosexual discourse, he in turn twists traditional epistemological categories for goodness, beauty, and godliness into contradictory figures which discredit the very grounds for shaping such categories.

Take, for instance, the following association of flowers and murderers from *Notre-Dame-des-fleurs*:

> Cette merveilleuse *éclosion de belles et sombres fleurs*, je ne l'appris que par fragments: l'un m'était livré par un bout de journal, l'autre cité négligemment par mon avocat. . . . *Ces assassins maintenant morts* sont pourtant arrivés jusqu'à moi. (N.D.F.; 9. italics added)

> I learned only in bits and pieces of that wonderful *blossoming of dark and lovely flowers*: one was revealed to me by a scrap of newspaper; another was casually alluded to by my lawyer. . . . *These murderers*, now dead, have nevertheless reached me. (O.L.F.; 62, italics added)

The traditional symbolic association of flowers with beauty and innocence is contravened by the identification of flowers with the personifications of evil in the discourse. A shift in gender complicates the figure further: "fleurs" is marked for feminine in French, "assassins" is marked for masculine. A term marked for masculine, "fragments," forms a transition between the two. Genet reiterates this metaphor shortly thereafter, eliminating the transitional term. The parenthetical reminder that "flowers" refers to thugs is so casual as to insinuate the reader's own complicity in this crime against language.

> Les journaux arrivent mal jusqu'à ma cellule, et les plus belles pages sont pillées de leurs plus belles fleurs (ces macs), comme jardins en mai. (N.D.F.; 10)
> The newspapers are tattered by the time they reach my cell, and the finest pages have been looted of *their finest flowers, those pimps*, like gardens in May. (O.L.F.; 63, italics added)

Such "analogies" resist assimilation into a poetic image or metaphorical meaning, leaving bare the movement of difference implied in metaphor, while submitting the "natural" meaning of symbols to the effects of that difference. In other words, Genet *uses a symbol for one thing to name something else*, thus introducing a movement of metaphor, the "to be or not to be" of metaphorical naming, into the symbols of dominant culture. He in turn places in question the claims of dominant discourse to truth, knowledge, and power.

In *Miracle de la rose* Genet pushes the creative power of metaphor to its limits. The association of his anti-hero, Harcamone, with a rose, initiates a process of metaphorical transformation which finally destabilizes the very difference between reality and hallucination.

> Harcamone comparut devant un directeur affolé d'être en face d'un mystère aussi terrible que celui que propose une rose dans tout son éclat. (M.R.; 132)

> Harcamone appeared before a warden who was dismayed at being confronted with a mystery as absurd as that of a rose in full bloom. (M.R.; 202)

Eventually we discover that the "rose," symbol of beauty and mystery, refers to Harcamone's member, marked for feminine in argot terms such as "la queue," "la verge," and "la bite."

> Si j'ai rêvé d'une queue, ce fut toujours celle d'Harcamone.... La queue se confondait avec Harcamone, ne souriant jamais il était lui-même la verge sévère d'un mâle, d'une force et d'une beauté surnaturelles. (M.R.; 134)

> When I dreamed of a prick, it was always Harcamone's.... The prick merged with Harcamone; never smiling, he was himself the stern organ of a supernaturally strong and handsome male. (M.R.; 206)

By naming Harcamone's sex in terms marked for feminine, then identifying him with that part of the body, the narrator is able to address his hero in the feminine, as the object of his own virile desire. Since Harcamone is in reality untouchable, Genet uses metaphor to create a fiction about Harcamone and to place himself in that fiction.

> La vérité, c'est qu'Harcamone appartenait à un prince-forban qui avait entendu parler de nous. De sa galère, entre ses gueux cuivrés, ... il nous avait envoyé sa bite admirable, aussi mal dissimulée sous les traits d'un jeune maçon que pouvait l'être l'assassin lui-même sous les traits d'une rose. (M.R.; 135)

> The truth of the matter is that Harcamone belonged to a pirate prince who had heard about us. From his galley, among his coppery riffraff... he had sent us his superb organ, which was as ill-concealed in the guise of a young mason as the murderer himself would have been in the guise of a rose. (M.R.; 206)

The analogy between "rose" and "murderer" violates the traditional association of flowers with innocence and beauty, while creating a new order of the beautiful with reference to the underside of society. The

narrator even composes a poem in praise of Harcamone's member, perverting the sacred symbolism of romantic love in figures for homosexual
desire. In the translation I have italicized words marked grammatically
for the feminine in French. (This poem was censored from the Gallimard
edition of Genet's *Oeuvres complètes*, and consequently from the English
translation as well.)[36] I quote the third and sixth quatrains:

O ma sainte Harcamone, ô vierge de nos lits
Vous parcourez le ciel, errante, et seriez nue
Sans le chant qui vous couvre et surtout sans ces plis
De clarté qui vous font d'innocence vêtue. . . .

Posez-vous sur mon front, portez-vous à mes dents,
O gaule enténébrée et montez à ma bouche,
Entrez au fond de moi où la mort vous attend
Pâle fille étendue sur sa fragile couche. (M. R.; 135)

Oh *my holy Harcamone*, oh virgin of our beds,
You cross the sky, *wandering*, and would be *naked*
Without the chant which covers you and especially without those folds
Of light which make you *clothed* with innocence. . .

Place yourself on my brow, bring yourself to my teeth,
Oh *Gaul plunged* in darkness, and rise to my mouth,
Enter my depths where death awaits you,
Pale maiden *stretched* out on her fragile bed. (my translation)

As I said before, Genet has mastered the art of metaphor. In Aristotle's
terms, Genet has acquired rhetorical skills which separate men from animals and distinguish poets and philosophers from ordinary men. In his
sexual orientation, however, Genet is both a man and not a Man, and
this paradox shapes his performance of poetic discourse. He thus borrows
the language of Romantic poets only to twist it into figures which violate
the underlying values separating male and female in romantic love.

Critics such as Pierre de Boisdeffre recognized the danger posed by
Genet's work for French culture.[37]

What is serious is that such a work—so completely 'lacking in that preoccupation with the universal which seems inseparable from great works'—far
from remaining clandestine, is offered for the admiration of the crowds. The
outlaws that Genet celebrates, the vices he stages, the praise . . . given the
French Gestapo, the intolerable *ennui* provoked by these erotic litanies, would
be, if taken seriously, the condemnation of our literature. (Boisdeffre; p.284,
my translation)

Boisdeffre seems not to criticize Genet so much for paying homage to
the devil as for doing it in the language of mainstream culture. Genet

typically attacks conventional morality and the sanctity of "our litera-ture" by employing sacred symbols in displaced representations of homo-sexual desire. Furthermore, and perhaps more dangerously, Genet challenges the very notion of universal truth, the cornerstone of the "great works," when he submits the symbols of dominant culture to the violence of metaphorical difference.

The "miracle" scene from *Miracle de la rose* is a case in point. The movement of metaphor perverts the symbols of heterosexual discourse, including references to Catholic liturgy, female sexuality, and courtly romance, into figures for homosexual acts. The miracle begins as the narrator describes the transformation of Harcamone's chains into a gar-land of white roses.

> Mais la ferveur de notre admiration avec la charge de sainteté qui pesait sur la chaîne serrant ses poignets—ses cheveux ayant eu le temps de pousser, leurs boucles s'embrouillaient sur son front avec la cruauté savante des tor-sades de la couronne d'épines—fit cette chaîne se transformer sous nos yeux à peine surpris, en une guirlande de roses blanches. La transformation com-mença au poignet gauche qu'elle entoura d'un bracelet de fleurs et continua le long de la chaîne, de maille en maille, jusqu'au poignet droit. (M.R.; 14–15)

> But the fervor of our admiration and the burden of saintliness which weighed on the chain that gripped his wrists—his hair had had time to grow and the curls had matted over his forehead with the cunning cruelty of the twists of the crown of thorns—caused the chain to be transformed before our scarcely astonished eyes into a garland of white flowers. (M. R.; 15)

Once again opposites attract. Guilt and crime are associated with in-nocence and beauty as roses replace the murderer's chains. This figuration differs from that mentioned earlier, in that metaphorical substitution here produces poetic metamorphosis, moving the speaking subject between reality and fantasy. The chains both are and are not roses, implying that the speaking subject both is and is not seeing what he "sees." Included in this passage is a metaphor comparing Harcamone's curly locks to the crown of thorns, a figure which sanctifies the suffering of a common thug by means of implication with the crucified Christ.

In the course of the transformation, the symbol "roses" acquires a new, sexual referent. The "miracle of the rose" veils the narrator's fantasy of deflowering his hero.

> J'avançai deux pas, le corps penché en avant, les ciseaux à la main, et coupai la plus belle rose qui pendait à une tige souple, tout près de son poignet gauche. La tête de la rose tomba sur mon pied nu et roula sur le dallage parmi les boucles de cheveux coupés et sales. Je la ramassai et relevai mon visage ex-

tasié, assez tôt pour voir l'horreur peint sur celui d'Harcamone, dont la nervosité n'avait pu résister à la préfiguration si sûre de sa mort. (M.R.; 15)

I took two steps, with my body bent forward and the scissors in my hand, and I cut off the loveliest rose, which was hanging by a supple stem near his left wrist. The head of the rose fell on my bare foot and rolled on the pavestones among the dirty curls of cut hair. I picked it up and raised my enraptured face, just in time to see the horror stamped on that of Harcamone, whose nervousness had been unable to resist that sure prefiguration of his death. (M.R.; 16)

The rose-cutting symbolizes, by means of convention, the violation of feminine innocence. This meaning is reiterated in the implied allusion to the erotic climax of the *Roman de la rose*, no doubt inspired by the medieval history of Fontevrault prison. By staging a scene whose symbolic meaning has even been codified in the lexicon (to "deflower" a maiden), Genet makes the stock symbol an obvious target of irony. The "miracle de la rose" culminates in the narrator's homosexual fantasy, bringing down an entire philosophical and literary tradition which places virtue, beauty, and innocence on the side of women; strength, sexuality, and experience on the side of men. Ironically, the "rose" in Genet's fantasy refers to Harcamone, a man convicted of raping and killing a little girl.

Pendant un instant très court, je me trouvai un genou en terre devant mon idole qui tremblait d'horreur, ou de honte, ou d'amour, et me regardait comme si elle m'eût reconnu, ou seulement comme si Harcamone eût reconnu Genet, et que je fusse la cause de son atroce émoi. (M.R.; 15)

For a very brief instant, I found myself on one knee before my idol, who was trembling with horror, or shame, or love, staring at me as if he had recognized me, or merely as if Harcamone had recognized Genet, and as if I were the cause of his frightful emotion. (M.R.; 16)

The irony of the rose-plucking symbolism derives in part from a reflection upon the gesture as a commonplace literary symbol, a reflection foregrounded by a metaphorical perversion of the referent, which slides between male and female. The movement of reference has a curious effect on the rhetorical function of metaphor. Rather than signify something new about the context (the association of Harcamone with the rose does not alter our opinion of his virtue), the symbolic image refers back to the figure as an end in itself, as an imitation of an imitation. In this kind of figure we discover yet another philosophical dimension of Genet's performance of dominant discourse. The self-referential movement of metaphor turns the symbol into an empty trace for the movement of semiosis, forming a tautology of the sort, "a rose is a rose is a rose." The cancellation of the meaning of poetic discourse in this kind of figure exemplifies what

Sartre has remarked, that "Genet's poems draw their substance from famous poems whose blood they suck."[38]

Genet has discovered the power of metaphor to move the speaking subject between reality and fantasy, logic and desire, meaning and nonsense. He shows that metaphor not only disguises the literal meaning of one thing behind a signifier for something else, but constitutes an act of performance, a means by which subjects represent themselves for other subjects in discourse. To the extent that the "to be or not to be" of metaphor cancels out meaning as soon as it emerges, metaphor constitutes an act of pure performance, a kind of mime-play which transcends the imitation of meaning in the form of language.[39] It is this very suspension of the reference of representation which would later characterize Genet's style of "theater about theater" and shape the spectator's implication in the events on stage.[40]

In the following example from *Notre-Dame-des-fleurs*, analogy creates an image of something only to erase it by means of another, contradictory image:

> Des capitales surgissaient au milieu de son enfance sablonneuse. Des capitales comme des cactus sous le ciel. Des capitales comme des soleils verts, rayonnants de rayons aigus, trempés de curare. Son enfance, comme un sahara, tout minuscule ou immense—on ne sait—abrité par la lumière, le parfum et le flux de charme personnel d'un gigantesque magnolia fleuri qui montait dans un ciel profond comme une grotte, par-dessus le soleil invisible et pourtant présent. Cette enfance séchait sur son sable brûlé, avec, en des instants rapides comme des traits, minces comme eux, minces comme ce paradis qu'on voit entre les paupières d'un Mongol, un aperçu sur le magnolia invisible et présent. . . . (N.D.F.; 44)

> Capitals rose up from his sandy childhood. Capitals like cactuses beneath the sky. Cactuses like green suns, radiating pointed rays and steeped in poison. His childhood, like a sahara, quite tiny or immense—we don't know—a childhood sheltered by the light, the scent, and the flow of personal charm of a huge flowering magnolia that rose into a sky deep as a grotto above the invisible though present sun. This childhood was withering on its broiling sand, with—in moments swift as pencil strokes and as thin, thin as the paradise one sees between the eyelids of a Mongol—a glimpse of the invisible and present magnolia. (O.L.F.; 151)

"Capitales" can either mean cities or letters of the alphabet. The commonplace expression, "cities sprout up" initially leans in the direction of the first interpretation, cities. However, the "desert" in which the capitals emerge is not a geographical location but a metaphor for a state of mind. Therefore, we must suspend our first interpretation and think of "capitales" in less concrete terms. As the passage continues, the movement between two ideas—the aridity of a desert and the emergence of language as a creative resource—focusses attention on the less obvious meaning of "capitales," letters of the alphabet.

The series of analogies beginning with "des capitales comme des cactus" ("capitals like cactus beneath the sky") and ending with "trempés de curare" ("steeped in poison"), the first, fairly accessible analogy between sprouting capital letters and cactus is upset by the next comparison between cactus (and by extension, the "capitales" to which they are compared) and green suns. In reality, suns do not "sprout up" from below but cast down life-giving light from above. Genet's suns contradict our expectations: they are green and cast poisonous rays.

The commonplace comparison of a desert with existence recurs in the next sentence in a simile: "Son enfance, comme un sahara." The paradoxical indications for the size of the desert, "minuscule ou immense," and the substitution of a giant magnolia for the sun, upset the analogical relation between the two terms of the original simile, since "desert" has lost its conventional semantic make-up in the process. Once more the magnolia, which should grow under the sunlight, surpasses the height of the sun and casts down its own light, odor, and charm. Moreover, the sky into which the magnolia rises is "deep as a cave."

The work of analogy in this figuration inhibits the rhetorical function of the symbols, namely to give sensorial qualities to abstract states of being, by reducing the symbols themselves to abstractions. The sun exists (it is "present"), but we cannot see it directly without being blinded (it is "invisible"). It casts down rays, but is sheltered by the shade of a giant magnolia. In other words, the movement of metaphor works against the immediate presentation of meaning to perception in symbols, replacing representation with the tracing of semiotic performance.

The third segment of the passage begins with a repetition of the existence/desert metaphor: "Cette enfance séchait sur son sable brulé" ("This childhood was withering on its broiling sand"). It then continues the reference to vision begun in "invisible" with the words "un aperçu sur le magnolia invisible et présent." The magnolia parallels the sun, since it symbolizes those "presences" which disappear as soon as we attempt to apprehend them by means of perception.

The "unseeable," in this case, has the "lumière, le parfum, le flux de charme personnel" which we associate with Baudelaire's synesthetic visions. Unlike the figuration in this passage, Baudelaire's metaphors usually create parallels between concrete experience, like the perception of a woman's hair, body, or perfume, and consistently developed imagery depicting a fantasy.[41] The perception of light, perfume, and charm in Genet's vision occurs in "instants," rapid moments which cannot be fixed on the retina. They occur in flashes ("traits") across the mind's eye. They also resemble pencil strokes ("traits"), marks inscribed by the poet on the blank page, since they evoke no signified, no concrete image. These "instants" trace a movement of poetic imagination in search of a new language.

Genet evokes Baudelaire's poetics of synesthesia in a type of language which defies synthesis in a poetic image. The contradictory work of analogy in this passage reduces the figure to an empty trace for the work of metaphor, without producing the substance of metaphorical meaning. In place of synesthesia, Genet's manipulation of metaphor produces kinesthesia, a playful staging of the subject in the folds of figurative discourse. In this regard Genet's poetics reverberates with Antonin Artaud's cry for the triumph of mise-en-scène over speech in contemporary theater and culture.[42]

In borrowing Baudelaire's imagery only to "suck its blood" in this way, Genet pushes aside a tradition of poetry based on the metaphysical ideal of the "proper sense" of metaphor, making room for a new poetic order based upon the politics of non-sense.

Throughout my discussion, I have returned to the idea of how an author speaking from the margins of dominant culture and ideology manages to be a man though excluded from the notion of Man universalized by metaphysical philosophy. Genet's difference—his homosexuality, his marginality—prevents him from appropriating the language of dominant discourse, much less the privileged language of the French literary canon, as an ordinary man. Genet's strength, his "man-hood," rests in the fact that he chose neither to remain silent nor to mask his difference behind the discourse of heterosexual culture, but to impose his difference on the signs and symbols of dominant discourse. By using metaphor against metaphor, Genet exposes cracks and crevices in the monolithic order of Man, while opening poetry and poetics to the rich plurality of voices speaking for our humanity.

FOUR

The Perversion of I/Eye in *Un Chant d'amour*

The indexical pull of metaphor in Genet's novels parallels the indexical focus of the image in Genet's film, *Un Chant d'amour*. The cinematic image is both an icon and an index: it produces a perfect copy of its object, and points both to the former presence of the object before the camera and to the place of the spectator's look behind the camera eye. While dominant, narrative cinema produces films which mask the work of reference and subject-address in film discourse in order to assure the spectator's immersion in the plenitude of the visual field, Genet's film draws attention to the spectator's implication in the events on screen.

Since cinematic representation is not simply a signifier *of something* but a signifier *for someone*, the question of cinema is inseparable from the question of performance, a process which determines the subject's implication in social and ideological discourses. As Stephen Heath has said,

> An important—determining—part of ideological systems is then the achievement of a number of machines (institutions) that can *move* the individual as subject, shifting and tying desire, realigning excess and contradiction, in a perpetual retotalization—a remembering—of the imaginary in which the individual-subject is grasped as identity. It is in terms of this 'double bind'— the statement of social meanings and the holding of the individual to those meanings, the suturing of the enounced and the enunciation, what was called above 'the vision of the subject', that the institution of cinema can be understood.[1]

Heath identifies film performance with the subject's psychological implication in narrative, a system of codes for ensuring closure between the "I" of the enunciation and the "I" of the enounced in the imaginary-symbolic realm. Heath, following the example of Christian Metz in "The Imaginary Signifier, "[2] situates the spectating subject in the framework of Lacanian psychoanalysis. In Lacan, the subject of the "mirror phase" is originally divided into a subject which speaks and a subject which is "spoken" in language.[3] The imaginary integration of these two faces of the subject occurs by means of the subject's participation in discourse, a symbolic medium in which the subject's projections are held and returned in the form of a coherent image. Cinema is a type of social institution in which the subject's desire is staged; narrative is a socially determined structure which regulates and perpetuates that staging. Heath says,

> The film is figured out by its narrative as a totality, the imaginary relation of the spectator to an undivided present full of images of the accomplishment of desire, . . . of fictions of wholeness . . . exactly a memory-spectacle in which the elements of production are bound up and resolved; the representation of unity and the unity of representation.[4]

In Heath, "classic narrative film" performs the relation between representation and the subject in cinema, while non-narrative films or filmic figures which disturb narrative closure are not, in the first instance, a function of film performance. Though Heath suggests at the end of his discussion that certain avant-garde practices, rather than destroy performance simply perform "differently," he tends to divide cinema into classical narrative performance and its "other," namely, transgressive, avant-garde practice.

By defining performance as the act of being something for someone else, a function of the subject's moment by moment construction in discourse, we manage to transcend the boundaries separating dominant cinema from its others. The point of the previous chapter was to show that performance is inseparable from the movement of figures in discourse, rather than a kind of master code structuring specific styles or modes of representation to the exclusion of others. Likewise, all kinds of films engage the subject's desire to identify with the fiction, but certain film practices, including Genet's, place in question the terms of the contract binding the spectating subject to the voice of authority in dominant film discourse. It is in this framework that my analysis of performance in Genet's novels leads directly to questions of film performance raised by his only original film, Un Chant d'amour.

Jean Genet has been associated with the cinema in one way or another since the 1950s. His film projects include directorial collaboration on scripts he did not write, film adaptations of his plays, and an original screenplay he did not direct. Genet directed Nico Papatakis's film Les Abysses in 1963. Joseph Strick filmed Genet's play The Balcony in 1963, and Christopher Miles filmed The Maids in 1973. Genet wrote the script for Tony Richardson's Mademoiselle in 1966, and his poem, "Le Condamné à mort," is the basis of a film by Albert-André Lheureux, entitled, "Possession du condamné" (1967).

Un Chant d'amour, a silent, black and white film made in sixteen millimeter and lasting thirty-five minutes, is singular in that it is neither an adaptation nor a collaboration. Though Jean Cocteau assisted Genet with the technical aspect of the film, as Jean Mitry says, *Un Chant d'a-mour* is "entièrement réalisé par Jean Genet."[5] Moreover, unlike the other films in which Genet was engaged, this film transcribes into cinematic terms Genet's ideal of textual performance along the lines of the index, the sign function which traces relations of reference and subject-address in discourse.

Un Chant d'amour has been generally avoided in scholarly studies of Genet, perhaps because of the pornographic aspects of the film, which caused it to be banned in France and the United States for some twenty years. The nature of the film medium and the disposition of the spectator in front of the film might explain why scholars discuss Genet's quasi-pornographic literature and not his film. Film images present characters "in the flesh." Therefore the explicit representation of sex organs on screen is more susceptible to the label "pornographic" than the same representation in literature. This very statement about the difference between cinema and literature was used to uphold the court decision to ban Genet's film from screening in Berkeley, California, in 1966:

> Because of the nature of the medium, we think a motion picture of sexual scenes may transcend the bounds of the constitutional guarantee long before a frank description of the same scenes in the written word.[6]

Moreover, the potential for spectator identification is greater in cinema than in literature or theater, because of the difference between the disposition of the spectating subject of cinema and the reading subject or the theater spectator.[7] The film spectator is isolated, passive, his attention more or less captive in the darkened theater. The reader can emerge from the book; the theater spectator can recognize the difference between the on-stage fiction and off-stage reality by merely looking beyond the sets to the spaces back-stage. Also, as Metz points out in "The Imaginary Signifier," it is the very absence of the reality traced on the film image which invites the spectator's projections into the film, thereby determining him or her as the locus of cinematic discourse, a voyeur constructing the film according to his or her own desire.[8]

Ironically, the little critical acclaim given *Un Chant d'amour* in the United States, primarily by American avant-garde filmmakers and critics, commits a type of censorship by idealizing the work on esthetic grounds. Justifying the pornographic aspects of the film in the name of high art, critics such as Jonas Mekas and Anaïs Nin ignore the perversely ironic nature of Genet's eroticism, which victimizes rather than gratifies the spectator.[9]

There is a movement in Genet's film between the explicit representation of sexual perversions, including fetishism, onanism, and voyeurism, and the displaced representation of the same in fairly commonplace symbols, such as a flower being plucked or a pistol being shoved into a prisoner's mouth by a guard. As we discovered in the novels, Genet's original contribution to erotic literature consists in neither the explicit nor the symbolic representation of sexual perversions, but in a perversion of the subject's performance of dominant discourse. Genet eroticizes the cinematic signifier, as it were, engaging directly the question of the spectator's desire of and in the film. In *Un Chant d'amour* he frustrates the spectator's voyeurism by perverting normal relations between the subject of the enounced and the subject of the filmic enunciation.

Un Chant d'amour can be divided into five segments: an opening scene which is to be read in symbolic terms and which prefigures the rest of the film; two more or less realistic scenes in a prison depicting the actions of the main characters, two prisoners and a guard; a departure from the prison setting in fantasy sequences; and a closing which recapitulates the various motifs of the film.

In the opening a prison guard walks forward, looking up at something off-screen. Cut to a medium close-up of two barred (prison) windows. Out of the window on the left, a hand attached to a virile arm swings a garland of flowers to another hand attached to a virile arm hanging out of a window on the right. After several attempts the hand on screen right fails to catch the garland.

It should be noted that the garland is an important symbol in Genet's novel *Miracle de la rose*. As I discussed in chapter 3, the transformation of Harcamone's chains into a garland of white roses is a precondition of the narrator's symbolic intercourse with him. One is also reminded of the systematic representation of bodies by arms and hands in the novel, *Pompes funèbres*. In *Un Chant d'amour*, as in the novel, the isolation of arms and hands from the body symbolizes the imaginary fragmentation of the body in castration anxiety, a theme which links homosexuality to figures of desire in Genet's work. These metonymies also invite the spectator to imagine what is not directly represented on screen, the absent bodies, thereby projecting his or her imaginary into the film.

The symbolism of the opening sequence is developed throughout the film in the themes of alienation and frustrated desire. The prison walls, penetrated by virile arms attempting union by means of arms, hands, and the garland of flowers, constitute paradigmatic elements which are later replaced by straws passed through holes in the wall, smoke passed through the straws, and a flower passed between the mouths of two lovers. All symbolize the unfulfilled desire for homosexual possession.

Most of the second segment consists of cuts from a well-lighted cell with a fair prisoner in a white T-shirt, to a darker cell with a swarthy, hairy prisoner in a dark uniform. The fair man is dancing slowly, caressing a tattoo of a woman on his upper arm with one hand and his crotch with the other. The man in the dark cell attempts to contact his neighbor. He knocks on the wall, then penetrates a small hole in the wall with a straw from his mattress and blows cigarette smoke into the fair man's cell. The latter ignores these signals. The swarthy man, angry and frustrated, seals up the wall with bread paste and masturbates against the wall. The fair man next door falls onto his own cot in orgasm. Meanwhile the guard from the opening shot has entered the prison: he peeps in on the dark man's climax, then spies on the fair man.

In the third segment of the film, the guard walks to other cells and spies through peep-holes in the doors at various half-naked prisoners masturbating. In these shots the prisoners gaze directly into the camera, evidently taking pleasure in being placed on exhibit. In the first shot, a white man dressed only in a striped T-shirt smiles into the camera. In the next cell, a black man in white pants masturbates in rhythm to a calypso he performs for the camera. He finally collapses on his cot in a climax of pleasure. Their gazes into the camera are intercut with close-up shots of the guard's eye penetrating the peep-holes of the cell doors and long-shots of the guard, obviously excited, walking from one cell door to the next in the hallway.

The guard, returning to the two original men, peeps in on the fair man caressing his own foot and on his swarthy neighbor. The fair man, tired and frustrated by his solitary eroticism, knocks on the wall separating him from the swarthy man. The latter responds by caressing the wall. The fair man takes a straw from the mattress and penetrates the hole in the wall, inviting the other man to pass him smoke from his cigarette. A series of shots alternating between the two cells represents the two men finally making contact: the fair man inhales the smoke exhaled through the straw by the swarthy man.

The guard, meanwhile, has been spying on their "intercourse," visibly aroused and grabbing his crotch. The swarthy man, observing the guard's look, signals a warning to his neighbor to stop their communication. Deprived of his scopic gratification, the guard acts out his sadism by entering the cell of the swarthy man and beating him into submission. This scene is intercut with two sequences depicting the inner visions of the guard and his victim.

It is worth noting that the motif of the voyeur peeping through key-holes of doors along a hallway figures prominently in Cocteau's *Le Sang d'un poète*. This motif is significantly transformed in Genet's film, and does not put into question the authorship of *Un Chant d'amour*.

The guard's scopic relation to the prisoners defines a perversion of the erotic drive toward union or continuity, since the scopic drive demands a physical distance between the voyeur and the object of desire. Freud says that voyeurism not only displaces the sexual drive from the genitals to the eyes, but is accompanied by sadism, since the object of desire is subjugated by the controlling look of the subject.[10] The prisoners are trapped in their desire, captives of the guard's look. Solitude characterizes all of the perversions shown in the film. However, none of the other perversions, such as the fetishistic substitution of the sex organs by feet, straws, and flowers, or the onanism of the prisoners, contains the element of sadism implicit in the guard's voyeurism.

Where the other perversions are substitutes for sexual contact—means of transcending the distance separating the prisoners—voyeurism is a drive based on the distancing (the "garde," or psychic defense) of the voyeur from the erotic object.[11] The voyeur engages the physical presence of the other only to keep him at a distance, behind the wall, beyond the door or window. The complicity of the onanists who look complacently back at the guard as he peeps into their cells defines a type of masochism intimately related to scopophilia: exhibitionism.

The fourth segment consists of two inner visions, the guard's and the prisoner's. The guard's fantasy begins when the guard closes his eyes and the image fades to black. One is reminded of the association of blindness, or closing the eyes to physical reality, with the generation of inner visions in Genet's novel, *Notre-Dame-des-fleurs*. In the film the guard "sees" himself in various erotic postures with anonymous nude men, including the swarthy prisoner. In the guard's fantasy, several motifs represented early in the film recur: a garland of flowers is swung into the image from the left side of the screen, a hand from the right attempts to grab it. Two men chew on a flower uniting/separating their mouths. A third scene refers directly to the guard's violence toward the swarthy prisoner: a symbolic rape is performed as the guard forces his gun into the man's mouth. This and the other scenes of the fantasy are played against a black backdrop in an undefinable space. The guard's fantasy ends and we are returned to the prison cell in which the guard is beating the swarthy prisoner to his knees.

The prisoner's fantasy begins as an image of him looking up at the guard fades to black and cuts to a country scene. In this shot, he and his fair neighbor are free, playing chase in a woods. Attached to the fair man's belt is a garland of flowers from which he offers a flower to the dark man. This action is a variation of the rose-plucking figure in *Miracle de la rose*, which I discussed in chapter 3. In the novel the narrator's gesture symbolizes his desire to rape Harcamone. In the film the object of desire offers the lover his "flower." The film sequence ends as the swarthy man caresses his friend, lying on the ground. No nudity or explicit sex are included in this scene. The prisoner's fantasy, ironically, represents the ideal of "normal" love in the film, homosexual desire. This sequence ends and we are returned to the prison scene. Ashamed and defeated by the guard, the swarthy man throws himself on the cot and buries his head in the mattress.

The final segment takes up and resolves the various motifs of the film. The guard walks away from the prison as he entered the film: looking up at something as he did in the opening of the film. This time he looks behind him. Inside the prison, the swarthy man knocks on the wall, in hopes of communicating with the prisoner behind it. Outside, the arms continue to play toss and catch with the garland of flowers. The hand on screen right catches the garland.

The composition of the images themselves reiterates the theme of unresolved desire in terms of formal oppositions—between left and right of frame, left and right sides of the prison wall, inside and outside of the prison cell, and in the contrast of light and dark. This last contrast dominates the illumination of every shot. The fair prisoner wears a white shirt and his cell is well lighted; his swarthy neighbor wears a dark uniform and his cell is dim. The contrast of light and dark in the scenes of exhibitionism and voyeurism reiterates the theme of alienation and solitude associated with those perversions. The first prisoner wears a black and white-striped T-shirt; the second, a black man, wears white trousers.

The strong contrast of light and dark in the scenes depicting the guard's inner vision reiterates, in formal terms, the perverse nature of the guard's desire. He sees himself in various erotic postures with men, but in each one physical union is either mediated by an object, such as a flower or a gun, or defines a perversion of heterosexual intercourse, such as fellatio. The motif of the two arms swinging and attempting in vain to catch the garland recurs here, again against a black backdrop. For the guard, intercourse with other men is impossible, since his desire to dominate replaces love with sadism.

The contrasts of light and dark and left and right of frame are resolved in the swarthy prisoner's fantasy, which represents the consummation of the erotic ideal of the film, homosexual love. The pastoral setting of the scene and the absence of pornographic detail serve to legitimize this traditionally "perverse" relation between men. Here, flowers are a natural part of the diegesis, rather than simply sexual symbols. In the film, as in the novels, the explicit representation of sex acts serves not to add realism or even sensationalism to erotic discourse, but to implicate the spectator in the perverseness of representation. The innocence of the prisoner's fantasy denies the spectator voyeuristic participation in the characters' desire.

It could be argued that this scene depicts a homosexual version of romantic love. For the only time in the film the contrast of light and dark is resolved in a spectrum of grey tones. The barriers separating the two men in reality (in prison) have disappeared, and a wealth of realistic detail relieves the image of the sharp formal conflicts which characterized earlier shots of flowers and prisoners.

The symbolic representation of eroticism and frustrated desire serves to expand the meaning of desire in *Un Chant d'amour* beyond the purely sexual, physical realm to an esthetic and psychological one. This kind of displacement permits our reflection on the eroticism of poetic discourse and the place of the spectator in that eroticism. It is no coincidence that the pornographic parts of the film are organized according to a tightly woven cross-cutting montage between the voyeur looking and the object of his look. In Genet the pornographic is inseparable from the manipulation of intersubjectivity (I/you, he/she) in discourse. Genet dares the spectator to desire the film, then perverts this desire by implicating the spectator in the sadism of the guard. It is precisely in this sense, and not simply with regard to the explicit representation of sexual perversions on screen, that *Un Chant d'amour* is an exercise in perversion, the perversion of the cinematic subject or "I" by means of displacements of the camera "eye".

Christian Metz and Jean-Louis Baudry argue that in order to discuss the eroticism of spectating we need to redefine an ontology of cinematic representation in terms of the spectator's desire to identify with the film, rather than focussing primarily on the eroticism of the filmic signified.[12] In defining the "essence" of the cinematic medium, traditional film theories privilege the reproduction of physical reality in the photographic image and the simulation of movement in the projection. This tradition stems from the criterion of mimesis shaping literary and artistic criticism from the classical period: works of art were (and still are) judged, classified, and censored with reference to their modes of and techniques for imitating reality. André Bazin goes so far as to say that the invention of the camera, and with it the ability to mechanically reproduce visual reality, relieved the other arts of their aspiration to mimesis:

> In achieving the aims of baroque art, photography has freed the plastic arts from their obsession with likeness. Painting was forced, as it turned out, to offer us illusion and this illusion was reckoned sufficient unto art. Photography and the cinema on the other hand are discoveries that satisfy, once and for all and in its very essence, our obsession with realism.[13]

The reality principle that has dominated film theory from the earliest days of the film industry focusses on the film object and the mimetic relation between cinematic representation and its object. As Baudry points out, the technical achievement of the camera to reproduce physical reality on film only partially explains the famous "illusion of reality" experienced by the spectator.[14] The spectator is disposed in advance to believe or desire to believe that the projections of light and dark on the film screen represent "reality." In other words, the illusion of reality can also be defined in terms of the disposition of the spectator. The current psychoanalytic bent of semiotic theory aims at redefining the "essence" of cinema in terms of the dialectic interaction of the spectator's own psychological projections with the mechanical projection of recorded reality on screen. According to this approach, advanced by Baudry, Metz, and others, the illusion of reality resides not simply in the technical ability of the camera to record physical reality, but also in the play of presence and absence in the representation itself, which implicates the spectator's desire in the film.[15] This approach also shifts attention from the iconic aspect of the film image to its indexical function.

Umberto Eco refines Peirce's classification of signs into icons, indices, and symbols (Saussure's "sign") by replacing the notion of "sign" with "semiotic function," saying that an element of discourse may have a mimetic function or an indexical function without being a "sign" per se.[16] This change permits explaining the semiotic function of nonlinguistic systems such as cinema, composed of both indexical and iconic aspects. Eco's "trace," as exemplified in hoofprints discovered in a roadway, illustrates the semiotic specificity of the cinematic signifier, which not only resembles its object more perfectly than any other type of representation, but points to the former presence of the physical reality it represents. The film image is thus an indexical icon, functioning within cinematic discourse as a trace of an absent reality.

In "The Imaginary Signifier," Christian Metz initiated the current shift of film theory from esthetic and strictly semiological concerns to the psychoanalytic question of the subject of cinema. Metz, modelling his ontology of cinema after Jacques Lacan's theory of the subject of the mirror phase of psychological development, focusses on the spectator's implication in the look of the absent camera. The indexical nature of the cinematic image permits Metz to define cinematic representation as an "imaginary signifier," a signifier of absence, which invites the spectator to invest the film with his own desire:

> In order to understand the fiction film, I must both 'take myself' for the character (= imaginary procedure) so that he benefits, by analogical projection, from all the schemata of intelligibility that I have within me, and not take myself for him (return to the real) so that the fiction can be established as such (= the symbolic): this is *seeming-real*. Similarly, in order to understand the film (at all), I must perceive the photographed object as absent, its photograph as present, and the presence of this absence as signifying. The imaginary of the cinema presupposes the symbolic, for the spectator must first of all have known the primordial mirror. But as the latter instituted the ego very largely in the imaginary, the second mirror of the screen, a symbolic apparatus, itself in turn depends on reflection and lack. However, it is not fantasy, a 'purely' symbolic-imaginary site, for the absence of the object and the codes of that absence are really produced in it by the physis of an equipment: the cinema is a body (a corpus for the semiologist), a fetish that can be loved.[17]

Metz employs the Lacanian division of psychological experience into the imaginary (the configurations of the individual's desire for the object, based on the movement between projection and identification), the symbolic (the displacement of the imaginary onto secondary, objective representations, such as images), and the real (the social situation of the subject and his entourage).[18] As a signifier or representation, the film is a symbolic apparatus, a socially determined system of semiotic codes. As a signifier of absence (a trace of physical reality), the film is an imaginary apparatus, inviting the participation of the spectator. As a physical, technical object, the film is a real apparatus. Metz points out that while all experience tends to oscillate between these three moments, the experience of cinema leans heavily to the side of the symbolic-imaginary, or the spectator's identification with the film by means of psychological projection.

Psychological projection is a defense mechanism which displaces an unconscious conflict (in the imaginary) onto the object of desire.[19] Through projection, the original relation to the mother (Melanie Klein's "good object"), is transferred to subsequent objects in the subject's erotic life, including displacements such as art objects (the realm of symbol formation). In Klein's corollary to the Freudian notion of projection, the sequel to projection is identification. Once invested with the spectator's projections, the film screen becomes a sort of mirror for the subject, a reflection of the self.[20]

The cinema industry, Metz's "capitalist apparatus," strives to produce films which will exploit the spectator's desire to merge with the film in a quasi-hallucinatory state. Though some films permit greater degrees of identification and scopic gratification than others (to this extent they are "good objects"), the industry does not promote films which remind the spectator that "it's only a film" and thrust him back into the reality of the moment (to this extent they are "bad objects").

The cinema is not simply a technological phenomenon, a mechanical apparatus for reproducing physical reality, nor simply a subjective phenomenon, consisting of the spectator's projections into the film, but a "series of mirror effects [between the film screen and the spectator's psychological screen] organized in a chain."[21] Furthermore, as Metz says, the institution of cinema is primarily an erotic apparatus, preserving and perpetuating the ideal of the film as "good object," as guarantee of the subject's closure with the Other in the imaginary realm.[22]

There is a sexual meaning to this movement of the subject in the film, a meaning turning around the figure of castration. The child's entrance into the symbolic order, the awakening of the drive to project the lost object of desire into substitutions, occurs at a stage in psychological development when the (male) child recognizes the sexual difference between the parents and between (him)self and the mother. The recognition of difference provokes castration anxiety, the fear of one's own cleavage as a result of the real separation from the Other.[23] The Oedipal scenario is played out repeatedly in adult life as the endless fluctuation between the constitutional division of the subject from its other, and the imaginary closure of the subject with its other and Others across the imaginary/symbolic realm.

As Stephen Heath points out, in Lacanian theory the term "castration" covers two distinct regimes of meaning. It describes both the division of the subject in the symbolic order and the real division between the sexes.[24] Dominant discourse reduces the dual notion of "lack" to the second meaning, the lack of a specific organ: the penis. Lack, in dominant discourse, is modelled after the biological difference between male and female.

Cinematic representation perpetuates the monolithic order of castration. As substitute for the erotic object, the film performs as a fetish. In Freud the fetish is a figure for the lack, a substitute for the penis the male subject projects into the mother's body to make up for an organ she is presumably missing.[25] By projecting the "same," the phallus, into the Other (the image of woman), the male subject defends himself against the fear of his own castration. The fetishistic function of cinema demands that the spectator be confirmed as "whole" subject through projective identification with the fiction.[26] Masking the fragmentation of the enunciation (including the film's articulation into shots and the disjuncture between sound and image tracks) through semiotic operations in the discourse, classical narrative films suture the subject's own lack and confirm his recognition of (identification with) himself in the Other, the film. In this sense discursive practices in dominant cinema repress the reality of castration as the division of the subject in the imaginary/symbolic order.[27]

Next, dominant cinema poses the solution to the original division of the subject in terms of the organization of subject-address in narrative discourse. The positions of looking and being looked at parallel the opposition of male and female in the diegesis. The man is usually the voyeur, the woman the object of the look, whose own ability to look and to shape discourse is lacking. Projecting the lack into woman's body guards against the (man's) recognition of difference, of bisexuality, as condition of possibility of the constitution of the subject.[28]

To the extent, then, that films perform as fetishes, they guarantee a male order of the symbolic, an ideology of the "same" turning around the phallus (and its lack). Moreover, by representing sexual difference as the opposition between male voyeur and female object of the look, classical narrative films confirm the omnipotence of the male gaze, the voice of authority in cinematic discourse. Such cinematic practices in turn define the spectator—man or woman in reality—as "he" in the imaginary/symbolic order. For this reason, women often take pleasure in films which represent the sexual exploitation of other women.

For the semiologist, cinema represents the institutionalized practice of perversion, controlled by the technical/economic/political structure of the film industry. In *Un Chant d'amour* Genet underlines the fundamentally perverse nature of dominant cinema by representing a voyeur, isolated prisoners of desire, and fetishistic displacements in the image. This diegetic (iconic) representation is but an overdetermination of the more crucial manipulation of (indexical) relations of subject-address in the discourse. By displacing the "normal" practice of scopophilia from the imaginary/symbolic realm to a conscious reflection upon that practice, Genet prevents the spectator's imaginary closure with the film, reminds him of his real separation from the erotic object, and disturbs the fetishistic function of the film. This brings us back to the ideological threat posed by Genet's film.

If the cinematic apparatus is essentially perverse, then what constitutes a more or less "perverse" film discourse? *Un Chant d'amour* is "perverse" not simply because it represents sexual perversions on screen, but because it displaces the normal practice of cinematic scopophilia from the realm of the imaginary to the realm of the real. Semiotic practices in the discourse upset the spectator's identification with the film and transform the film into a "bad object."

It could be argued that the critical and legal resistance to *Un Chant d'amour* mentioned earlier determines in advance the film's undesirability, its stature as "bad object." However, the film has been canonized in *film d'art* circles, as evidenced in its inclusion in the highly selective collections of the Anthology Film Archive and the Museum of Modern Art in New York. The film's lack of commercial distribution indicates that "mainstream" audiences do not seek out the film in the first place; therefore, we can only discuss the privileged audience of museums and archives. For this narrow public, *Un Chant d'amour* constitutes à priori a "good object," since it fulfills certain esthetic priorities of the art film crowd. An example of privately financed, independently made "countercinema," Genet's film explores the symbolic and poetic possibilities of cinematic representation, expresses a personal vision at the expense of commercial appeal, celebrates one-man authorship, and so on.

The semiotic practice of perversion in *Un Chant d'amour* derives from a disturbance of the classical narrative closure between primary and secondary identification in the spectator (the looks of the camera and of the characters, respectively). Primary identification can be explained by analogy with the inscription of subjectivity in linguistic discourse, along the lines of indices defined by linguistic code, the personal pronouns "I" and "you."

As Emile Benveniste explains, subjectivity is not a metaphysical essence but a function of discourse.[29] "I" is uttered, therefore I am. There can be no "I" of discourse without its corollary "you," the receiver of the message. The implication of "I" and "you" in turn permits the eventual identification of the subject with "he" and "she" in narrative discourse. For Benveniste, this convention puts into play shifts between the linguistic categories of person and non-person.

Benveniste's observations about linguistic discourse can be used to describe the inscription of subject-address in cinema, and the shifts between primary and secondary identification in Genet's film. The camera eye, defined by the parameters of the frame on the screen, resembles the speaker of linguistic discourse, the "I" and organizer of cinematic discourse, with one important difference: the positions of I and you do not shift between two subjects in cinema as they do in a dialogue between two speakers. The spectator's look is implicated in film discourse according to psychological identification with the camera I/eye: cinematic discourse cannot exist without a viewer to perceive and read it. This initial inscription of the spectator in the film defines primary identification.[30]

Primary identification is a condition of secondary identification, through which the spectator is implicated in the looks of the characters. In the cinema the shift from primary to secondary identification entails the identification or matching of the look of the camera with the look of the character, achieved primarily but not always by means of crosscuts joining shots of a character looking and the ostensible object of his look. Eye-level matching and diegetic contiguity between the character and the object of his look support the logic of the cross-cut.[31]

In classical narrative films, we are not usually disturbed by the shift from primary to secondary identification in the cross-cut, because the look of the camera transcends any particular identity in the diegesis. This shift is similar to the movement between the discourse of an omniscient, transparent narrator of the third-person novel and the reported speech of characters speaking in the story. The omniscient narrator pretends to represent characters "speaking in their own voices." Convention dictates that we ignore the mask assumed by the narrator to produce characters with whom we can identify.

As I discussed in chapter 2, something quite different occurs in certain postwar novels, such as *Pompes funèbres*, in which the narrator reveals himself as "I," an anonymous narrating presence, who occasionally trades places with his characters and speaks through their mouths. In *Pompes funèbres*, the narrator, named "Jean Genet," moves in and out of the roles of Erik and Hitler at different moments of the narrative. This kind of duality draws attention to the cleavage of the narrating subject, to the difference between "I" and "he," person and non-person of discourse, in the conventional representation of reported speech. This cleavage of the subject of modern literature is announced in Rimbaud's famous statement, "I is an other" ("Je est un autre").

In *Un Chant d'amour*, Genet transcribes the figure of the mask into cinematic terms, creating an awareness of a first-person cinematic narrator. By this means, Genet disturbs the shift between primary and secondary identification in the spectating subject.

We identify primarily with the narrator along the lines of the dialectical implication of "I" and "you." As narrative "I" identifies with "he," that is, with first one and then another character speaking in the novel, the reader can only identify with the characters across the intermediary of the mask. Furthermore, unveiling the mask worn by the narrator in his various impostures interferes with the reader's identification with the characters. If the reader is implicated in the discourse along the dialectical relation between "I" and "you," and if "I" has a dual referent (I = he), then the reader is divided in turn, as he identifies with the narration, denied the illusion of closure with the fiction. The disturbance of the shift between primary and secondary identification constitutes a "critical space" in which the reader moves between identification with and reflection upon his place in the discourse. This kind of movement defines a major source of tension, not only in the novels of Genet, but of Samuel Beckett and Marguerite Duras, for instance.[32]

First-person cinema, a genre which has been inadequately explained by recent film criticism,[33] is a problematic issue which requires careful study. Metz has said, both in early and recent essays, that the difficulty of distinguishing the camera eye from the diegesis it brings into view prohibits our discussing a narrating subjectivity or self-conscious "I" of cinematic discourse, one independent of the looks of the characters viewed on screen.[34] If this were true, there could be no "first-person cinema" comparable to the novel from which the term derives. Metz recently suggests that "strange camera angles" might draw attention to the fact of the camera,[35] but he does not examine how such self-conscious techniques change the spectator's relation to the discourse.

In *Un Chant d'amour* Genet creates awareness of the camera by mismatching the looks of the camera eye and the voyeur in the diegesis in a cross-cutting figure. He also addresses the looks of the characters to the fact of the camera as a presence within the diegesis. Such figures trace the intervention of a narrating I/eye into the film and disturb the shift between primary and secondary identification in the spectator.

First, there is a recurring disparity between the distance from the guard looking to the object of his look, and the distance from the camera eye to the object it observes in the subsequent shot. Moreover, the eye levels of characters looking off-screen and of the camera looking at the object of their looks are mismatched. For instance, the guard looking up in the opening shot is seen in medium long-shot. The prison exterior is not visible in the frame. The subsequent shot of prison windows is in close-up and from a different eye-level than the guard's look. Later, inside the prison, the guard peeps in on the swarthy prisoner, who is subsequently viewed in medium shot. When the guard returns to peep in on the same prisoner masturbating, a cut from the guard looking through the key-hole to an extreme close-up of the prisoner's body disturbs the logic of the cross-cut. We have difficulty inferring that the prisoner's body is seen from the guard's point of view. In the scenes of exhibitionism, the prisoners are shown in medium long-shot, looking back at the guard spying on them. Yet we see the object of their looks, the guard's eye penetrating the peephole, in extreme close-up.

Such interferences in the normal function of the cross-cut derive from a movement between the code (the assumption that a shot following a shot of a character looking off-screen represents that person's point of view) and a figure of lack (the implication that the matching shot in fact represents the point of view of the camera, the locus of the absent spectator). Such modifications in the code do not disturb the continuity and coherence of the diegesis as much as they draw attention to the look of the camera as an autonomous narrating presence (independent of the looks of the characters).

In the same way that the enunciation of "I" in the novel constitutes a reflection both on the production of discourse and on the complicity of the reader in that discourse, so awareness of the camera eye in *Un Chant d'amour* constitutes a reflection both on the cinematic apparatus and on the spectator's place in that apparatus. The interruption of the cross-cut by the imposing "look" of a narrating I/eye makes visible the spectator's primary implication in the discourse as an absent voyeur.

Awareness of the camera is reiterated in the shots of the onanists looking directly into the camera. As Metz says, in ordinary cinema the complicity between the voyeur and the exhibitionist, a relationship characteristic of most voyeurism, is short-circuited, since the actors are not only absent from film representation as such, but are forbidden by convention to look into the camera, to acknowledge the presence of the camera eye and the spectator's look.[36] The success of the average pornographic film derives from the spectator's sense of anonymity and denial of complicity in the events on screen, resulting from the inscription of lack and absence in the cinematic signifier. In *Un Chant d'amour*, recognition of the camera as an index for the absent voyeur of film discourse, the spectator, implicates the specator in the perversion of the film.

As Metz has said, spectator identification with (desire of) the film demands that the spectator both "take himself" for the character by means of psychological projection (in the realm of the imaginary), and not (mis)take himself for the character by comparing himself with the person on screen (in the realm of the real). Thus in *Un Chant d'amour*, reflection on the spectator's primary identification (with the camera) perverts the normal practice of cinematic scopophilia. The cross-cutting code shaping cinematic voyeurism opens the film to the spectator's projections, permitting him to participate in the film *qua* fiction (the realm of the imaginary/symbolic). The figure of lack created by the transgression of this code, which leads to the recognition of the camera eye, invites the spectator to recognize his situation in front of the film (a return to the real) and take himself for the guard, the voyeur in the film. This movement from the imaginary to the real along semiotic operations in the discourse transforms the film into a bad object and twists the scopic drive into feelings of bad conscience.

Recognition of the camera as autonomous narrating presence causes a doubling of the reference for the look, the "I" of the discourse. We recognize that I/eye refers to the autonomous narrator and the guard at the same time. This marks a cleavage in the normal closure of person and non-person in cinematic discourse, when "I" shifts into identification with "he," a character in the story. Since "you," the spectating subject, is constructed by dialectical implication with "I," and since "I" is here split into a doubled reference to subject and other, the spectator is taken up in a figure of the double, making visible the real division of the self in the symbolic order. "I" is an o/Other.

Thus, the movement between the realms of the imaginary/symbolic and the real of cinema in *Un Chant d'amour* "defetishizes" the film object and produces displeasure. As Serge Daney puts it:

> Every time the spectator, forgetting his situation, his posture, starts to respond with pleasure to what is playing in this little theater of desire . . . he is simply transformed into a guard.[37]

Genet not only implicates the spectator in the voyeurism of the guard in the diegesis, but reflects on the "garde," the scopic drive as defense against the real of castration. As Metz says, "What defines the scopic realm of cinema is not as much the distance kept ["gardée"], the defense ["la garde"] itself, (primary figure of lack, common to all voyeurism) as the absence of the object seen."[38] The implication of the spectator in the dual figure of the narrating subject (I = he) is inscribed with the identification of male and female, since the guard in the film desires not women but men subjected to the position of the feminine by his sadistic gaze. In other words, the fetishistic function of the film breaks down. Rather than recuperate the missing penis by projecting it into woman's body (creating the figure, he = [imaginary] he), the guard's sadistic looks at men in the throes of solitary pleasure effectively castrate the men in the film. These looks open up a gap in the imaginary there where the phallus is supposed to be, creating the figure he = (imaginary) she.

Genet reiterates this twist on the conventional representation of women in the sequence where the swarthy prisoner fantasizes himself in the countryside with the fair man, plucking a flower from the latter's garland. As Ken Kelman observes, this scene approaches a parody of the Hollywood boy-pursues-girl scenario, culminating in an ironic perversion of the literary cliché of "deflowering" the maiden, a figure I discuss in chapter 3 with regard to *Miracle de la rose*.[39]

Displacements of the look, from the narrating camera to the guard and to prisoners looking back, also problematize the sexual identity of the gaze as organizing principle of the discourse. The guard's own look and sometimes his organ of vision are the objects of the gazes of camera and prisoners. Sexuality is therefore represented in the film in terms of a constant shifting of positions between voyeurs and erotic objects (masculine and feminine being constructed thereby), rather than along the biological division between men and women in the diegesis. In this way, Genet constructs the subject of discourse around a figure of bisexuality, the spectator (s)he.

Jean Cocteau once defined cinema as the act of looking at events through a key-hole, implying that the voyeur is a metaphor for the spectator.[40] Genet characteristically twists this metaphor into an ironic reflection on the spectator's own perverseness, on the dubious sexuality of the subject of the look, and on the sadistic origins of scopic pleasure. By violating the law of the "same" as ontological support of the cinematic image, Genet, himself a former prisoner, effectively imprisons the spectator in his own dark cell of desire. Thus the spectating subject becomes the victim of Genet's irony. In chapter 2, I discussed similar operations in the novels which implicate the reading subject in the narrator's irony by perverting relations between narrative voice and the voices of characters speaking in the story.

In *Un Chant d'amour* Genet succeeded, in a rudimentary way, in exposing the terms of film performance, that is, the moment by moment identification of "I" with "eye" in film discourse, by foregrounding a first-person narrative "voice." By disturbing the spectator's dreamlike state during the film, by introducing a disquieting reflection on the cinema's predisposition to voyeurism, Genet stages the spectating subject in an ironic play of (self-)reflections. In this sense, Genet anticipated the dialectical cinema of avant-garde filmmakers of the 1960s through the 1980s, including Godard, Straub-Huillet, Duras, and Ackerman, whose work problematizes the spectator's relation to film discourse by exposing the distance between the voice of the enounced and the voice of the enunciation. Unlike those filmmakers, who take advantage of the material disjuncture of sound and image in order to stage the division of the subject in film narrative, Genet was limited by working only with the visual track. He nonetheless transcribes into cinematic terms the figure of the "double," originating in the novels in the form of the intrication of voices in narrative discourse (see chapters 1 and 2 of the present book). He also anticipated the conditions of representation which would characterize his "theater of the double."[41]

Un Chant d'amour might be viewed as an esthetic exercise for Genet, who had, by 1950, written *Haute Surveillance* (1947) and *Les Bonnes* (1948), but had not yet realized a theatrical production of either play. Theater is not primarily text but the *performance* of a text. Moreover, theatrical performance includes visual and spatial dimensions which can only be imagined in narrative. In the course of adapting his notion of textual performance to the needs of the spectating subject, Genet was forced to examine problems of spectator identification and transcribe his poetic vision into concrete, plastic images.

As I discuss in chapter 5, Genet created a style of theatrical performance which exposes the double at the origin of mimesis, thus destroying the illusion that a fixed reality precedes and even transcends representation. Following Artaud, Genet viewed reality as a house of illusions, as an imitation of theatrical performance.[42] As in the film, the staging of the spectating subject of Genet's theater constitutes a kind of recuperation of the imaginary by the real, since the spectator participates in the performance as an actor on the stage of life.

If cinematic representation exists as an imprint of absent realities, theatrical representation exists as an illusion of total presence: the presence of the spectators and actors in a single time and space; the presence of the place of production of the representation (the stage); and the visibility of the costumes, make-up and props employed by actors to create their roles.[43] The polemical movement between the representation as a symbolic-imaginary apparatus (as a fiction which invites our participation) and a real, technical apparatus is crucial to Genet's ideal of "theater about theater."

The kinds of doublings we discovered in Genet's novels—in the dual identities of the narrator, in ambiguous indications for narrative space and in the endless mirroring of narrative discourse and reported speech, are the bases for Genet's ideal of theatrical performance. These doublings are possible in the novel because of the conventional separation of narrator and narrating event from characters and the narration. They are possible in the theater because of the autonomy of the verbal text from mise-en-scene, the distance between the fiction and the means of representation, and so on. Such doublings are somewhat more difficult to articulate in cinema, especially silent cinema, because of the conjunction between the look of the spectator, the look of the camera, and the diegesis it brings into view. While Genet might have chosen the route of filmmaker-authors such as Duras or Robbe-Grillet, who place the spectating subject on stage by means of disjunctions between sound and image, he evidently discovered that the theater was a more powerful medium in which to explore the psychological and philosophical question of performance than the cinema. Genet made only this film before devoting himself to the theater, with its vast repertory of means for staging the subject in the drama of performance.[44]

FIVE

Passion: Between Text and Performance

While Genet earned a certain *succès de scandale* from his early poems and novels, he won worldwide notoriety from his plays. Genet clearly did not develop his radical style of theater overnight, yet critics and scholars have failed to explain the development of Genet's theater out of his earlier work with problems of subject-address and narrative point of view in the novels. Moreover, when critics discuss Genet's film as a kind of side show to the main event of his theatrical career, they underestimate the continuities between the novelistic, the cinematic, and the dramatic modes in Genet's work. These kinds of continuities characterize the work of Genet and his contemporaries, including Duras, Beckett, and Robbe-Grillet, and place in question semiotic theories based upon the autonomy and specificity of any given mode of representation with regard to the others.

In this chapter, I challenge the philosophical and semiological assumptions underlying such theories in order to account for the evolution of Genet's theater out of the novels and film. By examining the merging of text, theater, and film in the framework of a general semiotics of performance, I both place sign theory in a new philosophical key and advance the state of the semiotics of theater and drama. The heterogeneity of theatrical representation, which includes both text and mise-en-scène, eludes the ontological model underlying sign theory. As a result, this potentially rich area of semiotic study has been fraught with difficulties from the start.

My approach goes against the grain of semiotic theories derived from the Saussurian sign, theories which begin by delimiting the ontological and structural specificity of the mode under investigation. Since sign theory posits the marriage of signifier and signified as the origin of signification, the extension of sign theory to poetic systems such as literature and cinema perpetuates the assumption that each type of signifying system is discrete and self-sufficient.

The practice of separating representational modes for purposes of analysis and criticism shapes the structuralist tradition. The Czech esthetician Jan Mukarovsky, for instance, writing in the 1930s, defines structuralism as the investigation of the "possibilities [of every art form] provided by the character of its material and the way in which the given art masters it."[1]

In attempting to differentiate poetry from ordinary language, or dramatic action from everyday actions, the Prague School estheticians, including Mukarovsky, Otakar Zich, and Jiri Veltrusky, developed the notion of "foregrounding" or *ostranenij* advanced by the Russian Formalists.[2] They define the semiotic specificity of a given art form with reference to the means which that form employs to draw attention to aspects of language or other media as ends in themselves. Thus for Veltrusky, speaking about theater, "as soon as an act by itself attracts the attention of the perceiver, its properties become signs. It then enters consciousness by means of signs and becomes meaning."[3] The Prague School lacked a theoretical model for a general semiotics of the poetic text, however, and is characterized by positivistic descriptions of the *means* of sign production rather than by a scientific elaboration upon relations between signs and meanings in discourse. Thus the elements contributing to foregrounding in poetic discourse cannot be applied directly to drama, or vice versa, but remain tied to the specific material and mode of represenation under investigation.

In the 1940s Louis Hjelmslev formulated the question of the specificity of signifying systems in terms of a sign function producing a dialectical relation between the form of the expression and the form of the content of discourse.[4] His theory has shaped modern semiotics by virtue of the scientific rigor of his approach and the broad implications of the notion of sign function.[5] Since the Saussurian sign joins a phonetic element, the "image acoustique" and a concept, it is only by means of a metaphorical leap that the Saussurian sign can be used as a model for semiotic systems other than language.[6] The Hjelmslevian sign function, however, defines relations between the expression plane and the content plane of a given system, whether the material be words, images, figures, or anything else.

In order to determine which sign functions are specific to a given system, the analyst must first articulate relations between the larger and smaller segments of the material under investigation (the first and second articulations). This articulation or segmentation would be governed by corresponding relations between the form of the expression and the form of the content. In other words, a relation such as the contrast between two phonemes would not be distinctive to a semiotic system unless it entailed a corresponding contrast on the content plane.

Hjelmslev's dialectic influenced the semiotics of Christian Metz, who, in *Langage et cinéma*, examines the specificity of cinema in terms of codes structuring relations between units of the film chain.[7] Nowhere is the inseparability of the expression plane and the content plane as clear as in the cinema, which does not merely stand for something else but produces a copy of the object seized by the camera. Cinema not only produces a mechanical reproduction of visual reality but interprets that reality by means of relations between images and sounds, and eventually between shots and sequences in the signifying system.

Rather than investigate the multivalent interpretations opened up by the structure of meaning in any given film, Metz focusses on an ideal set of codes shaping the cinematic signifier. He avoids reducing the abstract notion of cinema to its material properties such as cellulose, light, and movement, insisting on the role of codes in determining the semiotic specificity of cinema. For instance, a code such as the dissolve serving as a transition from one shot to the next requires certain manipulations of the film material. These include the superimposition of two layers of film and changes in exposure of the film to light entering the camera lens. Metz insists that such technical manipulations of the material define the system "cinema" only to the extent that they shape formal relations on the expression and content planes.

Furthermore, Metz goes to great lengths in *Langage et cinéma* to distinguish purely cinematic codes such as the dissolve, whose meaning is inseparable from the expression plane of cinema, from extra-cinematic codes such as the language of film dialogue. The result is a kind of ontology of the cinematic signifier, since the delimitation of the field of investigation leads to questions as to the relation of cinema to reality, to a metaphysical interpretation of mimesis, to the closure of meaning and being in cinematic discourse.

In *The Imaginary Signifier* (1981), which I discussed in detail in chapter 4, Metz moves beyond the linguistically oriented semiotics of the cinematic signifier to a psycho-semiotic study of the spectating subject's relation to the film image. He nevertheless perpetuates the phenomenological assumptions of his earlier work, basing his theory of spectator identification on a delineation of the ontological and technical "apparatus" of cinema. Metz's theory of the subject derives from a static conception of the image as origin, as minimal unit of signification and model for the subject's closure with the cinematic signifier. Here, the "subject" constitutes a unifying function of an ideal, closed system rather than an effect or production of specific discourses or textual performances. As I demonstrated with regard to Genet's film, *Un Chant d'amour*, Metz's theoretical stance underestimates the philosophical implications of disruptions in the closure between spectator's look and the look of the camera, disruptions produced by the manipulation of the codes of dominant cinema.

Even when Metz analyzes filmic figures such as metaphor and metonymy, he chooses not to theorize about the place of the subject in specific textual figures, as I have in chapter 3. Metz focusses instead on the formal construction of such figures in theory. He therefore overlooks the subject's moment by moment construction in the dynamic organization of sound and image in textual performance.[8]

The tendency to elaborate theoretical systems at the expense of a deep analysis of individual texts has led to the marginalization of writers such as Genet, who address the problem of spectator identification within the dialogue or the staging of a play, or within the organization of looks in a film, by disturbing the spectator's hypnotic engagement in the psycho-semiotic apparatus of the discourse. Rather than modify theory to account for such textual practices, critics such as Metz establish oppositions between conventional and avant-garde authors, the latter defined in terms of transgressions or violations of poetic norms.

The metaphysical bent of semiotics can be traced both to Saussure and to Hjelmslev, whose impact on current semiotic theory must not be underestimated. Hjelmslev excludes the question of the individual performance of a code, the "purport" or "substance" of discourse, from the realm of linguistic theory altogether, suggesting that this aspect of language be taken up by anthropology or psychology. He states:

> Such a linguistics . . . would be one whose science of the expression is not a phonetics and whose science of the content is not a semantics. Such a science would be an algebra of language, operating with unnamed entities, i.e. arbitrarily named entities without natural designation, which would receive a motivated designation only on being confronted with the substance.[9]

In order to maintain an ideal of closure between the content and the expression in the notion of sign function, Hjelmslev must exclude questions raised by the speaking event, including the speaker's intentions and the reference of discourse. Such context-bound features point to the vulnerability of language to the force of performance, a force which constantly threatens the meaning and coherence of discourse with the forces of passion, irony, and ambiguity.

One generally associates performance with the theater, specifically with the actor's negotiation of a dramatic role on stage, or a director's interpretation and mise-en-scène of a written text for an audience. Thus, in this sense, performance implies a movement between a more or less stable, transcendent element, the dramatic text, and a living, dynamic, and more or less contingent element, the theatrical interpretation of the text. In linguistic and poetic theories, the "performers" have changed, but the philosophical implications of their claims about textual performance have been handed down from the theater. In authors as varied as Otakar Zich, Jan Mukarovsky, Benveniste, and Austin, performance defines the speaking/spectating subject's participation in the contract binding meaning to being in discourse. Linguistic codes make up the fixed, transcendent elements by means of which individual subjects participate in language. Semiotic codes govern the subject's particpation in artistic representation.

In the 1930s Mukarovsky anticipated Benveniste's focus on the subject of discourse when he defined theater as a set of "immaterial relations" and an "immaterial interplay of forces moving through time and space, pulling the spectator into its changeable tension, into the interplay we call a production, a performance."[10] Mukarovsky conceives the spectating subject as the locus of meaning, a transcendental "I" which shapes the performance by means of a dialectical movement between the system of the text and the spectator's consciousness. Mukarovsky differs from his predecessor, Otakar Zich, for whom the dialectical relation between spectator and actor alone produced the unifying force of theater.[11] For Mukarovsky, the actor's work constitutes but one element among many which the spectator assimilates through the unifying logic of perception.

Emile Benveniste led semiotics out of the structuralist impasse it faced in the 1960s when he introduced the philosophical question of the speaker's relation to discourse into debates about the form of meaning.[12] "I" and "you" constitute codes for inscribing intersubjectivity in language and transcend any specific instance of textual performance. As in Kant's metaphysic, the transcendental subject of Benveniste's semiotic thus precedes representation as such, is a condition of the very possibility of meaning, without which discourse could not take place. Benveniste warns that any perversion of the contract binding "I" and "you," such as the identification of "I" and "he," would cause a break-down of communication and a misrepresentation of the speaker's identity. Benveniste cites a line from Rimbaud's *Une Saison en enfer* as an example of this kind of perversion: "Je est un autre."[13] As I discussed in chapter 1, Benveniste overlooks the rich implications of this kind of statement by reducing it to a figure for alienation. When Rimbaud announces that I is an other, he not only creates a figure for the cleavage of the subject of poetic discourse, but sets the stage for a modern poetics of performance. As I prove in the course of my analysis of three plays by Genet further on in this chapter, the staging of the subject in a figure of the double constitutes a model for contemporary poetry and poetics.

John Austin's notion of "performative utterances" would appear to have little in common with the theories of Benveniste and the Prague School estheticians, since Austin deliberately excludes poetic and dramatic discourses from the set of normative statements in question. In *How to Do Things with Words*,[14] Austin criticizes metaphysical philosophy for marginalizing statements which are neither true nor false but derive their force from a reference to the speech act itself. Austin then defines the conditions a statement must meet in order to belong to the linguistic category of performatives, namely that the speaker's intentions and the speaking situation must be "serious." In his famous debate with the advocates of speech act theory, Jacques Derrida points out that Austin sustains the very kind of hierarchy he criticizes in metaphysical philosophy when he excludes certain kinds of speech acts from the category of performative utterances.[15]

For example, if a speaker performs a promise or enters into a contract with an interlocutor, the speaker's intentions and the existential context of the statement must be compatible with the meaning of the statement. Thus a promise to wed uttered at a wedding rehearsal is not serious, nor is an ironic statement, since they both, in different ways, produce conflicts between the meaning of the utterance and the frame of reference or the intentions of the speaker. They constitute exceptions to, rather than examples of, the rule of performative utterances.

Derrida locates the weak point in Austin's argument in the question of iterability. For a performative to have force and meaning in "serious" situations, it must conform to a set of conventions which the interlocutor recognizes based on previous experience. In other words, for a statement to be "serious" in a given context, it must also be recognizable and operative in "non-serious" contexts such as irony and role-play. If the compatibility between signification and reference is a condition of the force and meaning of an utterance, then the possibility of a disjunction between signification and reference is a condition of the serious statement. To paraphrase Umberto Eco, a sign is anything that can be used in order to lie, therefore the "non-serious" is inscribed in the very definition of signification.[16]

Another source of irony in Austin concerns the relation of serious (pragmatic) discourse to poetry and poetics. On the one hand, the very definition of performatives or the performative function in terms of a focus on the speech act itself, parallels Roman Jakobson's definition of the "poetic function" of language.[17] By projecting the paradigmatic onto the syntagmatic axis, the poetic function derives its force from a focus on the form of discourse rather than from the truth value of the message. On the other hand, unlike Jakobson, who insists upon the importance of the poetic function as a linguistic feature of practical as well as poetic discourse, Austin excludes performative statements made within poetic discourse, such as drama, from the realm of linguistics. Where Jakobson's poetic function "deepens the fundamental dichotomy of signs and objects" (separates the study of signs from metaphysical questions about reality), Austin's performative function remains tied to the study of empirical relations between discourse and pragmatic reality.

Austin's exclusion of poetics from linguistics not only perpetuates the very philosophical standard which he claims to circumscribe, the standard of truth vs. non-truth. It also discourages our extrapolating the question of performatives into a general semiotics of performance. Such a semiotics would resist formulation into the signifier/signified model shaping structuralism and structuralist poetics in its turn. A semiotics of performance would be based on those aspects of language which do not "signify" per se, but point to referents in a pragmatic or discursive context, along the lines of deixis.

In a recent attempt to define the semiotic specificity of the dramatic text, Serpieri et al. cite Austin among various theorists who focus on relations of subject-address and reference to shape a model for semiosis. The authors, setting aside Austin's criterion of empirical validity for the moment, claim that "the theater is entirely performative: indeed, performativity, which is realized in deixis, makes up what might be termed the specific theatrical language."[18]

Performativity would be characterized by the index, that category of signs Peirce defines in terms of aspects of language which simply point to referents in the discursive or pragmatic ("real") context rather than signify transcendent meanings.[19] An example of an index tied to the pragmatic context would be the demonstrative pronoun, accompanied perhaps by a gesture of the hand, in the statement "Look at that." The interlocutor must look in the direction of the referent established by the gesture and the pronoun in order to infer meaning from this statement. In a literary text, indices point to referents which have been established by the discursive context. The statement "We did it!" can only move the plot forward if the context has clearly established the reference of the pronouns.

Benveniste identifies the philosophical implications of these kinds of markings in the notion of deixis. Deixis, shaped by indexical relations in discourse, traces the presence of the speaking subject of discourse, without which speech would not be possible. Thus the personal and demonstrative pronouns and adverbs pointing to the here and now of the speaking event not only raise the question of the semantic context of discourse, but put into play the complicity of speaker and interlocutor, of I and you, in the speaking event.[20]

As it must be clear by now, theatrical performance can be defined as a play of indexical relations pointing both to a pragmatic and a discursive context and inscribing the spectator's implication in the dramatic text. The spectator must not only be able to read the gestures of actors pointing to people, places, and objects on stage, gestures which are often included in the verbal text itself in the form of stage directions. The spectator must also infer referents for the dialogue, when characters on stage narrate information about people and events off-stage. Such information is provided by the context of the dialogue itself, rather than the immediate setting of the action. In both cases the force of the dramatic text derives from the speaking event itself, i.e., from dynamic interrelations between speaker and interlocutors on-stage, between the text performed and the spectator, between on- and off-stage space. In the notion of deixis as a poetic function which defies assimilation into the signifier/signified model, one discovers the basis for a poetics of performance, a poetics which would place the spectator in question as subject or consciousness whose production/deconstruction is "staged" in the dramatic text.

Unfortunately, rather than take poetics or semiotics in this direction, one which would question the very metaphysical foundations of structural linguistics, Serpieri et al. formulate a hypothesis which grants a *signifying function* to deixis in theatrical representation. That is, rather than question the ability of sign theory (à la Saussure or Hjelmslev) to account for the force of deixis in theatrical performance, the authors declare that in the dramatic text indices acquire an iconic dimension. That is, they not only *point* to elements in the pragmatic or discursive contexts, they *display* themselves as speech acts. Segmentation, the overriding criterion of structural analysis, can therefore occur along the lines of signifier/signified relationships produced by this display. "Utterances can be segmented at every change in performative-deictic orientation by one speaker with regard to the other."[21]

Serpieri et al. thus add a new twist to Austin's category of performative utterances. Rather than exclude "non-serious" performatives such as dramatic dialogue from the realm of linguistics, the authors grant them a *signifying function*! They are thus able to contain the deictic dimension of theater within structural poetics, built upon an ideal of closure between signifier and signified on every level of the text.[22]

Seeking means of framing theatrical representation into a signifier/signified has been a main theme of semiotic theories leading up to Serpieri's segmentation of the dramatic text. Benveniste explains the "véritable problème sémiologique" in the following terms: "The truly semiological question is how the transposition of a verbal enunciation into an iconic enunciation is achieved."[23] For Eco, a semiotics of theater would center on the iconization of the body of the actor by means of "showing":

> The properly semiologic element of theater consists in the fact that the human body is no longer a thing among things, because someone shows it by separating it from the context of real events and constitutes it as sign; constituting at the same time as signifiers the movements that this body accomplishes and the space in which these movements are inscribed.[24]

For Hjelmslev the scientific validity of semiotics is based upon the practice of segmenting the text into units modelled after the sign function.[25] The "science" of performance has run into difficulties throughout the history of semiotics because performance resists the kind of internalization of meaning which sign theory demands. Thus, as recently as 1976, long after the semiotics of narrative, cinema, and other arts had advanced, Patrice Pavis underscores the urgency to articulate a semiotics of theatrical performance, heretofore fraught with blind spots.[26]

When Serpieri et al. grant an iconic dimension to deixis in their semiotics of the dramatic text, they do not take into account the effects of staging on the constitution of the indexical icon, which delays and utterly defies static formalization into the structural linguistic model. Moreover, by insisting on the ontological specificity of the dramatic text, they foreclose investigation into the work of deixis in narrative and cinematic texts. As I proved ealier in this book, Genet's novels and film are witness to the merging of different representational modes in contemporary literature.

As Kristeva argues so forcefully in *Desire in Language*,[27] structuralism obscures the philosophical question of the speaking subject of discourse by modelling semiosis after the closure of meaning and being in the sign. By taking for granted the presence and unity of the speaking subject in the present of theatrical performance, Serpieri et al. lose sight of the drama being staged in the spaces between the segments of discourse, the drama of the spectator's identification with the representation.

In *Dissemination*[28] Jacques Derrida shifts the focus of poetics from the metaphysical closure between representations and their objects in mimesis, to the reading/spectating subject's "performance" of a poetic text. Particularly in the section titled "The Double Session," Derrida brings to light those aspects of representation which structural poetics obscures. In his critique of the ontological interpretation of mimesis, Derrida raises the issue of performance in the context of a deconstruction of the poetic sign. He twists the mirror joining poetic signifier and signified to reveal the endless movement of the subject in a play of reflections in the poetic text. While Derrida, in this essay and in *Of Grammatology*,[29] would seem to discredit the semiological enterprise by insisting on the fundamentally unscientific and contingent nature of man's performance of discourse, there is a point at which deconstruction and semiotics intersect. As I have argued throughout this book, by expanding the notion of semiosis to a general theory of how subjects become something for other subjects in discourse, we trace the movement of the subject in textual performance along the lines of semiotic codes shaping the speaker's inscription in socially determined discourses. We change the philosophical framework of semiotics, while making use of distinctions such as enunciation and enounced, index and icon, signifier and signified, and so forth.

The mime-play is a useful model for describing Genet's work, since the mime suspends the traditional primacy of the written text over performance and reveals a weak point in the classical interpretation of mimesis as the imitation of living speech. Since the mime does not breathe life into dramatic discourse but creates meaning by manipulating contortions of his body and face, his performance suspends the ideal closure between being and meaning in speech, placing in question the unity and the identity of the speaking and spectating subject.[30]

Mallarmé, the focus of the "Double Session," describes this movement as a play of passion, "tainted with vice yet sacred, between desire and fulfillment, perpetration and remembrance; here anticipating, there recalling, in the future, in the past, under the false appearance of a present."[31] The mime-play thus serves as a model for a semiotics of performance. This kind of staging also symbolizes the violence of passion joining/separating narrator and character, characters and actors, camera eye and narrating I, in Genet's novels, plays, and film.

As I now examine three of Genet's plays, Les Bonnes, Le Balcon, and Les Nègres, I shall focus on the semiological and philosophical issues at stake in the texts themselves, including Genet's directions concerning the performance, rather than on the stage productions of individual directors. Though it is important to note the variety of styles which directors as different as Roger Blin, Peter Brooks, and Richard Schechner have brought to bear on the problem of the double in Genet, it is simply beyond the scope of this essay to describe or judge the quality of one production or another.[32]

Sartre proposed a relation between Genet and the Passion, the suffering and crucifixion of Christ, even before Genet produced the plays. But Sartre, commenting on Genet's novels, considers only the theme of violent crime in the story and Genet's existential experience as author/criminal/homosexual, rather than the philosophical issue of the subject's construction in discourse. For Sartre, "Creation will then really be a Passion: a passion because the author suffers, in the realm of the imaginary, with the sufferings of his heroes and because his characters' crimes will entail further persecutions in real life."[33]

Applying Sartre's observation to the plays, we might say that Genet performs a kind of passion by creating characters whose rage pushes them to extremes of self-effacement and violence. In Les Bonnes Claire and Solange love one another and share their hate of Madam. Their role-play fails to free them from the social and emotional prisons which hold them, leading instead to the ritualistic murder/suicide of Claire. In Le Balcon Genet stages the sadomasochistic fantasies of clients in a bordello. Characters play out their private scenarios of desire behind borrowed identities. In Les Nègres Genet exposes murder as the ultimate gesture of the slave revolting against his master. A cock crows three times to signal the transformation of slaves into masters, judges into accused, and spectators into victims.

Looking closer at the plays, we observe an intimate relation between plot and theme and Genet's radical interpretation of the notion of passion as a process of dramatic metamorphosis.[34] This modern passion rewrites the Christian Passion in terms of our contemporary concern with the ritualistic function of drama. Genet shapes this passion by deconstructing, rather than abandoning, the classical unities of time, place, and action.

In the "Discours des trois unités," Corneille debates the value of the unities of time, place, and action for French theater of the classical period.[35] The action must occur within twenty-four hours, the location of the action should be limited to the space which could be travelled within the time of the action, and the action itself should not digress from a single dramatic event structured according to the initiation, the climax, and the dénouement of a conflict. The importance of such prescriptions for classical French writers reflects not so much a respect for classical Greek poetics in seventeenth-century France, as an interpretation of that poetics which served the Cartesian ideal of closure between thought and being.

This philosophical stance explains, moreover, the problematic assimilation of the three unities (governing the believability of the performance) into Aristotle's poetics of tragedy (governing the structure of the verbal text). As Corneille points out, Aristotle discouraged references to the performance in the text of the play: "Aristote veut que la tragédie soit belle et capable de plaire sans le secours des comédiens et hors de la représentation."[36] Yet in seventeenth-century *querelles* about theater, the question of the purity of the dramatic text comes up in the framework of the discussion of the three unities.

Aristotle's exclusion of performance from his defense of tragedy not only achieves for dramatic poetry the "purity" of the epic form, but it betrays the same kind of distrust of representation which Derrida finds in Plato.[37] Though written dialogue is one step removed from spoken discourse, in the realm of poetry dialogue constitutes the most immediate form of imitation because it mirrors living speech. Performance would threaten the inner coherence and transcendence of the verbal text with the exteriority and contingency of representation, of textual "writing" in the sense named by Derrida.

Since mise-en-scène affects the meaning of the dialogue, theatrical representation cannot be said simply to copy the unity of being and meaning in mimesis, but to determine its formation. For this reason the question of performance and all that it implies, including exteriority, supplementary, and difference, take center stage in a semiotics of dramatic discourse. Furthermore, the importance granted to mise-en-scène in the theater of Genet and his contemporaries challenges the metaphysical ideal of closure between voice and meaning in speech, an ideal from which the Aristotelian tradition in French theater derived.

In one sense Genet's plays conform rigorously to the letter of the three unities. The action unfolds in a time period which almost matches the real time of the performance, and even transcends the unity of place by foregrounding the stage as the primary locus of the action. *Les Bonnes* takes place in Madam's bedroom and the time of the action parallels the time of the performance. *Le Balcon* begins at night in a bordello and ends in the same place as the cock's crow announces the dawn. *Les Nègres* resembles a primitive ritual in which the stage transforms before our eyes into a courtroom, a funeral parlor, and an African jungle. The time of the action matches the time of the performance.

Though the three unities structure the time and space of the action, Genet disturbs the ontological mission of the three unities by revealing the interdependency of speech and "writing," between text and performance, at the origin of mimesis.[38] The effects of this "deconstruction" produce what has been referred to as the "structure of the double" in Genet's theater.[39]

Les Bonnes opens on a play within the play. Claire and Solange, two maids, go through a routine they have evidently rehearsed before, in the absence of their Mistress. In a game of role-play which clearly parallels the merging of I, you, and he/she in the novels, Claire plays Madam and Solange plays Claire. "Claire" attends to "Madam," dressing her in an extravagant gown and acting as a mirror in which Claire projects herself. Claire directs this play, occasionally dropping her role to give directions to Solange on how to play Claire.

The scene not only reveals the sadomasochistic tone of the maids' relationship to one another, but exposes the situation of the action. Claire and Solange have conspired to denounce Madam's lover to the police by means of anonymous letters. In the course of this scene the lover phones, announcing his release from prison, and, by implication, the inevitable discovery of Claire as the author of the letters.

The mask falls as the maids prepare for Madam's return and scheme to murder her by poisoning the tilleul. Madam returns, but upon hearing of her lover's release, departs without drinking the poisoned brew. Thus caught in their own conspiracy and trapped in a play of mirrors which binds Madam to Claire and Claire to Solange, the maids give a fatal twist to their theatrics which breaks the circle of desire. Claire, playing Madam, directs Solange, playing Claire, to serve the poisoned tilleul. Thus "Claire" murders Claire. We might say that Claire's reflection transcends Claire by both murdering and surviving the original.

In Le Balcon our sense of time and place is mystified by the absence of an anchoring of the action in a coherent diegetic framework. The play is divided into nine tableaux, including four opening "plays" within the play which depict the sadomasochistic dramas enacted by clients and prostitutes in different salons in the bordello. The connection between passion and ritual is explicitly marked in this play. The clients, and by implication, the spectators, act out their erotic fantasies by means of identifying with fictional roles. The travesties they assume elevate the clients to roles of social power unknown to them outside the bordello and allow them to assume masterful roles with the prostitutes. Like the maids, the clients and girls in Le Grand Balcon transgress the boundaries of their social and sexual identities in theatrical games. Unlike Claire and Solange, however, the Bishop, the General, the Judge, and other figures in Madam Irma's house of illusions do not renounce their lives but merely lose track of their identities in the fields between reality and illusion, between on- and off-stage, between the inside and the outside of the bordello.

The scenes in the salons all contain references to Madam Irma's center of operations, her bedroom. Genet suggests that the stage be set with mirrors reflecting an unmade bed placed in the first few rows of the audience. We recognize this bed as a fixture in Madam Irma's bedroom, as the action changes locations in the fifth and ninth tableaux. Madam's bedroom contains, in turn, references to the salons. A small control board registers images of the events in those rooms, giving Madam a controlling look on the performances of her girls and clients. Moreover, two panels of mirrors form the back wall of the set.

The staging of looks connecting actors and spectators by means of mirrors and screens resembles the montage of looks implicating viewer and viewed in Genet's film, *Un Chant d'amour*. As I explained in chapter 4, cinema transcribes the implication of I and you in terms of the spectator's primary identification with the look of the camera, which permits secondary identification with the looks of characters in the fiction. In the film, Genet stages an intrusion of the Other into the dialectical closure of I and eye by unmasking the presence of the camera behind the looks (i.e., the "discourses") of characters. In this way Genet perverts the spectator's drive to merge with the film.

In *Le Balcon* the intrusion of off-stage space into the present and presence of the performance on stage interrupts the closure between spectator and spectacle by doubling the reference of indices shaping subject-address and contextuality. The place of the performance becomes confused with the place of the spectator viewing the performance, and leads to a general breakdown of the limits defining on- and off-stage space, spectator and spectacle, and the meaning and reference of the dialogue.

Verbal clues and sound effects refer to another dimension of the action, to a revolution raging outside the bordello. We hear machine guns firing off-stage. Clients interrupt their performances to inquire about the political situation. Madam Irma advises her clients about safe means of leaving the bordello. Characters enter from locations outside and report that the Royal Palace has been taken over and that the royal family has been arrested.

The only time the action moves outside the bordello occurs in tableau 6, in a scene between one of Irma's girls, Chantal, and her lover Roger, who apparently have taken sides with the revolutionaries.

In the fifth tableau, the merging of outside and inside begins to develop. The Chief of Police, a friend of Irma's, takes refuge in the Grand Balcon and exposes his plan of action. He will wait for the revolutionaries to oust the Queen and then try to assume power himself. His fate will be sealed in a matter of hours: either he will die at the hands of the revolutionaries or will become emperor of the realm.

In either case, the Police Chief's death is imminent. As a figurehead of state, his individual being will be replaced by endless representations of his being, including his picture and his name. His image has already been disseminated on posters and banners and will end up on coins and stamps. The Police Chief not only recognizes the relation between representation and death, but draws our attention to that relation as it structures the representation being performed for us. In language which reminds one of Derrida's reply to Austin about iterability and death, the Police Chief reminds us that the possibility of the extinction of the real is a condition of representation, in the same way that the possibility of representation is a condition of the real. Nothing can escape this permanent intrusion of representation into the inner spaces of being.

—J'obligerais mon image à se détacher de moi, à pénétrer, à forcer tes salons, à réfléchir, à se multiplier. Irma, ma fonction me pèse. Ici, elle m'apparaîtra dans le soleil terrible du plaisir et de la mort. [Rêveur] De la mort. (p. 85)

—I'll make my image detach itself from me. I'll make it penetrate into your studios, force its way in, reflect and multiply itself. Irma, my function weighs me down. Here, it will appear to me in the blazing light of pleasure and death. [Musingly] Of death. (Balcony, p. 48)

Between pleasure and death, between the illusion of closure and the recognition of division, the play turns the question of mimesis into a drama of the subject of desire. The death-by-representation of the Police Chief obeys the same rules that govern the erotic performances of characters in the brothel, since the clients and prostitutes must renounce their personal identities for the sake of their passions. Following the perverse logic which joins politics and prostitution, the revolution referred to off-stage moves on-stage, into the Grand Balcon. Madam Irma's bedroom becomes the headquarters of the new political regime, and Irma becomes Queen of the realm, with the Police Chief at her side. Thus the inside and the outside of the brothel, like the inside and the outside of representation, fold together in the difficult present and presence of the performance.

In a final stroke of theatrical genius, Genet deconstructs this promise of closure between text and performance, between the presence and absence inscribed in references to on- and off-stage space, by revealing a mirror there where we expect the presence of a stable diegetic "reality." As the ninth and final tableau opens, the Bishop, the General, and the Judge, who have tried to forget their personal identities in order to become ministers in the new government, pose for some photographers. By fixing their images in photographs, photographs aimed at seizing archetypical representations of religious, military, and judicial authority, the photographers produce "une image vraie d'un spectacle faux" (p. 113). The image is true because of an ontological fallacy which grants objectivity to mechanical reproductions, but dangerously false, because it conceals the possibility of the lie which is inscribed in the reference of the photographic image. A sign of a sign, the photograph says something of the instability of the transcendental signified of metaphysics.

Moreover, photography stages a scene of violence tantamount to murder. The photograph not only produces a likeness more perfect than the work of the human hand, but guarantees the symbolic destruction of the individual identity of the subject because of the possibility of infinite reproductions of the likeness. The photograph fixes on paper a moment which has ceased being as soon as it is recorded on film, and therefore anticipates the death of its referent.[40]

A sign of the lie and symbol of murder, the photograph forms a model for the ultimate theatrical figure in *Le Balcon*. The Queen/Irma invites the Police Chief to witness his own "death," that is, to witness his incarnation by an actor in Irma's Mausoleum salon. The Bishop, the General, and the Judge join the Police Chief as he watches the performance through an opening in a wall in Irma's bedroom. The voyeuristic staging of viewer and object of the look opens up into a metaphor for the spectator's own implication in the events on stage, as the wall opening widens and the salon scene occupies center stage. The set turns inside-out, as it were. The play-within-the-play replaces the original setting and engages the spectator directly as a voyeur.

Ironically, the actor playing the Police Chief is none other than Roger, the revolutionary from the sixth tableau, once again in Irma's employ (or had he ever left it?). Disguised as the Police Chief, Roger possesses powers he never knew as a mere revolutionary. Though he misses the revolution and his mistress, Chantal, he is mesmerized by the charm of the brothel and the force of his disguise, and would play out his borrowed identity indefinitely were it not for Irma's rules. Irma steps in and kicks him out of the brothel, preventing illusion from becoming a permanent presence.

The Police Chief understands this staging of himself as a metaphor for his own death by representation. Playing the part to its necessary end, he descends into the Mausoleum salon, not, however, without pausing to pose for the photographers:

—Vous, regardez-moi vivre et mourir. Pour la postérité: feu! (Trois éclairs presque simultanés de magnésium.) —Gagné! (p. 133)

—You! Watch me live, and die. For posterity: shoot! (Three almost simultaneous flashes.) I've won! (*Balcony*, p. 94)

His exit through the floor of the stage signals the end of the revolution "routine" and leaves the Bishop, the General, and the Judge hanging precariously between two histories and two identities, between life and death. Irma shows them the way out of the brothel and contemplates preparations for the next evening's performance. Machine guns fire and a cock crows off-stage, reminding us that the outside of the brothel is but another fold of its inside, another dimension of make-believe in which the spectating subject is held.

Just as Genet's novels incorporate an actor/narrator wearing the masks of characters in the story, so his plays incorporate actors speaking behind masks in the name of an absent narrator. The question of "who speaks?" in theatrical representation can be explored along the lines of the representation of narrative "voice" in theater and narrative. For Benveniste the voice of discourse is articulated in personal and demonstrative pronouns shaping subject-address and reference in discourse, and in verbs and adverbs signalling the present and presence of the speaking event.[41] The time and place of discourse shape the movement of deixis in performance—on stage or in the folds of textual writing. The time of discourse is the time of desire, since the implication of "I" and "you" in performance symbolizes the wrestling of two subjectivities to transcend the limits of their individual identities. Since Lacan and Derrida, we recognize that the present and presence of desire, of discourse, is an illusion. I am never there where "I" is objectified in language. The "now" is but a trace of a signified trying to catch up with a signifier in semiosis. As Derrida puts it:

> There is no present text in general, and there is not even a past present text, a text which is past as having been present. The text is not thinkable in any originary or modified form of presence. The unconscious text is already woven of pure traces, differences in which meaning and force are united; a text nowhere present, consisting of archives which are always already transcriptions. Always already: repositories of a meaning which was never present, whose signified presence is always reconstituted by deferment, *nachträglich*, belatedly, supplementarily: for *nachträglich* also means supplementary.[42]

When Genet subordinates the time and place of the story to the present and presence of textual performance, only to reveal the troubling duality of that place, that time, he makes performance the scene of a crime. Genet introduces passion into representation as a violent transgression of the authority of narrative voice. In *Les Nègres* Genet brings the question of passion to bear on the traditionally dialectical structure of didactic theater.

Genet's own sympathies with revolutionary groups such as the Black Panthers, the Baader-Meinhoff gang, and the Palestine Liberation Organization have been documented in statements published in political pamphlets, newspaper articles, and in the recent essay/novel, *Un Captif amoureux*.[43] In *Les Nègres* Genet proposes a political theater which exposes the master-slave relationship in terms of the inscription of authority in language and theatrical representation. The discourse of authority structures meaning around a transcendental "I" and organizes visual representation around the unifying center of monocular perspective. The I and eye of bourgeois art therefore nullify differences —between white and black, or between male and female, for instance—by relegating blacks and females to the margins of otherness, of supplementarity, in the order of the "same" of classical dialectics. Dialectical discourse is always a discourse of exclusion and reduction of difference. Therefore even Marxist theater, which, after Brecht, exposes the processes of its own production, presents revolutionary ideas in the form of a dialectical closure between the means and ends of theatrical representation, posits the marriage of poetic signifier and signified in the dramatic text. In other words, dialectical materialist theater employs the discourse of authority to combat institutions of authority.

Genet refuses the dialectical closure of didactic theater, replacing dialectics with an ironic staging of "différance," Derrida's term for the slippery movement between signifier and signified in textual writing. In Genet performance constantly erodes mimesis as soon as it promises to present a transcendental signified in the immediate presence of representation. In *Les Nègres* and in the later play *Les Paravents*, Genet comes closest to realizing Artaud's vision of a "theater of cruelty," theater which reverses the Aristotelian tradition of privileging text over mise-en-scène, and stages the spectating subject in a play of passion which eludes representation as such.[44]

Les Nègres opens on a frankly artificial setting with few indications for the location of the action.[45] Some iron scaffolds support platforms above the stage and create a spatial hierarchy which corresponds to relations of power between characters on stage. The white Court, including the Queen, her Valet, the Governor, the Judge, and the Missionary, sit on the platform surrounding the stage and look down on the actions performed by black characters. Typically Genet creates this hierarchy only to destroy it. All of the actors are black, and those who play whites in the Court wear white masks which reveal the black skin and frizzy hair of the performers. At some point in the play the masks fall and the Court descends to the stage level of the Blacks.

Throughout the play a white casket covered with flowers occupies center stage. It supposedly contains the corpse of a white woman supposedly murdered by a black man named Village before the beginning of the play. It is difficult to summarize the action, since the play does not represent anything as much as it struggles with the question of how to represent the murder of a white woman by a black man for a white audience. Genet states something of the difficulty facing a white author writing about blacks for a white audience in the preface to the play.

> One evening an actor asked me to write a play which would be played by blacks. But, what is a black? And, first of all, what color is that? (p. 8, my translation)

The structure of the play is equally difficult to summarize, since there are no traditional divisions between scenes. From beginning to end, characters move in and out of roles, in and out of fictional locations, in and out of costumes, without so much as pausing to reflect on the passages. Moreover, as so much of the force of *Les Nègres* derives from the performance itself, including the play with masks, sound effects, and the dances and mimes of characters on stage, Genet's instructions for the performance constitute an integral aspect of any written account of the play. As Corneille judged even in the seventeenth century, the author's remarks about the performance of the text are not mere intrusions into the original unity of dramatic dialogue, but contribute to an original tension between text and performance in theatrical representation.

In the opening scene, three black men and four black women, all in European evening dress which artfully exudes bad taste, dance a minuet to music by Mozart. A fourth black man, barefoot and dressed as a shoeshine boy, joins them. The music stops and Archibald, a kind of master of ceremonies, steps forward and introduces his troupe of actors to the audience by colorful sobriquets. These names, like the names in the novel *Notre-Dame-des-fleurs*, contribute to the masquerade as surely as the costumes, gestures, and dialogue of the actors. We meet Dieudonné Village, Adelaïde Bobo, Edgar-Hélas, Ville de Saint-Nazaire, Augusta Neige, Félicité Gueuse-Pardon, Dioup, and Etiennette-Vertu-Rose-Secrète. They have all come from daytime jobs among whites in order to stage this spectacle for a white audience.

Actors and spectators thus divide, in a first instance, along racial lines. This opposition is so important for the realization of the ritual that Genet insists, in the introduction to the play, that for every performance there be at least one white spectator in the audience. In the unlikely case that the play is performed for an all-black audience, at least one spectator should wear a white mask. If such a spectator cannot be found, Genet proposes placing a white mannequin in the audience.

A sharp irony tinges Archibald's opening address. He declares that the troupe has taken precautions to amuse rather than assault the white audience, but this entertainment turns around the savage murder of a white woman:

—Nous avons donc tué une Blanche,

and killed her violently,

—Seuls nous étions capables de le faire, sauvagement. (p. 25)

Archibald continues the litany of crimes they have committed, presumably to entertain the audience. Liars, they have given false names; thieves, they have stolen the French language.

In the Aristotelian tradition, drama entertains an audience by providing catharsis, the curative effects of emotional release, by means of the perfect coherence of plot structure. By identifying with the victims or victors of the play, spectators are moved to pity, sorrow, or wrath and form judgments about the characters. So indeed does the Court, in farcical imitation of the white audience, demand a good representation of the murder and an emotional catharsis of their own guilt. The Judge says,

—Vous nous avez promis la représentation du crime afin de mériter votre condamnation. (p. 37)

If they could only see the crime, identify with the victim, and resolve racial difference by means of oppositions such as us and them, good and evil, black and white, the Court (= the white audience) could justify their preconceived condemnation of the black race. In the same way, white spectators demand a mirror of themselves along the lines of the unity of meaning and being in mimesis. Not only must representation erase difference in the production of a good copy, it must employ the language of power, the language of whites. A play about blacks written and performed for a white audience is, therefore, first of all a lie, since blacks must mask their difference to achieve anything like a representation of themselves.

In the play the Blacks, like Genet, expose the lie by resisting the kind of representation the white Court demands. First of all, the players keep straying from the prepared text of the play-within-the-play to comment on their performances. In this way the players introduce the disturbing effects of staging into the closure of spoken dialogue and challenge the primacy of the dramatic text in classical poetics. Archibald constantly reminds his cast of their duties toward the written text:

—C'est à moi qu'il faut obéir. Et au texte que nous avons mis au point. (p. 29)

The actors, especially Village, claim that they can submit the text to their whims of the moment:

—Mais je reste libre d'aller vite ou lentement dans mon récit et dans mon jeu. Je peux me mouvoir au ralenti. (p. 30)

—D'ailleurs, je suis fatigué. Vous oubliez que je suis déjà éreinté par un crime qu'il me fallait bien accomplir avant votre arrivée puisqu'il vous faut à chaque séance un cadavre frais. (p. 31)

—But I'm still free to speed up or draw out my recital and my performance. I can move in slow motion, can't I? I can sigh more often and more deeply. (*Blacks*, p. 18)

—Besides, I'm tired. You forget that I'm already knocked out from the crime
I had to finish off before you arrived, since you need a fresh corpse for every
performance. (*Blacks*, p. 19)

Village also stumbles onto his real passion for a black woman, Vertu,
and is promptly told that love has no place in this play.

This kind of preoccupation with the effects of performance on the
ideal closure of text and voice in dialogue shapes the evolution of Genet's
theater. From *Les Bonnes* to *Les Paravents*, the primacy of the written
text over the staging of performance gradually declines. In *Les Nègres* the
theater of violence constitutes, in an important sense, the submission of
the word to the physical demands of mise-en-scène, the exposure of speech
to the exteriority of spectacle.

Almost half-way into the play the troupe manages to pull together a
recreation of the murder scene. They choose Diouf, a black man, to play
the white woman, disguising him in a blond wig, an extravagant white
mask, and a borrowed skirt. Village resists his part as long as possible.
Every time he tries to reenact his crime, his discourse assumes the distance and mediacy of a narration. He tells of how he entered a bar, saw
the white woman knitting behind the counter, ordered a drink, two
drinks. Village, the narrator of his own crime, then imitates the speech
of his victim in a high falsetto voice. Why does he speak in place of Diouf,
the actor dressed as the white woman? What better way to stage the lie
of representation than to present reported speech, presumably the mimetic element par excellence of narrative, as a function of the mask worn
by the narrator! Here Genet applies his discoveries about narrative directly to his concept of theatrical performance. In the novels and the film,
Genet disturbs the traditional transparency of narrative voice behind the
representation of character, in reported speech and in the organization of
looks, respectively. Genet introduces this difficulty into theatrical representation in terms of a movement between narration and imitation,
between diegesis and mimesis, a movement caught up in an endless doubling of reflections.

Moved by the insistence of his cohorts, Village assumes his role and
finally speaks to the "Mask," Diouf masquerading as the white woman.
In this speech he instructs Diouf/the white woman to move behind the
screen for the murder scene.

In the stage directions Genet states his respect for the traditions of
Greek tragedy and reminds the actors to assume the grandeur and alle-
gorical stature of classical performers (p. 15). Like the Greeks, Genet
stages violent scenes out of the sight of the audience, while the Blacks,
in chorus, narrate the action. Instead of the full representation of the
seduction and murder, the Blacks chant about the splendor of this crime
of black against white. Félicité calls for nothing less than the uprising of
the black continent.

—Tu es là, Afrique aux reins cambrés, à la cuisse oblongue? Afrique boudeuse, Afrique travaillée dans le feu, dans le fer, Afrique aux millions d'esclaves royaux, Afrique déportée, continent à la dérive, tu es là? Lentement vous vous évanouissez, vous reculez dans le passé, les récits de naufragés, les musées coloniaux, les travaux des savants, mais je vous rapelle ce soir pour assister à une fête secrète. (p. 111)

—Are you there, Africa with the bulging chest and oblong thigh? Sulking Africa, wrought of iron, in the fire, Africa of the millions of royal slaves, deported Africa, drifting continent, are you there? Slowly you vanish, you withdraw into the past, into the tales of castaways, colonial museums, the works of scholars, but I call you back this evening to attend a secret revel. (*Blacks*, p. 77)

The violence of non-representation gives voice to the silent rage of blacks, which white culture and representation have tried to contain. The crescendo of these chants signals a turning point in the play. The Blacks denounce their European identities and turn the stage into an African jungle. The Court, having left the stage in order to prepare the execution of the murderer, enters the jungle and meets not with the obedient reflections of white culture, but with blacks seeking revenge. One by one the Court members fall victim to this violence and die in a heap. Village and Vertu remain on stage and make plans for a new world according to a black model.

Throughout the play the Court mirrors the white ruling class and sends back to the audience a contorted image of itself. Not only do members of the Court wear white masks which betray their own blackness, but they employ staccato rhythms and artificial tones to render their performances as contrived as possible. Their gestures and their politeness and condescension to the Blacks form a caricature of official, white culture. Their attention to the play within the play is periodically interrupted by reports on the progress of their capital investments in Africa—in tobacco, coffee, and rubber.

If, as I have argued before, the movement of imitation effaces the existential identity of the referent, then white culture has petrified into extinction the moment it can be reduced to a caricature, a copy of a copy. The Governor thus speaks for the audience when he declares that the white Court has come to the performance to attend its own funeral, its own suicide:

—Et nous savons que nous sommes venus assister à nos propres funérailles. Ils croient nous y obliger, mais c'est par l'effet de notre courtoisie que nous descendrons dans la mort. Notre suicide. . . . (p. 24)

In Genet's theater, as we have already seen, death consists of the effects of representation on the personal identity of the subject of mimesis.

Perhaps more troubling than a physical death, murder-by-representation is not limited to the destruction of an individual life, but does violence to dominant culture and the order of mimesis.

The representation of blacks by a white author is thus posed as a question and staged as a masquerade. This strategy twists the spectating subject's drive to identify with the play. If the audience identifies with whites on stage, and if these characters obviously betray their true identities as blacks (whatever a black is), then the spectating subject enters the play only to find his own image duplicated infinitely. As the play unfolds and the Blacks assassinate the white Court, the spectator is drawn into a kind of ritualistic suicide, much on the order of Claire's or the Police Chief's in *Les Bonnes* and *Le Balcon*, respectively. What began as the murder of white culture by representation turns into the annihilation of the subject of dominant culture by means of performance. As oppositions between right and wrong, black and white, victim and victor become blurred in the constantly shifting roles and identities of characters on stage, the spectating subject is snared into a modern sacrifice which denies the participant catharsis and places him or her on the altar instead.

Since the question of black identity has formed the dark side of European history, both in the moral sense and in the sense that the question has inhabited the shadows of dominant white culture from the beginning, it eludes representation as such. White man invented the mirror in order to reduce difference to an endless return of the same, of the image, the copy. Classical mimesis is thus an instrument of power, since it defines black in terms of the underside of white culture, as a supplement to the primacy of white male discourse. By resisting the discourse of power, by approaching theater from the angle of performance rather than dialectics, Genet dismantles mimesis in order to present the color black, or rather the difference between black and white, as a force in the construction of being, and to present being as the endless pursuit of an illusion.

Derrida points out the moral implications of difference for linguistic theory in *Of Grammatology*. In Saussure the inversion of the hierachy which grants primacy to speech over writing and causes the troubling intrusion of the outside, the material representation, into the inside of meaning and being in spoken discourse, constitutes nothing less than a criminal act, a crime against nature, against the "natural" (metaphysical) balance between body and soul: a crime of passion (p. 34). Extending this notion to problems of literary and dramatic representation, we begin to understand the meaning of passion as the ritualistic deconstruction both of the present and presence of dramatic discourse and of the unity of speaking/spectating subject of mimesis. This interpretation of passion parallels the Biblical Passion, which names the struggle of Christ to quit his physical nature, with its flaws and limitations, with its promise of death, before returning to the Spirit, the Father and Origin of Being, the Word-Made-God.

On the way to find God, metaphysical philosophy, and structural po-etics in its turn, have contained the violence of desire and textual per-formance by granting primordial importance to the interior closure of body and soul in spoken discourse. Confronted with the work of Genet and his generation, we are forced to reconsider poetics and semiotics in terms of a staging of the subject as a question. Such a shift in the philo-sophical key of critical theory not only takes into consideration the force of desire in poetic texts, but challenges traditional boundaries separating representational modes. In Genet, the movement of the subject in the folds of textual performance transcends the material and ontological specificity of theatrical representation and traces the participation be-tween text, theater and film in his work. Theater is thus both a model for the movement of the subject in semiosis and a figure shaping the triumph of passion in Genet's literary imagination.

Conclusion

While the 1960s and 1970s witnessed a blossoming of the visual arts, especially film and video, the 1980s belong to the arts of performance. The proliferation of performance events in urban theaters and lofts, in rural fields and roadways, testifies to a revival of the spirit of medieval carnival and challenges the boundaries between art and life, representation and reality, performers and spectators, in contemporary culture.[1] The current interest in performance is not limited to theater, nor does it exclude film, video, or painting. Performance, in theory and in practice, defines a focus of the arts on the human subject as participant in a speaking, spectating, or reading event. Performance, in this broad sense, has far-reaching philosophical implications and accounts for trends in the arts which elude traditional categories naming genres, styles, and forms of representation.

Richard Schechner, director of the Performance Group and editor of the *Drama Review*, recently underscored both the importance of performance studies for humanistic and scientific inquiry, and the difficulty of containing performance within any given theoretical or esthetic framework:

> The expanding view of what performance is demands that people both in their art and in their thinking deal with politics, economics, and ritual. Performance—how people deconstruct/reconstruct their various experiential worlds—interrogates and affects social, political, economic, and ritual activities. Exactly how this process works is what we need to know more about.[2]

Performance has always tested the limits of theater built around the dramatic text, but in recent years the theory and practice of performance have expanded beyond the realm of theater and drama altogether, touching on problems of the subject's inscription in ideological and political discourses and engaging the studies of psychology and philosophy. By bringing together the discourses of Genet, Derrida, Bakhtin, and others, I have staged a kind of dialogue whose meaning should not be reduced to a simple thesis, but open onto larger debates concerning the place of representation in modern culture and the arts. Many of these issues are taken up by Genet himself in his final, autobiographical essay *Un Captif amoureux* (1986).

Though this is not the place for a lengthy discussion of *Un Captif amoureux*, published just after Genet's death and some twenty-five years after his last play, I mention it here to emphasize the continuity between Genet's properly literary work and his work of nonfiction with reference to the question of performance. *Un Captif* differs fundamentally from the works I discuss in my book, consisting as it does of a compendium of personal impressions, documentary reportage, and memories of Genet's experiences with the Black Panthers and the Palestinian guerillas, the Fedayeen. The discourse focusses on historical referents, including political events in the United States and the Middle East, and contrasts sharply with the closed fictional reference of literary discourse. Genet seems to have abandoned literary hallucination for political commentary, weaving a tale of autobiographical reflections with journalistic documentation and detailed, eye-witness accounts of torture, human misery, and personal triumph.

In spite of these differences, *Un Captif amoureux* forms a whole with the early work, extending Genet's ongoing preoccupation with the question of man's place in literary discourse into the broader question of the staging of political and historical discourses. Genet not only underscores the political meaning of marginal language and speech styles within the predominantly white European power structure; he questions the very relation between the meaning of words and the reference of discourse, placing in question the unity and coherence of the subject and signified of Western philosophy.

The book opens with a remark reminiscent of Derrida or Mallarmé, about the original division of signs into ideal signifiers of meaning and physical traces on the surface of representation.

La page qui fut d'abord blanche, est maintenant parcourue du haut en bas de minuscules signes noirs, les lettres, les mots, les virgules, les points d'exclamation, et c'est grâce à eux qu'on dit que cette page est lisible. Cependant à une sorte d'inquiétude dans l'esprit, à ce haut-le-coeur très proche de la nausée, au flottement qui me fait hésiter à écrire . . . la réalité est-elle cette totalité des signes noirs? (C.A.; 11)

The page which was blank at first is now criss-crossed from top to bottom with tiny black signs—the letters, the words, the commas, the exclamation points—and it is thanks to them that it is said that this page is legible. However, [thanks] to a kind of uneasiness in the mind, to this queasiness bordering on nausea, to the vacillation which makes me hesitate to write . . . is reality this totality of black signs? (my translation)

To the extent that the referent of discourse is as elusive as the movement of black traces on paper, the speaking subject struggles in a kind of ontological quicksand for a grip on reality. This existential dilemma explains the hold of the mass media on the imaginary of modern man. The media, especially film and video, replace empirical knowledge with an illusion of perceptual mastery over an image of absent realties.

Genet describes the Black Power and Palestinian resistance movements as spectacles built upon the duplicities of theatrical performance and having the ephemeral quality of mechanically produced images.[3] He documents how film, video, and photo-journalism create such movements, propagating an image of marginal culture which reflects the fears and desires of dominant culture and ideology—"a true image of a false spectacle," as he would say in *Le Balcon*. Representation obscures ideological difference under the guise of imitation, reducing the movement of political resistance to a performance without substance, to a mime-play turned in upon itself.

The mime-play forms a central figure of Genet's book. He says that the Fedayeen leaders denounced card-playing as a pastime of the bourgeois enemy. The soldiers play nonetheless, miming the gestures of a poker game right down to the last glance and grimace of competition *without cards* (C.A.; 38–39). Genet describes this staging as a metaphor for the Palestinian resistance, which plays at war without holding the cards of power, trading political change for a *répétition*, a rehearsal of representation.

Les joueurs de cartes, les doigts pleins de spectres, aussi beaux, aussi sûrs d'eux fussent-ils, savaient que leurs gestes perpétueraient—il faut aussi l'entendre comme condamnation perpétuelle—une partie de cartes sans début ni fin. Ils avaient sous les mains cette absence autant que sous leurs pieds les feddayin. (C.A.; 149)

The cardplayers, their fingers full of ghosts, however handsome and sure of themselves that they be, knew that their gestures would perpetuate—it also must be understood as a perpetual condemnation—a card game without beginning or end. They had this absence under their hands as well as under their feet, the Fedayeen. (my translation)

While many critics view *Un Captif amoureux* as a confirmation of Genet's political *engagement* and a kind of liberation from the yoke of *Saint Genet*,[4] it is also a work which questions the very notions of engagement and liberation. Though the "captive" of the title refers to the narrator, who admits to being a prisoner of his own love for the Palestinian people, the book returns time and again to the notion that modern man is the captive of representation, held hostage by the reflections of his own desire. In his final work Genet eludes the lure of representation by staging political discourse between speech and writing, between the text of history and the voice of lived experience, troubling the force of the image with the movement of performance.

Notes

INTRODUCTION

1. See, for instance, Odette Aslan, *Jean Genet* (Paris: Seghers, 1973); Peter Brooks and Joseph Halpern, *Genet: A Collection of Critical Essays* (Englewood Cliffs, N.J.: Prentice Hall, 1979); Richard Coe, *The Theater of Jean Genet: A Casebook* (New York: Grove Press, 1979); Sylvie Debevec Henning, *Genet's Ritual Play* (Amsterdam: Rodopi, 1981); Bettina Knapp, *Jean Genet* (New York: Twayne, 1968); Jean-Marie Magnan, *Pour un blason de Jean Genet* (Paris: Seghers, 1966); Kelly Morris, ed., *Genet and Ionesco: The Theater of the Double* (New York: Bantam Books, 1969); Camille Naish, *A Genetic Approach to Structures in the Work of Jean Genet* (Cambridge: Harvard University Press, 1978); and Jeannette L. Savona, *Jean Genet* (New York: Grove Press, 1983).

2. *Saint Genet: Comédien et martyr*, vol. 1 of *Oeuvres complètes de Jean Genet* (Paris: Gallimard, 1953). Hereafter I cite the translation by Bernard Frechtman, *Saint Genet: Actor and Martyr* (New York: American Library, 1963).

3. Much of the early Genet scholarship seems to have been generated by Sartre's study. Richard Coe, for instance, explains the evolution of Genet's work, including the novels and plays, according to the recurrence of a triangular metaphysical motif, including the *en soi*, the *pour soi*, and *autrui*. *The Vision of Jean Genet* (New York: Grove Press, 1968).

Claude Bonnefoy agrees with Sartre that Genet writes about social transgression in order to show the evil in all of us. Bonnefoy echoes Sartre when he describes the movement between sense certainty and language in Genet's symbols, insists upon the importance of Nature in Genet's spiritualism, and explains the dialectic of sacred and profane in Genet's existentialism. *Jean Genet*, (Paris: Editions universitaires, 1965).

Philip Thody, rejecting Sartre's existential explanation of Genet's call to crime, is nonetheless intrigued by the psychological impulse which transformed the thief into the poet and determined the development of Genet's self-abasement into enlightened self-criticism. *Jean Genet: A Study of His Novels and Plays* (London: Hamish Hamilton, 1968).

Joseph McMahon and Lewis Cetta are exceptions to the Sartrian trend. The former views Genet's homosexuality as the source of his creative urge and the basis for synthesizing opposite realms of experience in the formation of symbols, in *The Imagination of Jean Genet* (New Haven: Yale University Press, 1963). Cetta analyzes the recurrence of Jungian themes of creation and conflict in Genet's theater, in *Profane Play, Ritual and Jean Genet: A Study of His Drama* (University: University of Alabama Press, 1974).

4. For an analysis of text, theater, and film in Marguerite Duras, see Oswald, "Semiotics and/or Deconstruction: In Quest of Cinema," *Semiotica* 60, nos. 3/4 (1986): 315–41.

5. In vol. 2 of *Oeuvres complètes* (Paris: Gallimard, 1964), pp. 11–171.

6. Artaud, p. 133.

7. Derrida offers an interpretation of Artaud's metaphysics in "La Parole Soufflée," in *L'Ecriture et la différence* (Paris: Seuil, 1967). Artaud seeks a universal language of the stage which transcends oppositions between body and soul, reality and representation, voice and meaning, in a movement of performance *qua* phenomenological event (p. 291). On the other hand, Derrida explains, when Artaud calls for pure mise-en-scène at the expense of the closure of voice and meaning in

the poetic text, he reintroduces the problem of difference as a force structuring the theatrical event and challenges the very premise of metaphysical theater.

8. Quoted by Derrida in *L'Ecriture et la différence*, p. 276, from *La Cruelle raison poétique*, p. 69, my translation.

9. See Genet's Preface to *Les Bonnes* (Paris: Jean-Jacques Pauvert, 1954), pp. 11–17.

10. Trans. Mary Elizabeth Meek (Coral Gables: University of Miami Press, 1971).

11. Keir Elam refers to deixis as the particular characteristic of theater. *The Semiotics of Theater and Drama* (New York: Metheun & Co., 1980), p. 139.

12. Trans. Gayatri Chakravorty Spivak (Baltimore: The Johns Hopkins University Press, 1976).

13. Trans. Barbara Johnson (Chicago: University of Chicago Press, 1981).

14. Though in *L'Ecriture et la différence* Derrida warns against our generalizing Artaud's call for pure mise en scène into a general poetics of discourse, in *Dissemination* he debates the philosophical issues at stake in precisely such a project, shifting attention from mimetic to performative aspects of poetry.

15. Artaud, p. 106.

16. *L'Ecriture et la différence*, p. 344.

17. Ibid., p. 343.

18. Morris, op. cit.

19. I have placed abbreviations of the titles of works after the page number of citations, in those instances where I thought some confusion might arise. Genet's novels in French are abbreviated as follows: *Notre-Dame-des-fleurs*, N.D.F.; *Miracle de la rose*, M.R.; *Pompes funèbres*, P.F. The English translations are abbreviated as follows: *Our Lady of the Flowers*, O.L.F.; *Miracle of the Rose*, M.R.; and *Funeral Rites*, F.R. I abbreviate the titles of the theoretical works cited only when the full title of the work has been clearly referred to in the text. For example, quotations from Derrida's *La Voix et le phénomène* are marked V.P., and quotations from Ricoeur's *La Métaphore vive* are marked M.V.

20. Genet spent the last fifteen years or so of his life in the Middle East. He has an adopted Moroccan son and is buried in Tangiers. See "L'Homme que Genet n'a pas giflé," an interview with Mohamed Choukri, in *Jeune Afrique*, no. 1335 (1986): 50–51.

I. THE SCENE OF SILENCE

1. Trans. Bernard Frechtman (New York: New American Library, 1963), p. 81. Originally published as *Saint Genêt: Comédien et martyr* (Paris: Gallimard, 1951).

2. Jacques Derrida, *La Voix et le phénomène* (Paris: Presses universitaires de France, 1967), p. 108.

3. *The Critique of Pure Reason*, trans. J. M. D. Meiklejohn (New York: E. P. Dutton, 1942), p. 79.

4. "Que la perception accompagne ou non l'énoncé de perception, que la vie comme présence à soi accompagne ou non l'énoncé du *Je*, cela est parfaitement indifférent au fonctionnement du vouloir-dire. Ma mort est structurellement nécessaire au prononcé du *Je*" (V.P.; 107–8).

5. The notion of the subject's division into a being-for-itself and a being-for-others, a division symbolized in the reciprocal acts of giving and responding to names, forms the cornerstone of Jacques Lacan's psychoanalytic theory of the subject. "What I look for in speech is the response of the other. What constitutes me as subject is my question. In order to make myself recognized by the other, I only utter what *was* in view of that which will be. In order to find him, I call

him by a name which he has to either assume or refuse in order to respond to me" "Fonction et champ de la parole et du langage en psychanalyse," in *Ecrits I*, p. 181, my translation. The game of naming entails a threat of death as the subject offers himself up as an identity for others. *Ecrits I*, p. 205.

When Lacan traces the origin of the speaking subject in a developmentally marked stage in the biological life of the subject, in the "mirror phase," he differs fundamentally from Derrida, who discredits the notion of an ontological origin of being. In Derrida, the speaking subject is always and already divided in its relation to itself and this relation shapes the subject's relation to others in language.

6. Please note that John Searle uses the words "meaning" and "expression" somewhat differently. Searle distinguishes between the "utterance meaning"—what the speaker intended by a statement—and the "sentence meaning"—what the words signify by convention. Thus in Searle the "utterance meaning" includes indication, while the "sentence meaning" resembles Husserl's notion of "expression." See *Expression and Meaning* (New York: Cambridge University Press, 1979), p. 31.

7. "Tout ce qui, dans mon discours, est destiné à manifester un vécu à autrui, doit passer par la médiation de la face physique. Cette médiation irréductible engage toute expression dans une opération indicative. La fonction de manifestation (*kundgebende Funktion*) est une fonction indicative" (V.P.; 41).

8. Trans. James Strachey (New York: Penguin, 1960), p. 71.

9. "Ce mouvement de la différance ne survient pas à un sujet transcendental. Il le produit. L'auto-affection n'est pas une modalité d'expérience caractérisant un étant qui serait déjà lui-même (*autos*). Elle produit le même comme rapport à soi dans la différence d'avec soi, le même comme le non-identique" (V.P.; 92).

10. "Le concept de subjectivité appartient *à priori et en général* à l'ordre du *constitué*. Cela vaut *a fortiori* pour l'apprésentation analogique constituant l'intersubjectivité. Celle-ci est inséparable de la temporalisation comme ouverture du présent à un hors-soi, à un *autre* présent absolu. Cet hors-de-soi du temps est son *espacement*: une *archi-scène*. Cette scène, comme rapport d'un présent à un autre présent *comme tel*, c'est à dire comme représentation (*Vergegenwärtigung* ou *Repräsentation*) non dérivée, produit la structure du signe en général comme renvoi, comme être-pour-quelque-chose (*für etwas sein*) et en interdit radicalement la réduction. Il n'y a pas de subjectivité constituante. Et il faut déconstruire jusqu'au concept de constitution" (V.P.; 94).

11. Emile Benveniste, "Correlations of Tense in the French Verb," in *Problems in General Linguistics*, trans. Mary Elizabeth Meek (Coral Gables: University of Miami Press, 1971), pp. 205–15

12. See Albert Dauzat, *Les Noms de famille de France* (Paris: Payot, 1945), p. 36.

13. Dauzat, p. 180.

14. Derrida defines the relation between the proper and "le propre" or cleanliness, in Artaud in "La Parole Soufflée," in *L'Ecriture et la différence* (Paris: Seuil, 1967), p. 272.

15. In Derrida, the "innommable" is another name for the play of *différance* in which the speaking subject is held. *La Voix et le phénomène*, p. 94.

16. (Paris: Editions Gallilée, 1974), pp. 10–11. Gérard Genette discusses this function of names in Proust as well. See *Mimologiques* (Paris: Editions du Seuil, 1976), pp. 315–28.

17. In "Autobiography and the Case of the Signature: Reading Derrida's *Glas*," Jane Mary Todd points out the importance of naming for the question of authorship in Genet. In *Comparative Literature* 38, no. 1 (1986): 1–19.

18. Genette discusses the "diegetic motivation" of figures in "Métonymie chez Proust," in *Figures III* (Paris: Editions du Seuil, 1972), pp. 45–48.

19. Derrida points out the violence of metaphysical reduction in "Violence et métaphysique," in *L'Ecriture et la différence*, pp. 139–61.

20. Sigmund Freud, *Three Essays on the Theory of Sexuality*, in vol. 7 of *The Standard Edition of the Complete Psychological Works of Sigmund Freud*, trans. James Strachey (London: Hogarth Press, 1953), pp.155–58.

21. In Genet's last "novel," *Un Captif amoureux*, the warm relation of the mother and her son Hamza stands as an ideal of mutual devotion which illuminates the entire narration. Stripped of the irony of his youthful works, *Un Captif* betrays the childhood longing of Genet, an orphan. See p. 228, for example.

22. "A Case of Paranoia," in *Three Case Studies*, trans. James Strachey (New York: Collier, 1976), pp. 103–86.

23. See Keir Elam, *Semiotics of Theater and Drama* (New York: Methuen & Co., 1980), p. 139: "It will be noted that what allows the dialogue to create an interpersonal dialectic here within the time and location of discourse is the *deixis*. . . . What we have is not a set of propositions or descriptions but references by the speakers themselves as speakers, to their interlocutors as listener-addressees and to the spatio-temporal coordinates (the here-and-now) of the utterance by means of such deictic elements as demonstrative pronouns and spatial and temporal adverbs."

24. As Roland Barthes says "L'auteur (matériel) d'un récit ne peut se confondre en rien avec le narrateur de ce récit; les signes du narrateur sont immanents au récit et par conséquent parfaitement accessibles à une analyse sémiologique" (p. 19). Barthes explains the difference between author and narrator in terms reminiscent of Husserl: "Qui parle (dans le récit) n'est pas qui écrit (dans la vie) et qui écrit n'est pas qui est." "Introduction à l'analyse structurale du récit," in *Communications*, no. 8 (1966): 20.

25. Bettina Knapp restates this bit of legendary information in *Jean Genet* (New York: Saint Martin's Press, 1968), p. 23.

26. I disagree with Camille Naish, who perceives these discrepancies as figures for the doubling of narrative in Genet. *A Genetic Approach to Structures in the Work of Jean Genet* (Cambridge: Harvard University Press, 1978), p. 96.

27. François Rigolot, "Rhétorique du nom poétique," *Poétique*, no. 28 (1976): 466–83, and Gérard Genette, *Mimologiques*, pp. 315–28, privilege the mimetic relation between signifier and signified in the name.

28. "Ces quelques remarques ne sont pas seulement guidées par le souci de rappeler, après Claude Levi-Strauss, le caractère signifiant, et non pas indiciel, du nom propre. On voudrait aussi insister sur le caractère cratyléen du nom (et du signe) chez Proust: non seulement parce que Proust voit le rapport du signifiant et du signifié comme un rapport motivé, l'un copiant l'autre et reproduisant dans sa forme matérielle l'essence signifiée de la chose (et non la chose elle-même), mais aussi parce que, pour Proust comme pour Cratyle, 'la vertu des noms est d'enseigner.' " "Proust et les noms," in *Nouveaux essais critiques* (Paris: Editions du Seuil, 1972), p. 133.

29. *Glas* (Paris: Editions Galilée, 1974), p. 13.

30. Gérard Genette, for example, models the "poetic function" after the closure of signifier and signified in the linguistic sign. See "Langage poétique, poétique du langage," in *Figures II* (Paris: Editions du Seuil, 1969), pp. 49–70.

31. "Shifters, Verbal Categories and the Russian Verb," in vol. 2 of *Selected Writings* (The Hague: Mouton, 1971).

32. See, "Closing Statements: Linguistics and Poetics," in *Style in Language*, ed. Thomas Sebeok (Cambridge: MIT Press, 1960), pp. 350–77.

33. Dauzat says, "Le prénom est surtout usité d'une part dans les relations sentimentales, de l'autre, dans la famille." *Les Noms de famille en France*, p. 362.

34. In *La Voix et le phénomène*, Derrida speaks of the "mouvement innommable de la différance" (p. 94).

35. As Gérard Genette says, the "reader" is an instance of the fiction, as distinct from the historically constituted reader as the narrator is from the author. See "Discours du récit," in *Figures III* (Paris: Editions du Seuil, 1972), p. 265.

36. Sartre makes a similar observation about the reader. "Now, regardless of who the writer is, when the sentence starts with "I," a confusion arises in my mind between this "I" and my own. No doubt if I saw the other person, if I saw the words come out of his mouth, I would relate his speech to his person. But I am alone in my room, and if a voice somewhere utters the words that I read, it is mine; in reading, I speak in the bottom of my throat and I feel myself speaking. At the present moment, in this room, there is only one man who says "I," to wit, myself. Caught in the trap: since, in order to understand the sentence, I must relate the "I" to a subjectivity, it is to my own that I refer. That is the way in which a reader of novels spontaneously identifies himself with the character who is telling the story." *Saint Genet*, p. 498. The problem with Sartre's phenomenological approach is that he does not differentiate between the historically constituted reader and the "reader" as semiotic function, as trace of the other inscribed in every enunciation of "I."

37. See, for example, Patrice Pavis, *Problèmes de sémiologie théâtrale* (Montréal: Les Presses de l'université de Québec, 1976), and Alessandro Serpieri et al., "Toward a Segmentation of the Dramatic Text", in *Poetics Today* 2, no. 3: 163–200.

38. "Relationships of Person in the Verb," in *Problems in General Linguistics*, p. 199.

II. THE DISCOURSE OF THE OTHER

1. See Kelly Morris, ed., *Genet and Ionesco: The Theater of the Double* (New York: Bantam Books, 1969).

2. *Prolegomena to a Theory of Language*, trans. Francis J. Whitfield (Madison: University of Wisconsin Press, 1963), p. 79.

3. It has been argued that Bakhtin's debate with Russian Formalism in *The Formal Method in Literary Scholarship* (1929), trans. Albert J. Wehrle (Baltimore: The Johns Hopkins University Press, 1978) and in *Marxism and the Philosophy of Language* (1929), trans. Ladislav Matejka and I.R. Titunik (Cambridge: Harvard University Press, 1986), were published under the names of colleagues, Medvedev and Volochinov, respectively, in order to assert Bakhtin's refusal of the author's authority over the work. It cannot be denied, however, that these subterfuges might have resulted from the pressures of official censorship, which jeopardized Bakhtin's life and career. The publication of his doctoral thesis, *Rabelais and His World* (1965), trans. Hélène Iswolsky (Bloomington: Indiana University Press, 1984), was delayed for some twenty years, while other important essays remained unpublished until after his death in 1975. Not only was Bakhtin temporarily exiled to Siberia, but Medvedev and Volochinov "disappeared" during the reign of terror in the Soviet Union under Stalin. See Tzvetan Todorov, *Mikhail Bakhtine: Le Principe dialogique* (Paris: Editions du Seuil, 1981), pp. 13–26; Michael Holquist and Katerina Clark, *Mikhail Bakhtin* (Cambridge: Harvard University Press 1984), pp. 146–70; and Marina Yaguello, trans., Introduction to *Le Marxisme et la philosophie du langage* (Paris: Editions de Minuit, 1977), pp. 9–18. It must be added

that Matejka and Titunik are more reluctant than other critics to grant the authorship of *Marxism* to Bakhtin alone. See Introduction to *Marxism*.

4. Ed. Michael Holquist, trans. Caryl Emerson and Michael Holquist (Austin: University of Texas Press, 1981).

5. *Problems of Dostoevsky's Poetics*, ed. and trans. Caryl Emerson (Minneapolis: University of Minnesota Press, 1984).

6. *The Formal Method in Literary Scholarship*, pp. 75–103.

7. Thus Shklovsky perceived correlations between the style and composition of narrative, for example. See Victor Erlich, *Russian Formalism* 2nd rev. ed. (The Hague: Mouton, 1965), p.75. Peter Steiner emphasizes the philosophical diversity within Russian Formalism, which would seem to resist this broad and unifying characterization. However, in the three stages of Russian Formalism he describes, referred to in the metaphors of the machine, the biological organism, and the system, the diversity rests with the kinds of relations between parts of the form rather than with the overriding concern with the closure of form and meaning. *Russian Formalism: A Metapoetics* (Ithaca: Cornell University Press, 1984), pp. 9–43.

8. "Closing Statements: Linguistics and Poetics," in *Style in Language*, ed. Thomas Sebeok (Cambridge: MIT Press, 1960), p. 358.

9. Matejka and Titunik discuss the influence of Volochinov on the Prague School, which would explain the philosophical orientation of some of the Prague structuralists. See Introduction to *Marxism*. See also Jan Mukarovsky, "Structuralism and Literary Studies," pp. 65–82, and Jindrich Honzl, "Ritual and Theater," pp. 133–73, in *Prague School Reader*, ed. Peter Steiner (Austin: University of Texas Press, 1982).

10. See *Morphology of the Folktale* (Austin: University of Texas Press, 1968).

11. In *Figures II* (Paris: Editions du Seuil, 1969), pp. 49–70.

12. Of course, in book 3 of *The Republic*, Plato condemns poetry and rhetoric for deceiving the spectator with false images and for appealing to the emotions. He also claimed that the poet perverts the truth when he speaks through the mouths of characters in mimetic discourse.

13. "Frontières," p. 56.

14. In "Catégories du récit littéraire," Todorov examines the difficulty of classical poetics to explain the form and function of narrative discourse, pointing out that the diegetic is not automatically on the side of narrative discourse, nor is the mimetic automatically linked to character speech. To the extent that the narration of the story is conditioned by, indeed produced by, the discourse of the narrator, it is impossible to disengage mimesis from diegesis in the novel. The narrator represents himself in narrative discourse at the same time that he produces the story. Characters represent themselves in reported speech at the same time that their discourses are events occurring in the diegesis. *Communications* 8 (1966): 125–51.

With the notion of the interdependency of mimesis and diegesis in the novel, Todorov reveals something of the complexity and specificity of narrative, while leaving aside the crucial issue of the relation between the discourses of the narrator and the discourses of characters in the story. In early Todorov, the mimetic relation between direct discourse and the speaker transcends the dialogic relation between speakers in narrative representation. Thus a quotation, direct or indirect, produces an "image" of the speaker, just as a figure of speech produces an image of the narrator in narrative discourse.

While Todorov maintains the Aristotelian distinctions between mimesis and diegesis, he, like Genette, takes for granted the ontological unity of speech and voice, thereby circumscribing a problematic of the production of the subject speaking in dialogue. Todorov adopts Benveniste's notion of the subject as a transcendental given, as the very condition of possibility and the unifying voice of narrative. He thus overlooks the possible effects of alterity on the production of this unity in literary representation and leaves aside questions as to the relations between narrative discourse and reported speech. Early Todorov privileges instead the identification between narrating I and the reading subject (you) as the figure par excellence for relations of intersubjectivity in the novel. "Les Catégories du récit littéraire," p. 147.

In later work Todorov not only examines the contributions of Bakhtin to the theory of the novel (*Mikhail Bakhtine: Le Principe dialogique*), but studies the Spanish conquest of Mexico in terms of relations between the discourse of authority and the discourse of the other. See *La Conquête de l'Amérique* (Paris: Editions du Seuil, 1982).

15. In "Introduction à l'analyse structurale des récits," Barthes models discourse after the linguistic structure of the sentence. In the section titled "The Language of Narrative," he says, "If we need to give a working hypothesis to an analysis whose task is immense and materials infinite, the most reasonable approach would be to postulate a homological rapport between the sentence and discourse, to the extent that one and the same formal organization probably rules all semiotic systems, whatever might be their substances or dimensions." *Communications* 8 (1966): 3, my translation.

16. Emile Benveniste discusses differences between discourse and story in terms of markings for the narrator such as verb tense, voice, and adverbs pointing to the here and now of the narrating event. "Correlations of Tense in the French Verb," in *Problems in General Linguistics* (Coral Gables: University of Miami Press, 1971), pp. 205–16.

17. Pierre Guiraud distinguishes the *argot des malfaiteurs* from professional and popular *argots* on the basis of the secrecy of the codes governing the formation of its lexicon. See *L'Argot* (Paris: Presses universitaires de France, 1958), p. 19.

18. For instance, Vidocq, the ex-convict who figures prominently in *Les Misérables* as Jean Valjean, and in *La Comédie humaine* as Vautrin, exemplifies the Romantic project of bringing to life the underworld through language, even if that meant inventing a somewhat idealized portrait of that society. See Stephen Ullman, "Some Experiments in Local Color," in *Style in the French Novel* (Cambridge: Cambridge University Press, 1957), pp. 40–93.

19. The focus on dialogue as action resembles the performative utterance signalled by John Austin in *How to Do Things with Words* (Cambridge: Harvard University Press, 1962).

20. Austin defines the constative function of discourse, as opposed to the performative function, in terms of its focus on the information communicated by the words. In *How to Do Things with Words*.

21. See the Preface to *Les Bonnes* (Paris: Jean-Jacques Pauvert, 1954).

22. Melanie Klein examines the combined parental figure in "Envy and Gratitude," in vol. 3 of *The Writings of Melanie Klein* (London: Hogarth Press, 1975), pp. 197–98.

23. In "Les Ironies comme mentions," Dan Sperber and Deirdre Wilson, for example, define irony in terms of contrasts between the signification of an utterance (*l'emploi*) and reference to the context of discourse (*la mention*). In *Poétique* 36 (1978): 399–412.

24. "To describe his abjection he uses Racine's language." *Histoire de la littérature d'aujourd'hui* (Paris: Le Livre contemporain, 1959), p. 282.

25. *La Conquête de l'Amérique*.

26. See Roman Jakobson, "Closing Statements: Linguistics and Poetics", p. 353.

27. Alphonse Juilland points out similar implications of Céline's treatment of argot in *Voyage au bout de la nuit*: "D'après Céline, la crise de la littérature serait enracinée dans une certaine conception de la langue, aboutissment d'une longue évolution qui a suivi le tournant décisif pris par notre idiome lorsque le français 'Rabelais' s'est trouvé étouffé par le français 'Amyot', lorsqu'un français spontané a été remplacé par un français 'rabougri', un français populaire par un français précieux, un français démocratique par un français intellectuel, un français 'gras' par un français 'sec', un français 'vivant' par un français 'mort'. "Les 'Faux Amis' du vocabulaire de Louis-Ferdinand Céline," *Stanford French Review* 2, no. 3 (1978): 232–50.

28. *L'Argot*, p.9.

29. In *The Prison House of Language*, Frederic Jameson criticizes structuralism for modelling semiosis after linguistics, rather than the other way around, thus eliminating questions as to the desire of the speaking subject, questions which cannot be contained within linguistic codes, from epistemological concerns. In this regard Jameson echoes Bakhtin's point of view. (Princeton: Princeton University Press, 1972).

30. *The Poems of Saint John of the Cross*, trans. Robert Graves (New York: Grove Press, 1968), n. pag.

31. *Navire Night* (Paris: Mercure de France, 1982), n. pag.

32. Genet's support of the Black Panthers, for example, is discussed in the political pamphlet entitled "Here and Now for Bobby Seale" (New York: Committee to Defend the Panthers, 1970); his defense of the Baader-Meinhoff gang in "Violence et brutalité," *Le Monde*, 2 Sept. 1977, 1–2; and his sympathies with the Palestinian Liberation Movement in *Un Captif amoureux* (Gallimard: Paris, 1986).

33. Joseph McMahon is mistaken when he concludes that Riton was a defector from the Resistance. Not only is there no evidence of this in the novel, but the language Riton speaks forbids any association with the *maquisards* (in this novel), who speak bourgeois French. *The Imagination of Jean Genet*, p. 72.

34. Taking a clue from Thomas Bishop, *Pirandello and the French Theater* (New York: New York University Press, 1960), Edith Melcher points out the influence of Pirandello (*Six Characters in Search of an Author*) on Genet in "The Pirandellism of Jean Genet," *The French Review*, 39, no. 1 (1962): 32–35.

35. In *A Genetic Approach to Structures in the Work of Jean Genet*, Camille Naish performs a structuralist analysis of the genesis of Genet's work, by pointing out dualities in Genet's early poems which evolve into his entire oeuvre. Among the dualities Naish mentions are thematic oppositions and ambivalences, and the creation of "frames" within the narrative which double the narration itself. The "frame" theory includes the doubling of the narrator into a voice speaking within the secondary fiction and a voice speaking from outside of it. Naish's analysis of dualities in Genet fails to account for the dialogic interaction of voices in narrative discourse which contributes to Genet's esthetic of dissimulation and role-playing. Naish therefore fails to distinguish Genet's use of the double from the figure of the double as it appears in authors such as Proust. (Cambridge: Harvard University Press, 1978).

36. Martin Esslin uses this analogy regarding Genet's theater. "Genet—A Hall of Mirrors," in *The Theater of the Absurd* (New York: Doubleday-Anchor, 1962), pp. 140–67.

37. *Problems of Dostoevsky's Poetics*, pp. 106–37. Moreover, in the notion of dialogism, Bakhtin suggests means for theorizing about the merging of text, theater, and film in contemporary artistic production, along the lines of the speaking subject's inscription in representation.

38. *Un Captif Amoureux* (1986), the work Genet completed in his final years, resembles less a novel than an autobiographical reflexion upon his experiences with the Black Panthers and the Palestine Liberation Organization.

39. Preface to *Les Bonnes*, p. 13.

III. SEMIOSIS AS PERFORMANCE

1. MacMahon says, "If he had any literary cousin it would be Proust. . . . What gives the comparison a reasonable basis is the similarity between the benefits Genet derives from his memories and those Proust discovered in his." *The Imagination of Jean Genet*. (New Haven: Yale University Press), p. 63.

2. We must review with caution the various interpretations of Proust which privilege synthesis over the more difficult aspects of his style. In his close reading of Proust in *Allegories of Reading*, Paul de Man insists upon the intrusion of conflict and dissymmetry into Proustian metaphors, which goes against the grain of the apparent synesthesia holding together disparate elements of the discourse. (New Haven: Yale University Press, 1979), pp.57–78.

3. (Paris: Editions du Seuil, 1975).

4. Paul de Man points out that the tripartite structure of metaphor, including the literal meaning, the figurative usage, and the proper sense, is often obscured in English usage, as the proper sense, over time, replaces the literal sense of a word. If someone says, for instance, that an examination was a "real killer," we focus immediately on the meaning that the exam was "difficult," without fearing for our lives. *Allegories of Reading*, p. 65. De Man does not discuss how the tripartite structure of metaphor includes a movement between the semantic and semiotic planes of discourse.

5. Ricoeur (op. cit., p. 41) points out the importance of "making visible" in Aristotle's *Rhetoric*.

6. In *Figures III* (Paris: Editions du Seuil, 1972), p. 60.

7. *Speech Genres and Other Late Essays*, ed. Caryl Emerson and Michael Holquist, trans. Vern W. McGee, (Austin: University of Texas Press, 1986) p. 1.

8. Benveniste describes these two levels of discourse in "La Forme et le sens dans le langage," in *Langage*, Actes du XIIIe Congrès des sociétés de philosophie de langue française (Neuchâtel: La Baconnière, 1966), pp. 29–40.

9. "Two Aspects of Language, Two Types of Aphasic Disturbances," recently published in a second edition, under the title "The Linguistic Problem of Aphasia." In *Fundamentals of Language* (The Hague: Mouton, 1980), pp. 69–96 .

10. While Jakobson devotes an important essay to the nature of "shifters," indices such as the pronoun "I" whose reference shifts in the course of a dialogue, he does not consider the implications of this problem for poetic discourse. "Shifters, Verbal Categories and the Russian Verb," in *Selected Writings* (The Hague: Mouton, 1971), pp. 130–35.

Charles Sanders Peirce, who set the tone of current semiotic theories, including the work of Umberto Eco, defines index as "a sign, or representation, which refers to its object not so much because of any similarity or analogy with it, nor because it is associated with general characters which that object happens to possess, as because it is in dynamical (including spatial) connection both with the individual object, on the one hand, and with the senses or memory of the person for whom it serves as a sign, on the other hand." *Philosophical Writings of Peirce*, ed. Justus Buchler (New York: Dover Publications, 1955), p. 107.

11. Though John Searle describes metaphor as a "special case of the general problem of explaining how speaker's meaning and sentence or word meaning [the conventional meaning of words] come apart" in literal discourse, he does not show

the relationship between the performative function and the constative function. The performative function foregrounds the conventions invoked in a speech act (a promise, a threat, etc.). The constative function shapes the meaning of rhetorical figures, derived as they are from manipulations of the conventional meanings of words. *Expression and Meaning* (New York: Cambridge University Press, 1979), p. 77.

12. *How to Do Things with Words*, p. 115.

13. One is reminded of Eco's claim that a sign is anything which can be used to lie. *A Theory of Semiotics* (Bloomington: Indiana University Press, 1976), p. 58.

14. See Benveniste's definition of reference in "La Forme et le sens dans le langage," p. 37.

15. "Métonymie chez Proust."

16. See Jakobson, "Two Aspects of Language, Two Types of Aphasic Disturbances."

17. Christian Metz distinguishes between relations of contiguity in figures and in discourse by separating metonymy (and synecdoche) from syntactic alignment, but does not discuss indexation. While syntax defines the formal ordering of elements of discourse in the syntagm, indices define uncodified relations between the meaning and reference of discourse. See "Rhetoric and Linguistics: Roman Jakobson's Contribution," in *The Imaginary Signifier*, trans. Celia Britton, Annwyl Williams, Ben Brewster, and Alfred Guzzetti (Bloomington: Indiana University Press, 1982), pp. 174–82.

18. "Pour une reformulation du concept de signe iconique," *Communications*, no. 29 (1978): 146–48.

19. For Ricoeur, "The 'to see as' ['le voir comme'] is a factor revealed by the act of reading, to the very extent that the latter is 'the mode under which the imaginary is realized' . . . the 'to see as' is the intuitive relation which holds together the meaning and the image." Op. cit., p. 268, my translation.

20. Genette's notion of the "poétique du langage," for instance, privileges the "rapport actif entre signifiant et signifié." "Proust et le langage indirect," in *Figures II* (Paris: Editions du Seuil, 1969), p. 233. This idea is also implicit in his "Langage poétique, poétique du langage," in op. cit., pp.123–54.

21. Even Proust's "diegetically motivated metaphors," though inspired by a reference to the setting of the narration, do not point to the physical presence of the comparing term in the diegesis but create an atmosphere or semantic world which the reader must imagine for himself. In Proust movement in space is subordinated to the coherence of a mood or sensation. See Genette, "Proust et le langage indirect."

22. Camille Naish discusses the "circular effect" of this figure without elaborating on the indexical function of *comme* and *pareil*. *A Genetic Approach to the Work of Jean Genet* (Cambridge: Harvard University Press, 1978), p. 70 .

23. Herbert Read emphasizes the geometric, fragmentary, and kinesthetic priorities of Cubism. *A Concise History of Modern Painting* (New York: Praeger Press, 1968), pp. 67–104.

24. Ricoeur quotes Genette in *La Métaphore vive*, p. 189.

25. Genette makes a similar analogy between the *objet trouvé*, such as a real oyster shell placed on the canvas in a modern painting, and reported speech, in "Frontières du récit," *Figures II*, p. 54. Genette employs this analogy in order to describe the tautological relation between reported speech and its object, while I am referring to the indexical relation between an element of the diegesis and an event external to the diegesis.

26. Op. cit., p. 170.

27. Sartre suggests that Genet's literary "hallucinations" mirror hallucinations Genet experienced in his personal life. *Saint Genet*, trans. Bernard Frechtman (New York: New American Library, 1963), pp. 340–41. This biographical insight does not explain why authors like Nerval, who also hallucinated in real life, created literary "hallucinations" of quite a different sort.

28. Genet takes up this figure again in the film *Un Chant d'amour*, in a sequence which cuts between a prison cell and a romantic countryside.

29. Théophile Gauthier, for example, says that Genet's notion of poetry as a criminal act links him with surrealism. *Surréalisme et sexualité* (Paris: Gallimard, 1971), p. 328. Camille Naish (op. cit., pp. 122–26) compares the random ordering of events in *Pompes funèbres* with the narrative structure of Breton's *Nadja*. Jeannette Savona also associates Genet's style of theater with surrealists such as Alfred Jarry. *Jean Genet* (New York: Grove Press, 1983), pp. 14–15 .

30. Inez Hedges describes this aspect of surrealist metaphors in terms of the destruction and creation of semantic frames which the reader creates in order to make sense of the discourse. Through metaphorical "frame breaking" and "frame making," "man can evade the cage of language that imprisons him." "Surrealist Metaphor," *Poetics Today* 4, no. 2 (1983): 275–95 .

31. *Manifestes du surréalisme*, Collection Idées (Paris: Gallimard, 1969).

32. For an extended discussion of the dialectic of sexual difference, see Luce Irigaray, "La Tache aveugle d'un vieux rêve de symétrie," in *Speculum, de l'autre femme* (Paris: Minuit, 1974), pp.7–162 .

33. See Laura Oswald, "Figure/Discourse: Configurations of Desire in *Un Chien Andalou*," *Semiotica* 33, nos. 1/2 (1981): 105–22.

34. *Aristotle's Poetics*, trans. James Hutton (New York: W.W. Norton & Co., 1982), pp. 45–49 .

35. "White Mythology: Metaphor in the Text of Philosophy," trans. F. C. T. Moore, *New Literary History* 6, no. 1 (1974): 5–74 .

36. This poem is so important to the overall meaning and structure of *Miracle de la rose* that I will copy it as it appeared in the Marc Barbézat, L'Arbalète edition of 1946 .

> Dormir la bouche ouverte et l'espérer venir
> La lourde et la légère, attendre qu'elle passe,
> Attendre sur nos yeux son pied, le retenir,
> Car on sait qu'elle vibre et chante dans l'espace.
>
> Ni les fleurs ni la mort ni les portes de fer,
> L'ombre et ses gaffes noirs ne sauront, parfumée,
> Traçant son trait fatal empêcher que dans l'air
> Ne la portent vers moi ses ailes emplumées,
>
> O ma sainte Harcamone, ô vierge de nos lits
> Vous parcourez le ciel, errante, et seriez nue
> Sans le chant qui vous couvre et surtout sans ces plis
> De clarté qui vous font d'innocence vêtue.
>
> Mais vous êtes cruelle, ô verge du maçon!
> Pour vous, bouche parée, à bras tendus je chante
> Avec mes mains, avec mes doigts, mais du gazon
> Où vous dormez encore, ô ma belle méchante,
>
> Que vous portent chez moi, sur mon visage ouvert
> Vos ailes, vos parfums, votre musique folle!
> Fermez la porte et sur mes yeux, à mots couverts
> Chantez! Refusez-vous. Restez! Ou je m'envole!

Posez-vous sur mon front, portez-vous à mes dents,
O gaule enténébrée et montez à ma bouche,
Entrez au fond de moi où la mort vous attend
Pâle fille étendue sur sa fragile couche.

Hélas, les beaux maçons dont la queue par un trou
De la poche s'évade, échangent sur l'échelle,
Entre eux ces longs baisers plus chers que le Pérou
Pour le pauvre étendu dans l'ombre de leurs ailes.
(M.R.; 135)

37. *Une Histoire de la littérature d'aujourd'hui* (Paris: Le Livre contemporain, 1959), p. 284. John Leonard, reviewing the English translation of *Pompes funèbres* for the *New York Times*, seems to dismiss any threat to American values posed by Genet: "*Funeral Rites* is exemplary in its noxiousness. . . . It is actually (1) an exercise in cannibalism and necrophilia; (2) the proclamation of an esthetic of fascism; (3) a masturbatory fantasy that should shame Portnoy all the way to Sweden for an organ transplant; (4) an outrageous bore." "Portrait of the Artist as Narcissistic Hitler." Rev. of *Funeral Rites*, by Jean Genet, *New York Times*, 19 June 1969, p. 43.

38. *Saint Genet*, p. 305. Sartre also describes an "indexical" function of Genet's poetry as the participation between the "natural meaning" of words (their sounds and rhythms) and the things they refer to in the real world (pp. 302–9). Sartre's analysis of Genet's poetry is problematic, since poetry can only participate in the world of "things" to the extent that its structure is severed from the reference of discourse. Reference to "les choses" can participate in "le sens" only to the extent that the reference points to the verse itself as a "thing," a "mot-chose," a thing signifying "nothing" in Sartre's analysis.

39. In "The Double Session," Derrida uses the mime-play as a model for that aspect of poetry which transcends the relation between form and meaning and shapes the subject's performance of poetic discourse. *Dissemination*, trans. Barbara Johnson (Chicago: University of Chicago Press, 1981), pp. 175–226.

40. Genet, writing to Jacques Pauvert, the editor of *Les Bonnes*, has said, "Déjà ému par la morne tristesse d'un théâtre qui reflète trop exactement le monde visible, les actions des hommes, et non les Dieux, je tâchai d'obtenir un décalage qui, permettant un ton déclamatoire porterait le théâtre sur le théâtre." Preface to *Les Bonnes* (Paris: Jean-Jacques Pauvert, 1954), p. 13. "Already moved by the dire sadness of a theater which reflects too exactly the visible world, the actions of men, and not the Gods, I tried to obtain a distance which, permitting a declamatory tone, would bring theater to bear on theater" (my translation).

41. See, for instance, "Invitation au voyage" or "Parfum exotique" from *Les Fleurs du mal* (Paris: Garnier-Flammarion, 1964), pp. 77, 52.

42. "Le Théâtre et son double," in *Oeuvres complètes* (Paris: Gallimard, 1964), pp. 40–57 .

IV. THE PERVERSION OF I/EYE IN *UN CHANT D'AMOUR*

1. "Film Performance," in *Questions of Cinema* (Bloomington: Indiana University Press, 1981), pp. 126–27.

2. In *The Imaginary Signifier*, trans. Celia Britton, Annwyl Williams, Ben Brewster, and Alfred Guzzetti (Bloomington: Indiana University Press, 1982), pp. 1–87.

3. "Le Stade du miroir comme formateur de la fonction du Je," in *Ecrits I* (Paris: Editions Points, 1966), pp. 89–97.

4. "Film Performance," p. 118.

5. *Le Cinéma expérimental* (Paris: Editions universitaires, 1974), p. 35.

6. "Obscene Ruling Upheld," *San Francisco Examiner*, 25 October 1966, 16.

7. Jean-Louis Baudry develops this idea in "Le Dispositif," in *Communications*, no. 23 (1975), 56–72.

8. Op. cit.

9. Jonas Mekas, "Un Chant d'amour," in *Film Comment* 2, no. 1 (1964): 28. Anaïs Nin, rev. of *Un Chant d'amour*, by Jean Genet. *Los Angeles Free Press*, 24 December 1965, p. 5.

10. *Three Essays on the Theory of Sexuality*, in vol. 7 of *The Standard Edition of the Complete Psychological Works of Sigmund Freud*, trans. James Strachey (London: Hogarth, 1953), pp. 156–57.

11. Metz's definition of the "régime scopique" as "la distance gardée, la garde elle-même," loses something in Ben Brewster's translation of "garde" as "the keeping (of distance)." The French suggests the notion of distancing as a defense mechanism which underlies erotic displacement in all voyeurism. See "The Imaginary Signifier," p. 61, and the original French version, "Le Signifiant imaginaire," *Communications*, no. 23 (1976): 44.

12. Christian Metz, "The Fiction Film and Its Spectator," in *The Imaginary Signifier*, pp. 99–147, and Jean-Louis Baudry, "Le Dispositif."

13. "The Ontology of the Photographic Image," in *What Is Cinema?*, trans. Hugh Gray (Berkeley: University of California Press, 1967), pp. 9–16 .

14. "Le Dispositif," p. 68.

15. "The Imaginary Signifier," pp. 46–49.

16. "Pour une reformulation du concept de signe iconique," *Communications*, no. 29 (1978): 141–42.

17. "The Imaginary Signifier," p. 57; "Le Signifiant imaginaire," p. 41.

18. Jacques Lacan discusses this division both in "Le Stade du miroir" and in "Fonction de la parole et du langage en psychanalyse," in *Ecrits I*, pp. 111–208.

19. See Sigmund Freud, "Mourning and Melancholia," in vol. 14 of *The Standard Edition*, trans. James Strachey (London: Hogarth Press, 1917), pp. 243–58.

20. "On Identification," in vol. 3 of *The Writings of Melanie Klein* (London: Hogarth Press, 1975), p. 52.

21. "The Imaginary Signifier," p. 51 .

22. "The Imaginary Signifier," pp. 9–10.

23. Freud and Klein offer different explanations for the origins of castration anxiety. For Freud, it results from the recognition that the mother lacks a penis and the fear that she has been castrated. *Three Essays on the Theory of Sexuality*, p. 195. For Klein, castration anxiety results from the fantasy of a persecuting dual parental figure, i.e., fear of the father's penis inside the mother's body. "Early Stages of the Oedipus Conflict," in vol. 1 of *The Writings of Melanie Klein* (London: Hogarth, 1975), pp. 186–98.

24. "Difference," *Screen* 19, no. 3 (1978): 88.

25. "Fetishism," in vol. 22 of *The Standard Edition*, pp. 149–51 .

26. See Heath, "On Suture," in *Questions of Cinema*, p. 86.

27. See Heath, "Difference," p. 87 .

28. This argument runs through the first part of Luce Irigaray's *Speculum, de l'autre femme*, entitled "La Tache aveugle d'un vieux rêve de symétrie" (Paris: Minuit, 1974), pp. 9–162.

29. "Relations of Person in the Verb," in *Problems in General Linguistics* (Coral

Gables: University of Miami Press, 1971), p. 200, and "The Nature of Pronouns," in *Problems*, p. 218.

30. On the notions of primary and secondary identification, see "The Imaginary Signifier," pp. 45–57 .

31. For a detailed discussion of the effects of subject-address and cinematic point of view, see Edward Branigan, *Point of View in the Cinema: A Theory of Narrative and Subjectivity in Classical Film* (New York: Mouton, 1984).

32. Julia Kristeva describes this kind of disturbance of subjectivity in Lautréamont's *Les Chants de Maldoror*. In *La Révolution du langage poétique* (Paris: Editions du Seuil, 1974), pp. 315–35 .

33. Bruce Kawin calls "first-person cinema" those instances in which we view the story from the point of view of characters in the story. *Mindscreen* (Princeton: Princeton University Press, 1978).

34. "Sur la théorie classique du cinéma: A propos des travaux de Jean Mitry," in *Essais sur la signification au cinéma* (Paris: Klincksieck, 1972), p. 43, and "The Imaginary Signifier," pp. 50–51.

35. "The Imaginary Signifier," p. 55 .

36. "The Imaginary Signifier," p. 96 .

37. "Un Chant d'amour," *Cahiers du Cinéma*, no. 264 (1976): 60, my translation.

38. "Le Signifiant imaginaire," p. 44, my translation.

39. "Imagenations," in *Film Culture*, no. 32 (1964): 18.

40. Quoted by André Bazin in "Theatre and Cinema," in *What Is Cinema?*, p. 92.

41. *Genet and Ionesco: The Theatre of the Double*, ed. Kelly Morris (New York: Bantam, 1969).

42. Antonin Artaud, *Le Théâtre et son double*, in vol. 4 of *Oeuvres complètes* (Paris: Gallimard, 1964), p. 58.

43. See André Bazin, "Theatre and Cinema," p. 95.

44. According to Peter Brooks, Genet was working on another film project in the 1970s, which so far has not come to fruition. *Genet: A Collection of Critical Essays* (Englewood Cliffs, N.J.: Prentice Hall, 1979), p. 6 .

V. PASSION: BETWEEN TEXT AND PERFORMANCE

1. "A Note on the Esthetics of Film," in *Structure, Sign, and Function*. (New Haven: Yale University Press, 1977), p. 179. For more on Mukarovsky, see Jiri Veltrusky, "Jan Mukarovsky's Structural Poetics and Esthetics," *Poetics Today* 2, no. 1 (1981): 117–59 .

2. See Victor Erlich, *Russian Formalism* 2nd rev. ed. (The Hague: Mouton, 1965), p. 190.

3. "Man and Object in the Theater," in *Prague School Reader*, ed. and trans. Paul L. Garvin (Washington: Georgetown University Press, 1964), p. 83.

4. *Prolegomena to a Theory of Language*, trans. Francis J. Whitfield (Madison: University of Wisconsin Press, 1963 .)

5. See for instance, Umberto Eco, *A Theory of Semiotics* (Bloomington: Indiana University Press, 1976).

6. *Cours de linguistique générale* (Paris: Payot, 1971).

7. (Paris: Larousse, 1971).

8. Metz, 1981, pt. 2.

9. *Prolegomena*, p. 79.

10. "The Current State of the History of Theater," in *Structure, Sign, and Function* (New Haven: Yale University Press, 1977), p. 201.

11. "The Prague School Theory of Theater," *Poetics Today* 2, no. 3 (1981): 225–37.

12. "Correlations of Tense in the French Verb," in *Problems in General Linguistics* (Coral Gables: University of Miami Press, 1971), pp. 195–204 .

13. "Relationships of Person in the Verb," in *Problems in General Linguistics*, p. 199.

14. (Cambridge: Harvard University Press, 1962) .

15. "Signature, Event, Context," trans. Samuel Weber and Jeffrey Mehlman, *Glyph*, no. 1 (1977): 172–97.

16. *A Theory of Semiotics* (Bloomington: Indiana University Press, 1976), pp.7, 58.

17. Roman Jakobson, "Closing Statements: Linguistics and Poetics," in *Style in Language*, ed. Thomas Sebeok (Cambridge: MIT Press, 1960), pp. 350–77 .

18. Alessandro Serpieri et al., "Toward a Segmentation of the Dramatic Text," *Poetics Today* 2, no. 3 (1981): 163–200 .

19. "Logic as Semiotic," in *Philosophical Writings of Charles Sanders Peirce* (New York: Dover Press, 1955), pp. 98–119.

20. "Subjectivity in Language," in *Problems in General Linguistics*, pp. 223–30 .

21. Serpieri et al., p. 169.

22. This kind of model shapes Anne Ubersfeld's interpretation of the space of theater in *Lire le théâtre* (Paris: Editions sociales, 1982; 1st ed., 1977). She says "L'univers scénique spatialisé *est construit pour être signe*" (p. 151). "Ainsi l'espace scénique peut-il être la transposition d'une poétique textuelle. Tout le travail propre de la mise en scène consiste à trouver les équivalents spatiaux des grandes figures de rhétorique, et d'abord la métaphore et la métonymie" (p. 161).

23. "Comment s'éffectue la transposition d'une énonciation verbale en une énonciation iconique." "Sémiologie de la langue," *Semiotica* 1, no. 2 (1969): 129. My translation in English appears in the text.

24. "L'élément proprement sémiologique du théâtre consiste dans le fait que ce corps humain n'est plus une chose parmi les choses, parce que quelqu'un le montre, en le détachant du contexte des événements réels, et le constitue comme signe, constituant en même temps comme signifiants les mouvements que ce corps accomplit et l'espace dans lequel ces mouvements s'inscrivent." "Paramètres de la sémiologie théâtrale," in *Sémiologie de la représentation*, ed. André Helbo (Brussels: Editions complexe, 1975), p. 35. My translation appears in the text.

25. *Prolegomena to a Theory of Language* .

26. *Problèmes de sémiologie théatrale* (Montréal: Les Presses de l'université de Québec, 1976), p. 3 .

27. "From One Identity to Another," in *Desire in Language*, trans. Leon Roudiez (ed.), Thomas Gora, and Alice Jardine (New York: Columbia University Press, 1980), pp. 124–77.

28. Trans. Barbara Johnson (Chicago: University of Chicago Press, 1981).

29. Trans. Gayatri Chakravorty Spivak (Baltimore: The Johns Hopkins University Press, 1976).

30. Jeannette Savona rejects a deconstructive reading of Genet, modelling a sociological interpretation of the plays after Michel Foucault's discussion, in *Surveiller et punir*, of the role of surveillance in the structure of modern prisons. While Foucault is a likely frame of reference for interpreting the prison motif in Genet's work, especially as one traces the role of the look in structuring subject-address in Genet's film and plays, Savona reduces the philosophical richness of Foucault to formal oppositions between dominator and dominated in the fiction. She over-

looks the question of performance in Genet as an ongoing struggle to transcend the structures of domination. "Théâtre et univers carcéral: Jean Genet et Michel Foucault," in *French Forum* 10, no. 2 (1985): 201–14. Savona is at her best when she describes the recurrence of themes and structures in Genet's work. See *Jean Genet* (New York: Grove Press, 1984).

31. *Dissemination*, p. 175.

32. Odette Aslan discusses "Genet, His Actors and Directors" in *Genet: A Collection of Critical Essays*, ed. Peter Brooks and Joseph Halpern (Englewood Cliffs, NJ: Prentice Hall, 1979), pp. 146–55. Recently Jonathan Kalb states that Genet's scripts lend themselves to a wide spectrum of interpretations, but he criticizes Joanne Akalaitis for changing the tone and structure of *Le Balcon* beyond recognition in order to express her own political and esthetic claims. "Whose Text Is It Anyway? *The Balcony* at A. R. T.," *Theater* 17 (1986): 97–99.

33. *Saint Genet*, trans. Bernard Frechtman (New York: New American Library, 1963), p. 81.

34. Sylvie Debevec Henning describes Genet's plays in terms of the satanic, sacrificial mass described by René Girard in *La Violence et le sacré*. Unlike the Christian striving for totalization or oneness in the Mass, the pagan ritual exposes the community to the regular destruction of social categories and relations. While Girard views this violence as a threat to the social order, Henning views it as a regenerating force in Genet's work. *Genet's Ritual Play* (Amsterdam: Rodopi, 1981), p. 4 .

35. In vol. 3 of *Oeuvres complètes* (Paris: Gallimard, 1984), pp. 174 –90.

36. Vol. 3 of *Oeuvres complètes*, p. 182 .

37. *Dissemination*.

38. Ironically, Anne Ubersfeld describes a similar kind of "deconstruction" of the unity of place in Racine's *Phèdre*. Characters are neither "here" nor "there," but in a kind of tragic limbo traced in ambiguous indications for the space of the action. While Ubersfeld offers convincing insights into the style of mise-en-scène most apt to represent the tragic void in Racine's play, she does not claim that Racine in any way threatened the "canons of classical representation" dictating styles of mise-en-scène in his time. "The Space of Phèdre," *Poetics Today* 2, no. 3 (1981): 201–10 .

39. See for example, Kelly Morris, ed., *Genet and Ionesco: The Theater of the Double* (New York: Bantam Books, 1963), and Martin Esslin, "Jean Genet—A Hall of Mirrors," in *The Theater of the Absurd* (New York: Doubleday-Anchor, 1962), pp. 140–67.

40. This theme runs through *La Chambre claire* by Roland Barthes (Paris: Gallimard, 1984).

41. "Correlations of Tense in the French Verb," in *Problems in General Linguistics*, pp. 205–16 .

42. "Freud and the Scene of Writing," trans. Jeffrey Mehlman, *Yale French Studies*, no. 48 (1975): 73–117.

43. See for example, the Introduction to *Soledad Brother: The Prison Letters of George Jackson* (New York: Coward-McCann, 1970), n. pag.; "Here and Now for Bobby Seale" (New York: Committee to Defend the Panthers, 1970); "Violence et brutalité," *Le Monde*, 2 Sept. 1977, 1–2; and "Quatre heures à Chatila," *La Revue d'études palestiniennes*, no. 6 (1983): 4–19.

44. *Le Théâtre et son double*, in vol. 4 of *Oeùvres complètes* (Paris: Gallimard, 1964), pp. 106–53. Derrida says that the theater of cruelty, "c'est la vie elle-même en ce qu'elle a d'irreprésentable" ("is life itself in its aspect as unrepresentable," my translation). *L'Ecriture et la différence* (Paris: Seuil, 1967), p. 343.

45. See *Les Nègres*, p. 15 .

CONCLUSION

1. RoseLee Goldberg surveys trends in performance art in *Performance Art: Live Art, 1909 to the Present* (New York: Harry Abrams, 1979).

2. From Schechner's inaugural "T. D. S. Comment," as new editor of the *Drama Review* no. 1 (1986): 6.

3. See p. 41, 63, 116, 209, 210, 217–22, 331, 343.

4. See for instance, René de Cessaty, "Rêve d'une révolution," *La Quinzaine littéraire,* no. 464 (1986): 5; Tahar Ben Jelloun, "Le Testament de Jean Genet," *Jeune Afrique,* no. 1328 (1986): 60; M. F. Otavj, rev. of *Un Captif amoureux,* by Jean Genet. *Europe: Revue littéraire mensuelle* 64, no. 691–92: 219–20; and Bernard Séchène, "L'Athéologie de Jean Genet," *Infini,* no. 17 (1987): 102–28.

Bibliography

WORKS BY JEAN GENET

NOVELS

Notre-Dame-des-fleurs. Lyon: L'Arbalète, 1944.
Notre-Dame-des-fleurs. Vol. 2 of *Oeuvres complètes*. Paris: Gallimard, 1951, pp. 7–208.
Our Lady of the Flowers. Translated by Bernard Frechtman. New York: Grove Press, 1963.
Miracle de la rose. Lyon: L'Arbalète, 1946.
Miracle de la rose. Vol. 2 of *Oeuvres complètes*. Paris: Gallimard, 1951, pp. 220–470.
Pompes funèbres. Offered for subscription only. N.p., 1948.
Pompes funèbres. Vol. 3 of *Oeuvres complètes*. Paris: Gallimard, 1953, pp. 9–192.
Funeral Rites. Translated by Bernard Frechtman. New York: Grove Press, 1969.
Gutter in the Sky. Trans. (?). Philadelphia: André Levy, 1955.

FILMS

Un Chant d'amour. Dir. with Jean Cocteau, 1950. Available through the Museum of Modern Art, New York.
Les Abysses. Dir. with Nico Papatakis, 1963.
The Balcony. Adapted to film by Joseph Strick, 1963.
Mademoiselle. Dir. by Tony Richardson. Script by Genet.
The Maids. Adapted to film by Christopher Miles, 1973.
Possession du condamné. Dir. Albert-André Lheureux, from Genet's poem, "Le Condamné à mort." 1967.

PLAYS

Haute Surveillance. Vol. 4 of *Oeuvres complètes*. Paris: Gallimard, 1968, pp. 177–214.
Les Bonnes. Vol. 4 of *Oeuvres complètes*. Paris: Gallimard, 1968, pp. 137–76.
Le Balcon, Vol. 4 of *Oeuvres complètes*. Paris: Gallimard, 1968, pp. 33–136.
The Balcony. Translated by Bernard Frechtman. London: Faber and Faber, 1957.
Les Nègres. Lyon: L'Arbalète, 1963.
The Blacks: A Clown Show. Translated by Bernard Frechtman. New York: Grove Press, 1960.
Les Paravents. Lyon: L'Arbalète, 1976.

MISCELLANEOUS

L'Atelier d'Alberto Giacometti. Lyon: L'Arbalète, 1963.
Un Captif amoureux. Paris: Gallimard, 1986.
"L'Enfant criminel" et "Adame Miroir." Paris: Paul Morhien, 1949.
"Lettre à Léonore Fini." Paris: Loyou, 1950.
"Lettre à Jean-Jacques Pauvert." Preface to *Les Bonnes*. Paris: Jean-Jacques Pauvert, 1954.
"Ce qui est resté d'un Rembrandt déchiré en petits carrés bien réguliers, et foutu aux chiottes." Vol. 4 of *Oeuvres complètes*. Paris: Gallimard, 1968, pp. 19–32.

"Here and Now for Bobby Seale." New York: Committee to Defend the Panthers, 1970.

Introduction to *Soledad Brother: The Prison Letters of George Jackson.* New York: Coward-McCann, 1970, n.p.

"Quatre heures à Chatila," *Revue d'études palestiniennes,* no. 6 (1983): 3–17.

"Violence et brutalité," *Le Monde,* 2 Sept. 1977, 1–2.

WORKS ON GENET

Aslan, Odette. *Jean Genet.* Paris: Seghers, 1973.

Bataille, Georges. *La Littérature et le mal.* Paris: Gallimard, 1957, pp. 199–244.

Bishop, Thomas. *Pirandello and the French Theater.* New York: New York University Press, 1966.

Boisdeffre, Pierre de. *Une Histoire de la littérature d'aujourd'hui.* Paris: Le Livre contemporain, 1959.

Bonnefoy, Claude. *Jean Genet.* Paris: Editions universitaires, 1965.

Brooks, Peter, and Joseph Halpern. *Genet: A Collection of Critical Essays.* Englewood Cliffs, N. J.: Prentice Hall, 1979.

Cessaty, René de. "Rêve d'une révolution." *La Quinzaine littéraire,* no. 464 (1986): 5–7.

Cetta, Thomas. *Profane Play, Ritual and Jean Genet: A Study of His Drama.* University: University of Alabama Press, 1974.

Choukri, Mohamed. "L'Homme que Genet n'a pas giflé," *Jeune Afrique,* no. 1335 (1986): 50–51.

Cocteau, Jean. "Preparatory Notes on an Unknown Sexuality." Introduction to *Gutter in the Sky* by Jean Genet. Trans. (?). Philadelphia: André Levy, 1955.

Coe, Richard. *The Theater of Jean Genet: A Casebook.* New York: Grove Press, 1979.

———. *The Vision of Jean Genet.* New York: Grove Press, 1968.

Cronel, H. Review of *Un Captif amoureux,* by Jean Genet. *La Nouvelle Revue française* 407 (1986): 81–85.

Daney, Serge. "Un Chant d'amour." *Cahiers du cinéma,* no. 264 (1976): 60.

Deguy, Michel. "La 'Piétà' de Jean Genet." *La Quinzaine littéraire,* no. 471 (1986): 14–15.

Derrida, Jacques. *Glas.* Paris: Editions Galilée, 1974.

Driver, Tom. "Jean Genet." *Columbia Essays on Modern Writers,* no. 20. New York: Columbia University Press, 1966.

Erhman, Jacques. "Genet's Dramatic Metamorphosis." *Yale French Studies,* no. 29 (1962): 33–42.

Esslin, Martin. "Jean Genet—A Hall of Mirrors." In *The Theatre of the Absurd.* New York: Doubleday-Anchor, 1962, pp. 140–167.

Genette, Gérard. *Mimologiques.* Paris: Le Seuil, 1976.

Gauthier, Théophile. *Surréalisme et sexualité.* Paris: Gallimard, 1971.

Hassan, Ihab. *The Dismemberment of Orpheus: Toward a Postmodern Literature.* New York: Oxford, 1971.

Henning, Sylvie Debevec, *Genet's Ritual Play.* Amsterdam: Rodopi, 1981.

Jelloun, Tahar Ben. "Le Testament de Jean Genet." *Jeune Afrique,* no. 1328 (1986): 57–60.

Kalb, Jonathon. "Whose Text Is It Anyway? The *Balcony* at A. R. T.," *Theater,* 17 (1986): 97–99.

Kelman, Ken. "Imagenations." *Film Culture,* no. 32 (1964): 16–18.

Knapp, Bettina. *Jean Genet.* New York: St. Martin's Press, 1968.

———. "Interview with Amadou." *Drama Review,* 11, no.4 (1967): 105–8.

———. "Interview with Roger Blin." *Drama Review* 7, no. 3 (1963): 111–25.

Leonard, John. "Portait of the Artist as Narcissistic Hitler." Review of *Funeral Rites*, by Jean Genet. *New York Times*, 19 June 1969, p. 43.

Les Nègres au port de la lune. Ed. C. D. N. Bordeaux. Paris: Editions de la différence, 1988.

Magnan, Jean-Marie. *Pour un blason de Jean Genet.* Paris: Seghers, 1966.

Markopoulos, Gregory. "Jean Genet's Only Film: *Un Chant d'amour.*" *Scenario* 2, no. 8 (1961): 8–10.

McMahon, Joseph. *The Imagination of Jean Genet.* New Haven: Yale University Press, 1963.

Mekas, Jonas. "Un Chant d'amour." *Film Comment* 2, no. 1 (1964): 28.

Melcher, Edith. "The Pirandellism of Jean Genet." *The French Review* 39, no. 1 (1962): 32–35.

Mitry, Jean. *Le Cinéma expérimental.* Paris: Editions universitaires, 1974.

Moraly, Jean-Bernard. *Jean Genet, la vie écrite.* Paris: Editions de la différence, 1988.

Morris, Kelly, ed. *Genet and Ionesco: The Theater of the Double.* New York: Bantam Books, 1969.

Naish, Camille. *A Genetic Approach to Structures in the Work of Jean Genet.* Cambridge: Harvard University Press, 1978.

Nin, Anaïs. Review of *Un Chant d'amour*, by Jean Genet, *Los Angeles Free Press*, 24 Dec. 1965, p. 5.

"Obscene Ruling Upheld." *San Francisco Examiner.* 25 Oct. 1966, 16.

Ottavj, M. F. Review of *Un Captif amoureux*, by Jean Genet. *Europe: Revue littéraire mensuelle* 64, no. 691–92 (1986): 219–20.

Sartre, Jean-Paul. *Saint Genet: Actor and Martyr.* Translated by Bernard Frechtman. New York: American Library, 1963. From the French *Saint Genêt: Comédien et martyr.* Vol. 1 of *Oeuvres complètes de Jean Genet.* Paris: Gallimard, 1953.

Savona, Jeannette. *Jean Genet.* New York: Grove Press, 1983.

———. "Théâtre et univers carcéral: Jean Genet et Michel Foucault." *French Forum* 10, no. 2 (1985): 201–14.

Séchène, Bernard. "L'Athéologie de Jean Genet." *Infini, no.* 17 (1987): 102–28.

Thody, Philip. *Jean Genet: A Study of His Novels and Plays.* London: Hamish Hamilton, 1968.

Todd, Jane Mary. "Autobiography and the Case of the Signature: Reading Derrida's *Glas.*" *Comparative Literature* 38, no. 1 (1986): 1–19.

THEORETICAL WORKS

Aristotle. *The Poetics.* Translated by James Hutton. New York: W. W. Norton & Co., 1982.

Austin, John. *How To Do Things With Words.* Cambridge: Harvard University Press, 1962.

Bakhtin, Mikhail M. *The Dialogic Imagination.* Edited and introduced by Michael Holquist. Translated by Caryl Emerson and Michael Holquist. Austin: University of Texas Press, 1981.

———. *The Formal Method in Literary Scholarship.* Translated by Albert J. Wehrle. Baltimore: Inc Johns Hopkins University Press, 1978.

———. *Marxism and the Philosophy of Language.* Translated and introduced by Ladislav Matejka and I. R. Titunik. Cambridge: Harvard University Press, 1986.

———. *Le Marxisme et la philosophie du langage.* Translated and introduced by Marina Yaguello. Paris: Editions de Minuit, 1977.

———. *Problems in Dostoevsky's Poetics.* Edited and translated by Caryl Emerson. Minneapolis: University of Minnesota Press, 1984.

————. *Rabelais and His World*. Translated by Hélène Iswolsky. Bloomington: Indiana University Press, 1984.

————. *Speech Genres and Other Late Essays*. Translated by Vern W. McGee. Austin: University of Texas Press, 1986.

Barthes, Roland. *La Chambre claire*. Paris: Gallimard, 1984.

————. "Introduction à l'analyse structurale des récits." *Communications*, no. 8 (1966): 1–27.

————. "Proust et le noms." In *Nouveaux essais critiques*. Paris: Le Seuil, 1972, pp. 121–34.

————. "Rhétorique de l'image." *Communications*, no. 4 (1964): 40–51.

Bazin, André. *What Is Cinema?*. Translated by Hugh Gray. Berkeley: University of California Press, 1967.

Baudry, Jean-Louis. "Le Dispositif." *Communications*, no. 23 (1975): 56–72.

Benveniste, Emile. "Sémiologie de la langue." *Semiotica* 1, no. 2 (1969: 120–39.

————. *Problems in General Linguistics*. Translated by Mary E. Meek. Coral Gables: University of Miami Press, 1971.

————. "La Forme et le sens dans le langage." In *Le Langage*. Actes du XIIIe Congrès des sociétés de philosophie de langue française. Neuchâtel: La Baconnière, 1966, pp. 27–40.

Branigan, Edward. *Point of View in the Cinema: A Theory of Narrative and Subjectivity in Classical Film*. New York: Mouton, 1984.

Dauzat, Albert. *Les Noms de famille de France*. Paris: Payot, 1945.

Derrida, Jacques. *Dissemination*. Translated by Barbara Johnson. Chicago: University of Chicago Press, 1981.

————. *L'Ecriture et la différence*. Paris: Le Seuil, 1967.

————. "Freud and the Scene of Writing." Translated by Jeffrey Mehlman. *Yale French Studies*, no. 48 (1975): 73–117.

————. *Of Grammatology*. Translated by Gayatri Chakravorty Spivak. Baltimore: The Johns Hopkins University Press, 1976.

————. "Signature, Event, Context." Translated by Samuel Weber and Jeffrey Mehlman. *Glyph*, no. 1 (1977): 172–97.

————. *La Voix et le phénomène*. Paris: Presses universitaires de France, 1967.

————. "White Mythology." Translated by F. C. T. Moore. *New Literary History* 6, no. 1 (1974): 5–74.

Eco, Umberto. "Paramètres de la sémiologie théâtrale." In *Sémiologie de la représentation*. Edited by André Helbo. Brussels: Editions complexe, 1975, pp. 33–41.

————. "Pour une reformulation du concept de signe iconique." *Communications*, no. 29 (1978): 140–91.

Eco, Umberto. *A Theory of Semiotics*. Bloomington: Indiana University Press, 1976.

Elam, Keir. *The Semiotics of Theater and Drama*. New York: Metheun & Co., 1980.

Erlich, Victor. *Russian Formalism*. 2nd rev. ed. The Hague: Mouton, 1965.

Freud, Sigmund. "Fetishism." Vol. 21 of *The Standard Edition of the Complete Psychological Works of Sigmund Freud*. Translated by James Strachey. London: Hogarth Press, 1953.

————. *Jokes and Their Relation to the Unconscious*. Translated by James Strachey. New York: Penguin Books, 1960.

————. "Mourning and Melancholia." Vol. 14 of *The Standard Edition*. Translated by James Strachey. London: Hogarth Press, 1975, pp. 243–58.

————. *Three Case Studies*. Translated by James Strachey. New York: Collier Books, 1976.

————. *Three Essays on the Theory of Sexuality*. Vol. 7 of *The Standard Edition*. Translated by James Strachey. London: Hogarth Press, 1953.

Garvin, Paul, ed. and trans. *Structure, Sign, Function.* New Haven: Yale University Press, 1977.
Genette, Gérard. *Figures II.* Paris: Le Seuil, 1969.
———. *Figures III.* Paris: Le Seuil, 1972.
Guiraud, Pierre. *L'Argot.* Paris: Presses universitaires de France, 1958.
———. *Dictionnaire érotique.* Paris: Payot, 1978.
Heath, Stephen. "Difference." *Screen* 19, no. 3 (1978): 51–112.
———. *Questions of Cinema.* Bloomington: Indiana University Press, 1981.
Hedges, Inez. "Surrealist Metaphor." *Poetics Today* 4, no. 2, (1983), 275–95.
Hjelmslev, Louis. *Prolegomena to a Theory of Language.* Translated by Francis J. Whitfield. Madison: University of Wisconsin Press, 1963.
Holquist, Michael, and Katerina Clark. *Mikhail Bakhtin.* Cambridge: Harvard University Press, 1984.
Irigaray, Luce. *Speculum, de l'autre femme.* Paris: Minuit, 1974.
Jakobson, Roman. "Closing Statements: Linguistics and Poetics." In *Style in Language.* Edited by Thomas Sebeok. Cambridge: Harvard University Press, 1960, pp. 350–77.
———, and Morris Halle. "Two Aspects of Language, Two Types of Aphasic Disturbances." Reprinted as "The Linguistic Problem of Aphasia." In *Fundamentals of Language.* The Hague: Mouton, 1980, pp. 69–96.
Jameson, Frederic. *The Prison House of Language.* Princeton: Princeton University Press, 1982.
Kawin, Bruce. *Mindscreen.* Princeton: Princeton University Press: 1978.
Klein, Melanie. "Early Stages of the Oedipal Conflict." Vol. 1 of *The Writings of Melanie Klein.* London: Hogarth Press, 1975, pp. 186–99.
———. "On Identification." Vol. 3 of *The Writings of Melanie Klein.* pp. 141 –75.
———. "Envy and Gratitude." Vol. 3 of *The Writings of Melanie Klein,* pp. 176 –235.
Kristeva, Julia. "From One Identity to Another." In *Desire in Language.* Translated by Leon Roudiez (ed.), Thomas Gora, and Alice Jardine. New York: Columbia University Press, 1981, pp. 124–77.
———. *La Révolution du langage poétique.* Paris: Le Seuil, 1974.
Lacan, Jacques. *Ecrits I.* Paris: Editions Points, 1966.
Man, Paul de. *Allegories of Reading.* New Haven: Yale University Press, 1979.
Metz, Christian. *Essais sur la signification au cinéma.* Pt. 2. Paris: Klincksieck, 1982.
———. *The Imaginary Signifier.* Translated by Celia Britton, Annwyl Williams, Ben Brewster, and Alfred Guzzetti. Bloomington: Indiana University Press, 1981.
———. "Le Signifiant imaginaire." *Communications,* no. 23 (1976): 3–55.
Oswald, Laura. "Figure/Discourse: Configurations of Desire in *Un Chien Andalou*." *Semiotica* 33, nos. 1/2 (1981): 105–22.
———. "Semiotics and/or Deconstruction: In Quest of Cinema." *Semiotica* 60, Nos. 3/4 (1986): 315–41
Pavis, Patrice. *Problèmes de sémiologie théâtrale.* Montréal: Les Presses universitaires de Québec, 1976.
Peirce, Charles Sanders. "Logic as Semiotic." In *Philosophical Writings of Charles Sanders Peirce.* New York: Dover Press, 1955, pp. 98–119.
Propp, Vladimir. *Morphology of Folktale.* Translated by Lawrence Scott. Austin: University of Texas Press, 1968.
Ricoeur, Paul. *La Métaphore vive.* Paris: Editions du Seuil, 1975.
Rigolot, François. "Rhétorique du nom poétique." *Poétique,* no. 28 (1976), pp. 466–83.
Schechner, Richard. "Comment." *Drama Review* 30, no. 1 (1986): 5–7.
Searle, John. *Expression and Meaning.* New York: Cambridge University Press, 1979.

Serpieri, Alessandro, et. al. "Toward a Segmentation of the Dramatic Text," in *Poetics Today* 2, no. 3 (1981): 163–200.
Sperber, Dan, and Deirdre Wilson. "Les Ironies comme mentions." *Poétique*, no. 36 (1978): 399–412.
Steiner, Peter, ed. *Prague School Reader. Austin: University of Texas Press*, 1982.
———. *Russian Formalism: A Metapoetics*. Ithaca: Cornell University Press, 1984.
Todorov, Tzvetan. "Catégories du récit littéraire." *Communications*, no. 8 (1966): 125–51.
———. *La Conquête de l'Amérique*. Paris: Le Seuil, 1982.
———. *Mikhail Bakhtine: Le Principe dialogique*. Paris: Le Seuil, 1981.
Ubersfeld, Anne. *Lire le théâtre*. 4th ed. Paris: Editions sociales, 1982.
———. "The Space of *Phèdre*." *Poetics Today* 2, no. 3 (1981): 201–10.
Ullman, Stephen. *Style in the French Novel*. Cambridge: Cambridge University Press, 1957.
Veltrusky, Jiri. "Jan Mukarovsky's Structural Poetics and Esthetics." *Poetics Today* 2, no. 1 (1981): 117–59.
———. "The Prague School Theory of Theater." *Poetics Today* 2, no. 3 (1981): 225–35.
Yaguello, Marina, trans. Introduction to *Le Marxisme et la philosophie du langage*, by Mikhail Bakhtin. Paris: Editions du Minuit, 1977, pp. 9–18.

GENERAL

Artaud, Antonin. *Le Théâtre et son double*. Vol. 4 of *Oeuvres complètes*. Paris: Gallimard, 1964, pp. 11–171.
Baudelaire, Charles. *Les Fleurs du mal*. Paris: Garnier-Flammarion, 1964.
Corneille, Pierre. "Discours des trois unités." Vol. 3 of *Oeuvres complètes*. Paris: Gallimard, 1984, pp. 174–90.
Duras, Marguerite. *Navire Night*. Paris: Mercure de France, 1982.
Goldberg, RoseLee. *Performance Art: Live Art, 1909 to the Present*. New York: Harry Abrams, 1979.
Graves, Robert. "A lo Dovino." Introduction to *The Poems of Saint Jean of The Cross*. New York: Grove Press, 1968.
Juilland, Alphonse. "Les Faux amis du vocabulaire de Louis-Ferdinand Céline." *Stanford French Review* 2, no. 3 (1978): 232–50.
Kant, Immanuel. *The Critique of Pure Reason* Translated J. M. D. Meiklejohn. New York: E. P. Dutton & Co., 1942.
Michelet, Jules. *Le Peuple*. Paris: Hachette, 1846.
Proust, Marcel. *A la recherche du temps perdu*. Paris: Gallimard, 1973.
Read, Herbert. *A Concise History of Modern Painting*. New York: Praeger, 1978.
Rimbaud, Arthur. "Une Saison en enfer." In *Oeuvres poétiques*. Paris: Garnier-Flammarion, 1964, pp.117–39.
Sue, Eugène. *Mystères de Paris*. Paris: Jean-Jacques Pauvert, 1963.

Index